Volume 5

ECONOMIC TRENDS IN
SOVIET RUSSIA

ECONOMIC TRENDS IN SOVIET RUSSIA

A. YUGOFF

Translated by
EDEN and CEDAR PAUL

Routledge
Taylor & Francis Group

LONDON AND NEW YORK

First published in 1930 in Great Britain by George Allen & Unwin

This edition first published in 2023
by Routledge
4 Park Square, Milton Park, Abingdon, Oxon OX14 4RN

and by Routledge
605 Third Avenue, New York, NY 10158

Routledge is an imprint of the Taylor & Francis Group, an informa business

© 1930

British Library Cataloguing in Publication Data
A catalogue record for this book is available from the British Library

ISBN: 978-1-032-48466-2 (Set)
ISBN: 978-1-032-48893-6 (Volume 5) (hbk)
ISBN: 978-1-032-48897-4 (Volume 5) (pbk)
ISBN: 978-1-003-39128-9 (Volume 5) (ebk)

DOI: 10.4324/9781003391289

Publisher's Note
The publisher has gone to great lengths to ensure the quality of this reprint but points out that some imperfections in the original copies may be apparent.

Disclaimer
The publisher has made every effort to trace copyright holders and would welcome correspondence from those they have been unable to trace.

ECONOMIC TRENDS IN SOVIET RUSSIA

By A. YUGOFF

Translated by
EDEN AND CEDAR PAUL

The German original of this book (a translation by A. Gurland from the author's Russian MS.) was published by the Verlag Kaden und Comp., Dresden, 1929, under the title "Die Volkswirtschaft der Sowjetunion und ihre Probleme"

The German text used by the translators had had various alterations and additions made in typescript by the author. Whenever necessary the translators collated the text with the Russian version printed by "Globus", Riga, 1929.

FIRST PUBLISHED IN THE U.S.A. IN 1930

AUTHOR'S PREFACE TO THE
ENGLISH EDITION

THIS is the English version of a work published in German and Russian during the spring of 1929. A few trifling changes have been made in the English edition. The most important of these are additions of statistical comparisons bearing on economic conditions in Great Britain and the United States. Wherever possible, the Russian statistics have been brought up to date. References have also been made to the latest economic measures of the U.S.S.R.

A. YUGOFF

August 1929

TABLE OF CONTENTS

CONTENTS

CONTENTS

CONTENTS

INTRODUCTION

As yet there has been little study of the economic position of contemporary Russia. Nevertheless the Union of Socialist Soviet Republics (U.S.S.R.) offers an abundance of material for analysis and for the demonstration of manifold economic and social phenomena and laws.

Above all, the economic life of the Soviet Union displays all the contradictions that cannot fail to arise in a country which throughout the period of war and revolution has been isolated from the world economy, in one where the old-established means of communication and exchange have been paralysed, and where there has arisen a disproportion between production and consumption.

Soviet Russia is a land of economic contrasts and oppositions. In the towns, there are huge factories and workshops; in the countryside, a natural economy is still almost exclusively dominant. Huge trusts and syndicates, embracing whole branches of industry and commerce, confront independent home workers and itinerant traders. Theoretically and as a matter of principle, all the economic life of the country is under State control; whilst in practice currency crises, crises of production, gluts, crises of demand, press hard on one another's heels, and are renewed ever and again by the spontaneous play of economic forces and by the lack of due proportion between the various branches of economic life.

Furthermore in latter-day Russia we can see a peculiarly vivid picture of the results of artificially cultivated socialist economic forms in a country where neither the economic nor the social conditions are ripe for anything of the kind; we can note what a caricature of true socialism such an enforced "socialism" must be; and we can discern the way in which the narrownesses and restrictions of individualist economic relationships are continually breaking through the socialist crust. In contemporary Russia we can see how stubbornly the body economic, social conditions, and even so dispassionate a

B

thing as technique, react against experimental endeavours to change them prematurely; and in how striking a fashion the development of the forces of production none the less continues.

We can watch the gradual reestablishment of the economic life of this mighty land, and the healing of the wounds inflicted by the civil and imperialist wars. We can study the manner in which a utopian policy, one that disregards the iron laws of economic evolution, repeatedly gives rise to irremediable crises.

Two conflicting tendencies are at work in Soviet Russia to-day. One of them has originated out of the new economic and social situation created by the revolution, the overthrow of tsarism, and the freshly created possibilities for a rapid unfolding of productive forces alike in industry and agriculture. The other, which communist policy has artificially introduced into the realm of economic reality, acts as a brake upon economic progress, rivets utopian fetters upon these same productive forces, and gives rise to a pendulum swing from "right" to "left" and then back to "right" again.

My aim in the present work is to paint an objective picture of the economic position of contemporary Russia, but my task has been rendered more difficult by the tendentious and incomplete character of the statistical material which is alone available for the purpose. In Soviet Russia, the only data are official, and they are often inaccurate and contradictory. Still, even in these circumstances the study of Russian economic life remains possible. Experience shows that when statistics have been cooked, their falsity is demonstrated by the first crisis that happens along, and that statistical truth is often brought to light by the mutual recriminations of the various Soviet authorities and press organs. Besides, there is an abundance of valuable and often quite objective material in the economic journals and official reports. One who is in search of such objective material, must check the official reports by comparing them one with another, and must analyse them methodically.

I have regarded it as my main task to put before the reader

the decisive developmental trends of economic life in Russia during the first decade of the existence of Soviet Russia, and to acquaint him with the present position of affairs. My subsidiary purpose has been to analyse the basic problems, the growth, and the future prospects of the Soviet economy. Considerations of space, of course, have made it essential to limit attention to problems of outstanding importance, and even these have necessarily been dealt with very concisely.

ECONOMIC TRENDS IN SOVIET RUSSIA

CHAPTER ONE

RUSSIAN ECONOMICS SHORTLY BEFORE THE GREAT WAR

WE have to study the economics of Soviet Russia. Nevertheless —however much economic conditions in Russia may have been modified by the revolution, the civil war, and the policy of the Soviet government—the foundation upon which Soviet economics were reestablished after the communist revolution, was the economic, social, and cultural situation of the pre-revolutionary epoch. Hence, if we are to understand the social and economic processes of the present day, it is essential that we should make ourselves acquainted with the condition and the chief developmental trends of Russian economic life before the war and towards the end of the year 1917—at least in broad outline.

Most people know that agriculture has always played the leading role in Russian economic life. Of the one hundred and seventy millions of the population of the Russian Empire in 1914, 18·3 per cent lived in the towns, and 81·7 per cent in the rural districts.[1] The number of industrial workers did not exceed three millions. Whilst the whole value of industrial production in the area which now comprises the Soviet Union was estimated at 7·7 milliards of roubles, the value of agricultural production (crops, cattle breeding, forestry, etc.), was estimated at 11·7 milliards of roubles.[2]

1. INDUSTRY AT THE OUTSET OF THE WAR

The rapid development of Russian industry dates from the eighteen-seventies, from the liberation of the serfs. The

[1] Professor V. Den [Course of Economic Geography], 1925, p. 10; N. Oganoffsky [The Renovation of Russia and Agrarian Policy], 1914, p. 46. —Titles in brackets are English translations of the titles of Russian books.
[2] V. Groman [The Economics of the U.S.S.R.], 1927, p. 47.

economy of the days of serfdom, which was mainly a natural economy, was speedily replaced by a monetary system and the production of commodities for the market. Russia had entered the path of capitalist development, and was soon drawn into the worldwide system of capitalist economy and subjected to the laws of the capitalist world market. Russian manufacturing industry had, by the beginning of the nineteenth century, made great advances, being stimulated by the extensive demands of the State for materials needed in railway construction and for army supplies, and also by a great influx of capital from abroad. Within the course of a single decade, there was a huge increase in the mining of coal and ores, in the extraction of petroleum, and in the production of iron, steel, and textiles. A process of industrial concentration accompanied this increase in production and in the number of industrial workers.

At the opening of the twentieth century, Russian industry was affected by a crisis of over-production. The main cause of this crisis was, of course, the working of the general laws of capitalist production, the Russian crisis being brought about by the general crisis in the world economy which occurred during the early years of the present century. But whereas elsewhere in Europe the crisis lasted only two years, and was followed by a period of expanding trade, in Russia the worst period of the crisis was succeeded by a long-lasting depression which continued until 1908. The reason for this protraction was that the growth of Russian industry had been artificially fostered by the State demand for manufactured products and by protective tariffs. It had thus been over-stimulated. In the home market, there was an insufficiency of effective buyers, for the Russian peasant was too poor and his methods of agriculture were too primitive. On the other hand, the Russian industrialists could not manufacture for the foreign market, being unable to compete with more highly developed industrial countries in respect either of price or quality of goods. Poor harvests, which reduced the export of agricultural produce; the disastrous war with Japan, which had involved heavy

State expenditure, lessening the amount available for the State purchase of the ordinary products of industry; and, finally, the revolution of 1905–1906—these were the main causes of the prolonged depression that followed the acute crisis. Not until 1908 was there a revival of Russian industry, but thenceforward it was in a flourishing condition until the outbreak of the Great War.

During these years, there were various changes which promoted the development of Russian industry. Considerable amounts of foreign capital were being invested in Russia; agricultural production was being reorganised, with the result that the agrarian reforms of Stolypin were inaugurated; for several years in succession the harvests were good; there was an increase in the home demand for the products of manufacturing industry. The following table shows the growth of the various branches of Russian industry from 1890 to 1913.[1]

Branches of Industry		1890	1900	1908	1913
Cast Iron	(Million Poods[2])	54·9	176·8	175·3	283·0
Iron and Steel	,, ,,	51·9	132·5	162·9	246·6
Petroleum	,, ,,	226·0	631·1	563·3	561·3
Coal	,, ,,	367·2	986·0	1590·7	2213·8
Cotton	,, ,,	7·9	16·0	21·3	25·9
Sugar	,, ,,	—	49·0	92·6	108·4
Power Production (Million Units)		—	—	200·0	1283·0
Railway Construction (Versts[3])		28,000	49,500	61,200	63,800
Workers in Large-Scale Industry		720,000	1,600,000	1,765,000	2,518,000

These figures show clearly that Russian industry was rapidly expanding in the last five years before the war. Especially rapid was the development of those branches of industry which worked for a large market. According to Professor

[1] L. Kafengaus [The Expansion of Russian Industry from 1909 to 1913], 1914; N. Vanag and Tomsinsky [The Economic Evolution of Russia], 1928. The table is also compiled in part from the reports of various government departments in tsarist days.
[2] 1 pood equals 36·11 English pounds.
[3] 1 verst is approximately equal to 1 kilometre, or about 5 furlongs. (Precisely, 0·6628 of an English mile.)

Grinevetsky,[1] during the years 1908 to 1912 the production of agricultural machinery increased seven to eight times, the production of rubber goods increased threefold, woodwork and chemical industry were doubled, and so on.

During the last years before the war, there were important changes in the organisation of Russian industry and in the methods of production. There was an increasingly rapid process of concentration, the improvement in technique was accelerated, the number of joint-stock companies and the amount of business done by them increased greatly, the importance of syndicates for the marketing of industrial products grew. Furthermore, the ties between Russian industry and financial capital, both Russian and foreign, became much closer.

According to N. Vanag,[2] at the beginning of the year 1913 banking capital dominated a number of joint-stock companies in the metal industries to the extent of 87·9 per cent of all the capital invested in the Russian metal industries. (The amount of this banking capital was 386·1 millions of roubles.) All the share capital of the locomotive works, 96 per cent of the capital of the shipbuilding works, 77 per cent of the capital of the machine-making works, 75 per cent of coalmining capital, and 85 per cent of the capital of the petroleum industry, were in the hands of the banks. According to the calculations of P. Ol,[3] in the year 1913 the foreign capital invested in Russian industry totalled 1750 millions of roubles, this being approximately one-third of all the capital invested in Russian industry. The same author tells us that, as between various foreign countries, the amounts of foreign capital invested in Russia (including investments in tramways, electrical works, gas works, and other municipal undertakings) were as in Table opposite:

Approximately 75 per cent of this foreign capital was owned by countries which formed the subsequent Entente, and 20 per cent was owned by Germany and Austria-Hungary.

[1] [The Post-War Perspectives of Russian Industry], 1919, pp. 5–9.
[2] [Financial Capital in Russia shortly before the Great War], 1925, p. 89.
[3] [Foreign Capital in Russia], 1922, p. 8.

Source of Capital.						Amount of Capital in Millions of Roubles.
France	..	..	..	..	..	731·7
Britain	..	..	..	..	..	507·5
Germany ..	..	..	..	..	..	441·6
Belgium ..	..	..	..	..	..	321·6
United States	..	..	..	..	..	117·8
Holland ..	..	..	..	..	..	36·5
Switzerland	..	..	..	..	..	33·5
Sweden ..	..	..	..	..	..	23·8
Denmark ..	..	..	..	..	..	14·7
Austria-Hungary	..	..	..	..	..	7·6
Italy	..	..	..	..	..	2·5
Norway ..	..	..	..	..	..	2·3
Finland ..	..	..	..	..	..	2·0
Total	..	..	..	..	..	2243·1

The following figures show the increased concentration of Russian industry during the last years before the war. In 1913, 38·9 per cent of all industrial operatives were working in enterprises employing more than 1000 persons each. In the year 1900, there were only 2 metal mines in Russia producing more than 10 millions of poods each, and these enterprises produced 17·2 per cent of all the ores mined. By 1908, there were already 5 such mines producing more than 10 millions of poods each (41·5 per cent of the total production); and by 1913 there were 9 such mines with a production of over 10 millions of poods each (53·1 per cent of the total production). In the petroleum industry, 6 great enterprises produced 65 per cent of the total amount; in the coalmining industry, in the year 1891, 47·8 per cent of the coal mined was produced by great enterprises (those producing more than 5 millions of poods yearly); but by the year 1912, 84·5 per cent of the total production was from large-scale enterprises.[1]

Nevertheless, though Russian industry had developed thus rapidly during the last years before the war, it remained poorly developed when compared with the industry of other European countries, and was extremely backward from the technical point of view.

In size, Russia comes second among the great powers of the

[1] Official reports of factory inspectors for the year 1913.

world, and in population it comes third. As regards natural
resources, Russia occupies a very high place. For instance, 38
per cent of the world's petroleum comes from Russia, and
78 per cent of the deposits of peat are in that country. The
Russian coal deposits are twice as extensive as the British.
In respect of supplies of manganese, Russia comes first;
and in respect of supplies of copper, she comes second. There
are vast Russian territories suitable for the growth of cotton.
The afforested area of Russia amounts to more than 27 per
cent of the forests of the world.

Despite this abundance of natural treasures, Russia, owing
to the deficient utilisation of her productive powers, occupies a
very low position in the scale of world industry. In 1913, she
held the fifth place in the production of iron ores (accounting
for 6 per cent of the world production); in respect of cast iron,
likewise the fifth place ($5 \cdot 8$ per cent of the world production);
in the matter of coal, the sixth place ($2 \cdot 5$ per cent); cotton
spinning, the fourth place (5 per cent); and only in respect of
petroleum did she occupy the second place (17 per cent).

Russia lagged yet more behind other countries as regards
technical development. In 1913, as regards mechanical power
units in industry, agriculture, and transport, Russia accounted
for only $2 \cdot 2$ per cent of the world production in this field. The
same year, the comparative average output per industrial
worker was: in Britain and the U.S., 80; in Germany, 65; in
France, 26; in Russia, 9.

Some of the branches of industry were much better developed
than others. The most developed were the textile industry (33
per cent of the workers, 25 per cent of the production); the
food-producing industry (14 per cent of the workers, 33 per
cent of the production); mining (16 per cent of the workers,
10 per cent of the production); and the metal industry (20 per
cent of the workers, 14 per cent of the production). Comparatively backward were the chemical industry, the paper-making
industry, and the printing industry. Comparatively insignificant was the development of machine-making, and especially

the production of delicate mechanical apparatus and machine-tools.

Still more backward was railway development in Russia. There were but 0·3 kilometre of railway track per 100 square kilometres of area, this being only one thirty-sixth of the railway development in Germany, and less than that of the most backward countries elsewhere in Europe.

2. AGRICULTURE AT THE OUTSET OF THE WAR

Just before the revolution of 1905–1906, Russian agriculture had experienced a grave crisis. In the eighth chapter, I shall discuss in fuller detail the obstacles to the advance in Russian agriculture, and the main causes of the impoverishment of the peasantry in tsarist days. Suffice it to summarise them here. The existence of the huge estates of the great landlords, the extremely small size of the peasant farms, high rents, heavy taxation, the ties which bound the peasant to the rural commune, and the persistence of quasi-feudal and quasi-servile conditions, were mainly operative.[1] The vestiges of serfdom, the backwardness of agricultural enterprise on the estates of the great landlords, and the primitive nature of peasant farming, were all hindrances to capitalist development in Russia. Land hunger, eagerness for the partition of the estates of the great landlords, a longing to secure fuller civic rights, were the causes of the revolutionary upheavals among the peasantry in the years 1905 and 1906.

Influenced by financial and economic considerations, and alarmed by the aforesaid disturbances among the peasantry, Stolypin inaugurated a number of agrarian reforms. Though these did not appease the land hunger of the peasants or give

[1] In most Russian areas, the lands assigned to the peasantry when serfdom was abolished in 1861 were not handed over to individual peasants, but to the rural communes. It was the commune which decided which areas of land should be cultivated by individual peasants. The peasant could not leave the commune, or sell his share of land. The commune, moreover, had to provide the large sums of money that were stipulated in the emancipation ukase as payable for the liberation of the serfs.

political rights to the rural population, they certainly stimulated the introduction of a more intensive culture upon the larger peasant farms, and consolidated the economic prosperity of the comparatively well-to-do stratum of the rural population. Stolypin's reforms made it easier for the peasants to rid themselves of feudalist ties, allowed them to transform their share in the communal land into private property, and gave individual peasants the right of selling their share in the communal land and of breaking away from the commune to run their farms independently. Under the ægis of these laws, the peasant banks proceeded to make advances to those peasants who were prepared to make private farms out of land which had belonged to the great landlords.

The result was, to begin with, that the area of land under cultivation was rapidly increased by the farming of new land in southern and south-eastern Russia and in Siberia. During the years 1906–1910, the average increase in the cultivated area throughout the country was 4·8 per cent, and in the period 1911–1915 it was 14 per cent. In northern Caucasia, the increase was 46 per cent, and in Siberia it was 75 per cent.[1] There was also a moderate increase in the harvests (rye, 7·5 per cent; wheat, 11·8 per cent). Furthermore, there was an increase in the produce sent by peasants to the market. Owing to the good prices obtainable in the world market for agricultural produce during this period, agricultural production in Russia paid almost twice as well as before. A considerable advance was made in the transition from more primitive methods of agriculture to the three-field system, and from the three-field system to a rotation of the crops. The peasants' use of agricultural machinery increased fivefold or sixfold between 1908 and 1912; and their use of manures increased fourfold. Thanks to all these circumstances, there was a marked increase in the export of grain, which amounted on the average during the years 1909–1913 to 727·4 millions of poods.

[1] S. Dubroffsky [Stolypin's Reform], 1905; P. Lyashchenko [History of Russian Agriculture], 1927.

Stolypin's reforms hastened the breaking-up of the rural communes. Furthermore, the comparatively well-to-do peasants made extensive use of their right of acquiring land from the great landowners. Of the 72·8 millions of desyatines[1] of land which in the year 1905 were in the hands of the great landlords, by 1913 approximately 5·2 millions of desyatines, comprising 7 per cent, had been taken over by the peasants.[2]

Side by side with the concentration of ownership in the hands of the richer peasants, there went on ever more rapidly a process of social stratification in the countryside. In general, the peasants were proletarianised. The poorer sections of the villagers, those who had neither draught beasts nor agricultural implements, availed themselves of their newly acquired legal right of selling their plots of land. Between 1908 and 1915, 1·2 millions of these small farms had been sold, those who had been the owners going to swell the ranks of the urban proletariat, or hiring themselves out as labourers to the great landowners and the richer peasants.

As previously indicated, it was impossible for Stolypin's reforms to solve the urgent problems of Russian agriculture, but they played the part of a safety valve, deferring the explosion of peasant dissatisfaction.

The ruling classes of Russia did not only keep the peasants in a condition of permanent subserviency and cultural darkness, did not only keep them deprived of all political rights, but also, since the welfare of the gentry was based upon cheap labour and half-servile conditions in the villages, they interfered with the development of the productive forces of agriculture, and imposed insuperable obstacles in the path of the adoption of more advanced methods. Although before the war Russia occupied the first place in the production of grain, Russian agriculture remained extremely primitive, lagging behind all other European countries in respect alike of working methods and profitableness. The steadily increasing export of

[1] 1 desyatine = 2·7 acres.
[2] [Statistical Handbook of the League for Agrarian Reform], 1916.

agricultural produce was only secured at the expense of the partial starvation of the peasants, who lived under the most miserable conditions. From what has been said it will be plain that at the time when the Great War began, Russian agriculture and industry were both on the up grade, but that alike in town and countryside the developing capitalist method of production was coming more and more into conflict with the dominant political regime and with the vestiges of serfdom. The reorganisation of peasant agriculture, the introduction of intensive culture, and the modernisation of industry, could only be effected if the estates of the great landlords were broken up and if the semi-servile dependency of the peasants were done away with. Industry could not strike firm roots unless within the boundaries of Russia—among the peasantry—there should come into existence a numerically large section of effective buyers, and unless the regime of continuous governmental tutelage were done away with.

Finally it was essential that, both in town and countryside, the general population should be granted full legal and political rights. But extensive strikes during the years 1910–1914; and the unrest among the peasantry in the years 1913 and 1914, showed that the development of the country was not proceeding along normal lines.

CHAPTER TWO

RUSSIAN ECONOMICS DURING THE GREAT WAR

1. INDUSTRY

THE war gave rise to extensive changes in all branches of industry. During the first year of the war, owing to the restriction of the market and to the scarcity of labour power (the workers having been for the most part called up for military service), a general limitation of production was essential. But by the time the second year of the war had begun, the needs of national defence made it necessary for a speedy transformation and reorganisation of production, which had to be adapted to the supply of munitions, etc., for war purposes. The State provided industry with abundant financial means, obtained by domestic and foreign loans. Almost the whole of the metal industry was devoted to the production of arms and ammunition, the chemical industry to the production of explosives and poison gases, the textile and leather industries to the production of soldiers' boots, clothing, and equipment generally. But the extant enterprises were not able to cope with the demands of the war Moloch. From 1915 onwards, the army administration, various unions for national defence, societies formed alike in the town and in the countryside, having switched over the already existing machinery of production to war purposes, was now engaged in the creation of new enterprises to supply the purposes of war. Large orders for the production of the necessary machinery were given to the metal industry in Russia and abroad. Great difficulties arose, however, owing to the lack of labour power, and especially of skilled workers. Not until towards the end of 1915 was the system of withdrawing from the front such workers and employees as were needed for munition making and the like, in full force. But even then, owing to the scarcity of highly-skilled workers and the general lack of technical efficiency, the quality of production for war purposes left much to be desired.

In these circumstances it was inevitable that other branches of production than those which were supplying the needs of the army, must suffer greatly, even when their products were essential to the needs of the broad masses of the population. On the other hand, during the war, there came into existence various branches of production which had been unable to flourish before the war owing to incapacity to compete with Germany and Austria-Hungary. Now import from these countries was interrupted, also there was an unsatisfied demand. Hence, during the war, Russia began to undertake the production of explosives and dyes; began to use the by-products obtainable in the manufacture of coke; undertook the making of electrical apparatus, medical instruments, etc., etc. Discussing the effect of the war upon Russian industry, Professor Grinevetsky, Professor S. Prokopovich, and others, declare that the production of tools, delicate instruments, and, of course, arms and ammunition, received an immense impetus in Russia. On the other hand, there was a great falling-off in the building of locomotives (about 50 per cent), the building of railway carriages and trucks (about 40 per cent), and, especially the production of agricultural machinery and tools (from 92 to 95 per cent).

A study of the development of Russian industry during the war, shows that the fixed capital of industry—above all, machinery, motor appliances, and equipment—underwent a very great increase. Estimated in gold, the total monetary value of the products also increased; but whereas there was an enormous increase in the production of munitions, there was a corresponding decline in the production of other necessaries. V. Groman, one of the most noted experts in the State Planning Commission of the U.S.S.R., estimates that the total industrial production within the area now comprising the Soviet Union, increased from 7·7 milliards of roubles in 1913 to 8·4 milliards of roubles in 1916.[1]

The concentration and trustification of industry, which had

[1] V. Groman [The Economics of the U.S.S.R.], 1927, p. 47.

already begun in the eighteen-nineties, continued more and more rapidly as foreign capital flowed into the country. At the same time, the subordination of industry to financial capital advanced with rapid strides during the war.

Coalmining, the petroleum industry, the extraction of ores, and smelting likewise, suffered most grievously as an outcome of the general disorganisation of industry caused by the war. The scarcity of fuel was especially disastrous to industry. The provision of timber for fuel ceased almost entirely, and there was a decline (though less considerable) in the supply of coal and petroleum. The import of coal had completely ceased, although the need for fuel had greatly increased both in the navy and in the railway service.

Towards the end of 1916, the disorganising effects of the decline in the production of fuel and metals began to make themselves felt even in those industries which had hitherto been functioning normally, or had been on the up grade. In the towns, moreover, a shortage of fuel for warming purposes and a scarcity of food became serious, accompanied by an increasing inadequacy of the transport system. Numerous enterprises in Petrograd, Moscow, and other industrial centres, had to close down owing to a lack of raw materials and fuel. Scarcity of food and the great rise in prices led to extensive strikes on the part of the workers.

The government made various attempts to deal with the situation by the rationing of fuel, metallic ores, and products generally. A fuel committee, a metals committee, etc., were inaugurated, and State commissaries with extensive powers were appointed. But the tsarist government, having close ties with the leading circles of the industrial bourgeoisie, was unable to undertake energetic measures which would have run counter to the interests of the great industrialists. After the revolution of March 1917, the provisional government undertook to regulate and control industry. Under pressure of the revolutionary organisations, a Chief Economic Committee was appointed, and to this the task of inaugurating a "purposive

c

regulation of economic life" was entrusted. But the Chief Economic Committee had at once to encounter the resistance of the industrial magnates, and pursued a vacillating policy. Consequently it failed to secure the confidence of the revolutionary soviet organisations, and was of little practical importance. Amid the general decomposition, and in an atmosphere of increasing revolutionary tension, it proved unable to regulate the economic life of the country. A greater revolutionary transformation was at hand.

2. AGRICULTURE

The effects of the war upon agriculture were still more momentous. By the end of 1914, about 6,500,000 men had been called up, and by the end of 1917 no less than 15,070,000 men were enrolled in the army. By this time, 36·7 per cent of the active male workers and peasants had been withdrawn from production.[1] Some statisticians tell us that from one-third to one-half of the pre-war labour power had been withdrawn from the countryside. This was a very serious thing for agriculture, and the loss could not be made good by the sending of a few hundred thousand prisoners of war to work on the land. Almost all agricultural operations had to be performed by women, children, and old men. Owing to the militarisation of industry, the production of agricultural machinery had been almost completely arrested. There was hardly any possibility of importing either agricultural machinery or manures. Owing to the ever-increasing demand of the army for horses, the number of these available for agriculture declined from 17·9 millions in 1914 to 12·8 millions in 1917. The result of all this was that by the beginning of 1917 the area of land under cultivation had been reduced by 16·5 per cent. This reduction in the cultivated area was more marked on the estates of the great landlords than on the peasant farms, the latter being more readily adaptable to war conditions owing to the possi-

[1] S. Prokopovich [The War and Economic Life], 1917.

bility of setting all members of a peasant family to work in the fields. Still, because of the scarcity of labour power, farm beasts, and manures, and because of the difficulty of replacing worn-out tools and machinery, there was a great falling-off in the yield from the land. During the last five years before the war, from 1909 to 1913, the average amount of grain produced annually was reckoned at 4642 millions of poods. A decline set in in 1914, and by 1917 the production was only 3987 millions of poods.

Obviously the cessation of the export of grain during the war, leaving as it did about 700 millions of poods of previously exported grain available for home consumption, must have mitigated the scarcity of foodstuffs in Russia. Nevertheless, by 1916 there was already manifest a great shortage of grain in the towns. The failure of industry to supply the tools, etc., needed by the peasants, had deprived these of the necessary stimulus to the sale of grain and other agricultural produce. The food crisis was intensified by the increasing disorganisation of the transport system. Towards the end of 1915, the needs of the army, the towns, and the rural areas producing an insufficiency of grain, compelled the Government to purchase grain in large quantities, to fix the price of this staple, and to adopt other war measures.

Immediately after the March revolution, the scarcity of food in the towns became yet more marked, and by the decree of March 25, 1917, the provisional government established a State monopoly for the sale of grain. To begin with, this measure, in conjunction with the State fixing of prices and with rationing, gave good results. Ere long, however, the general decay of industry, commerce, transport, and the governmental apparatus, had assumed such catastrophic proportions that the coalition government was no longer able to cope with the increasing hunger of the towns. The war and the economic collapse— these were the main factors of dissatisfaction among the broad masses of the workers and the peasants; and these were the pre-requisites to the success of the November revolution.

CHAPTER THREE

RUSSIAN ECONOMICS DURING THE PERIOD OF "WAR COMMUNISM", 1918–1920

DURING the years 1918–1920, the economic life of Russia was in a condition of decay and decomposition. The civil war, the economic blockade, foreign intervention, and the communist attempts to effect immediate socialisation (nationalisation and communalisation), disrupted the Russian economic system. Immediately after seizing power, the communists declared all the land, all the factories and workshops, all the enterprises, all the houses in the country, to be nationalised. All the banks were done away with; the money and securities in the banks, all the goods in storehouses, etc., were declared State property. Wherever they encountered resistance, whether passive or active, the communists destroyed the State apparatus, which had already in great measure been democratised by the March revolution; they broke up the extant systems of urban and rural self-government, made an end of the private trading and industrial enterprises, the cooperatives, all pre-existent social organisation. The entire administration and management of the multiform life of the population was handed over to the local soviets. Money was no longer a legal instrument of exchange. Work was declared to be every one's duty. "He who will not work, neither shall he eat." Almost the whole of the population became State workers and State employees. The State undertook to supply the population gratuitously with food, clothing, and shelter; to satisfy every one's needs in the matter of books, newspapers, hospitals, schools, and theatres.

Almost at once, however, it became apparent that this "leap into the realm of freedom" was a leap into savagery. Industrial production sank to nil owing to the lack of raw materials and fuel, the absence of technical and managerial experts, and owing to the replacement of wages by a starvation allowance of food. On the average, industrial production sank to 17 per cent of the peace level, and in some instances even as low as from 1 to 2 per cent.[1] The peasant, receiving nothing from the town, refused to supply the town with grain and other agricultural produce. When the State tried to secure the products of the peasant's labour by force, sending special "food sections" into the countryside for this purpose, the peasant rejoined, here and there by risings, and everywhere by restricting the area under cultivation, by a limitation of cattle breeding and dairy farming. Agricultural production was reduced to 40 per cent by the year 1921. The disorganisation of the transport system was intensified by the spontaneous demobilisation of the huge army, and, amid the general disorder, the inefficiency of the transport administration made matters very much worse. The supply of coal, wood for fuel, and food, was almost at a standstill. The trams ceased to run; the droshkys disappeared; in most of the towns the waterworks, the drainage system, the electrical power stations, and the gasworks ceased to function. Houses, with no one to look after them properly, and not even kept warm, began to fall into ruin. The communists declared that they were establishing "a new and unprecedented structure of working community".[2] They tried to set the world the example of a complete nationalisation of all social activities. The population was to receive, not only food, but all articles of consumption, at special depots, through the working of a system of food cards, etc. But despite the utopian endeavours to regulate the entire consumption of the community, and to distribute all kinds of commodities monopolistically by the working of its own apparatus, the State was incompetent to deal even with the distribution of bread. The State apparatus, hastily improvised and prematurely centralised, managed by inexperienced officials, was absolutely incapable of organising a rationed supply of perishable goods and seasonal products. Thus it came to pass that millions of poods of frozen potatoes were destroyed; huge consignments of horseflesh, fish, etc.,

[1] V. Groman [The Economics of the U.S.S.R.], 1927, p. 10.
[2] "Krasnaya Moskva", 1919.

went bad. Butter, milk, eggs, flour, etc., could only be obtained in exceptional cases on medical prescription. The exits from the towns were watched by officials who were instructed to impound any foodstuffs that were brought in by private individuals, even were it only for personal consumption. During this period an illicit trade in foodstuffs, carried on in secret markets, assumed gigantic proportions. A great deal of food was smuggled into the towns, and the townsfolk made excursions into the country in search of the necessaries of life.

In addition to supplies of bread, and in many cases also peas, salt, sugar, and coffee, which were obtainable by the holders of food cards, the whole population was given a mid-day meal gratuitously at public eating-houses. This dinner was unsavoury, unappetising, for it had the stamp of the factory upon it. Those persons, however, who had secret sources of wealth were able to supplement the public allowances by the purchase of food in the secret markets, or by dining in secret restaurants. The State distributive organisations had a cumbrous apparatus, which in most instances was diverted from its purpose, and sold considerable quantities of food to private dealers. Even the communist supervisors were not proof against this temptation. The State declared war against such defalcations. Prosecution followed prosecution, and those found guilty were shot, but it was all in vain. The theft of public property was a daily occurrence. Nor had the Soviet authorities any better success in the purposive distribution of other articles of general need, or of raw materials and half-manufactured goods. The distribution of all these articles was centralised. A utilisation committee was appointed, to register and distribute all commodities. A complicated system of "class cards" came into existence.

Nevertheless the extent of the available supplies was not known to the Soviet authorities—could not possibly be known, for during the headlong process of communalisation all the warehouses had been closed and sealed without taking stock of their contents. As late as the year 1923, a considerable time

after the introduction of the New Economic Policy, forgotten
storehouses containing extensive supplies were "discovered".
Since, under war communism, the production of new commodities had almost entirely ceased, the Soviet government (fearing
an absolute famine of wares) was extremely penurious in the
distribution of industrial products. Clothing, boots and shoes,
cutlery, etc., were supplied only on production of special
certificates, which were granted in exceptional instances alone.
By way of public distribution in Moscow, during three years,
one-third of the population was supplied with 7 arshins[1] of
textiles per head, while the remaining two-thirds got nothing.
At the same time these articles were distributed in other ways,
much less thriftily. On the principle of "you scratch my back,
and I'll scratch yours", costly furs, sets of furniture, carpets,
china, English cloth, and lace-trimmed underclothing, were
"distributed". This was the first little correction of the system
of "class distribution". The second correction was undertaken
by the employees in charge of the distribution centres and the
storehouses. Despite the strictest supervision, they sent articles
by the hundred-thousand to the illegal "underground"
speculative market.

As a result of cold, hunger, and insanitary conditions generally, unprecedentedly severe epidemics of typhus and cholera
raged throughout the country; scurvy became common, and
tubercular diseases grew more frequent. The hospitals were
practically out of commission, and medicaments were almost
unobtainable. The rate of mortality, especially child mortality,
increased alarmingly. In Odessa, Kiev, Petrograd, and Samara,
the annual death rate among children was more than 70 per
thousand. The schools were closed, and the town population
dwindled. Every one who could, took refuge in the country,
where there was a better chance of avoiding death from
starvation.

Disturbances among the peasantry, strikes among the urban
operatives, and finally the revolt in the navy at Kronstadt,

[1] 1 arshin = (approximately) 28 inches, or a little more than ¾ yard.

compelled the Soviet government, in the year 1921, to admit
that the policy of an immediate introduction of communism
had failed. Hastily the authorities abandoned the attempt to
expropriate the peasants' corn by force (the so-called food
levies), permitted free trade within the country, allowed private
capital to be used for the promotion of small-scale industry, and
admitted private capital to large-scale industry also upon a
concessionary basis. Certain rights were granted to domestic
industry. The system of completely expropriating private
property was abandoned, and so was the idea of managing
enterprise by workers' committees. Payment for national and
municipal services, for school attendance, and for medical aid,
was reintroduced. The exchanges and the banks were reopened,
taxation was once more inaugurated, and so on. But as "strongholds of communism", the nationalisation of the greater part
of industry, of the railway service, and of navigation, was
retained, together with the nationalisation of large-scale trade
in the homeland, and also the State monopoly of foreign
commerce. In exceptional instances, the local soviets were
granted permission to hand over small-scale enterprises to their
former owners. These concessions of the Nep[1] released the
hidden forces of the economic organism. The reconstruction
of agriculture, industry, and municipal activities began.

Some of the Soviet economists (Strumilin, Krumin, Sarabyanoff, and Eichenvald) have endeavoured to justify the policy
of war communism as "a necessary policy of self-protection
in the period of intervention and civil war". Such attempts
conflict with historical fact, for the program of the immediate
realisation of communism, the program which the Soviet
authorities put in force as soon as they assumed power, was
announced by the representatives of the Communist Party at
the sittings of the Petrograd and Moscow soviets before the
revolution of November 1917—that is to say, before the civil
war and before any foreign intervention. Indeed, the whole

[1] The word Nep is composed of the initials of the words "New Economic
Policy" (same words and same initials in Russian as in English).

political literature of the communists during these days, including Buharin's *A B C of Communism*, is filled with the belief that by means of the methods of war communism the proletariat would be able to establish its dictatorship and to upbuild socialism in Russia.

No less false is the contention of the communists that the disastrous but inevitable policy of war communism was replaced by the Nep immediately after the end of the war. The peace treaties with Latvia and Lithuania were signed in July 1920, and the treaty with Finland in October of the same year. The civil war in Siberia was finished by October 1920; the fight against Wrangel, Petlyura, Bulak-Bulahovich, and Mahno, in southern Russia, likewise came to an end in November 1920. In fact, by the end of November 1920 there was peace throughout the country. Nevertheless the policy of "forcibly expropriating the peasants' grain" was continued down to April 1921, and the "hundred-per-cent liquidation of capitalism" went on as late as August 1921. Nay more, shortly after the end of the civil war, the following decrees were issued: the decree for the complete nationalisation of all industries, including small-scale enterprise, under date November 30, 1920;[1] the decree that the levying of taxes was to cease, because "money no longer functioned as a means of payment", under date February 3, 1921. In December 1920, on the eve of the announcement of the Nep, the Eighth Soviet Congress passed the most utopian of all the resolutions of the days of war communism, the resolution concerning the socialisation of peasant agriculture. Special committees were appointed to prescribe the scope and the kinds of cultivation to be practised on every one of the twenty millions of peasant farms. "Peasant farming must be conducted in accordance with a unified plan and under a unified management", said this resolution. The transition to the new economic policy was not taken until March 1921, when the

[1] According to this decree, all enterprises without mechanical power employing more than 10 workers, and all those with mechanical power employing more than 5 workers, were to be nationalised.

revolts among the peasants and the dissatisfaction among the town workers had attained a climax, and even the communist leaders had become convinced that their rule would collapse unless they changed their policy. The dates are on record for every one to read. In the end of February 1921, there were extensive strikes and other disturbances among the workers of Petrograd. The Kronstadt rising began early in March. On March 16, 1921, at a congress of the Communist Party, it was decided to abolish the corn levies, and this decision was announced on March 21st by the All-Russian Central Executive Committee of the Soviets.

The attempt to organise Russian economic life upon the basis of war communism was described by Lenin in the following terms: "We made the mistake of deciding upon an immediate transition to communist production and distribution. . . . We counted (or, to speak more accurately, we assumed without counting) upon our ability to organise a system of nationalised production and nationalised distribution communistically in a petty-bourgeois country by means of a direct command on the part of the proletarian State. Life has shown us our mistake. . . . In the spring of 1921, on the economic front, our attempt at the transition to communism sustained a defeat more serious than ever before."[1]

In actual fact, the transition to the Nep was a defeat of the communists; it was not a voluntary change of policy at the close of the civil war.

The resolution of the Tenth Congress of the Communist Party of Russia to replace the corn levy by a tax in kind, a resolution adopted on March 21, 1921, may be regarded as the beginning of the "New Economic Policy". This resolution is in flat contradiction with the principles of communist policy during the previous four years. The corn levy implied, as Lenin phrased the matter, "a situation in which every pood of grain over and above what was indispensable to the peasant farmer for the maintenance of himself and his family and his farm

[1] Lenin [Collected Works], Vol. XVIII, pp. 369–373.

stock, together with what was needed for sowing—every super-fluous pood of grain must be taken over by the State".[1] The resolution of the Communist Party of Russia abolished the corn levy, replaced it by a tax in kind, and decided that "all the supplies of food, fodder, and raw materials remaining in the hands of the peasant farmers after the payment of the tax are to be at the peasants' full disposal, and can be applied by them to the improvement and consolidation of their farming industry, to the increase of their individual consumption, or may be exchanged for products of factory industry and domestic industry, and utilised for agricultural production". It is a matter of historical interest to note that this breach with the old ideology of the communists was not easily effected. The resolution of the Tenth Party Congress, full of internal contra-dictions, did not yet permit freedom of trade, but only "the exchange of goods within the limits of the local market". These timid reservations were soon over-ruled by the progress of events. On October 4, 1921, a decree was issued permitting the State enterprises to sell goods "in the free market"; and this was followed on October 27th by a decree allowing the free sale of the products of the State enterprises working to supply the general needs of the population. By degrees, the "freedom of trading in the local market", and the legally per-mitted "exchange of commodities", developed into a freedom of trade throughout the country, which was only interrupted here and there and from time to time by relapses into the methods of war communism (closing of markets and seizure of goods) on the part of this or that State department which had not yet accommodated itself to all the principles of the new policy.

The introduction of the Nep was a complicated and tedious business. Throughout the remainder of the year 1921 and the early months of 1922 there was going on a transformation of the whole economic system upon the basis of an endeavour to reconcile the continued occupation of the "strongholds of com-munism" with the increasing development of private enterprise.

[1] Lenin [Collected Works], Vol. XV, p. 332.

CHAPTER FOUR

PRESENT CONDITION OF RUSSIAN INDUSTRY

WHEREAS in the industrial countries of western Europe industry
outbalances agriculture, in Russia industry occupies a subordinate place, in respect both of the amount of products and of the
number of persons engaged in it. Of the 82·7 millions of the
working population of the U.S.S.R. during the economic year
1926–1927,[1] only 2·8 millions were operatives and employees in
manufacturing industry and mining, 1·3 millions in transport,
300,000 in the building industry, and 1·9 millions in domestic
industry and minor manual occupations. In agriculture, on the
other hand, 71·7 millions were engaged. Thus in large-scale
industry there were occupied 3·38 per cent of the working
population, and in agriculture 86·72 per cent.[2] We have to
remember, however, that a considerable proportion of the
industrial operatives and transport workers and most of the
domestic workers remain in touch with agriculture, and take
part from time to time in agricultural production.

Of the total production in Russia during the economic
year 1926–1927, 38 per cent is accounted for by large-scale
and small-scale industry, and 62 per cent by agriculture.
Nevertheless, the importance of industry is very great. This is
explicable, in part by the fact that the technical level of Russian
industry stands far higher than that of Russian agriculture; but
in part also by the fact that, since the beginnings of capitalist
evolution in Russia, industry has taken the lead in the development of the productive forces of the country, setting the time
and prescribing the forms for agricultural advance.

Besides, the figures of gross production fail to give us an
accurate idea of the respective parts played by industry and
agriculture in the national turnover of goods. Whereas the

[1] The Russian economic year extends from October 1st to September 30th.
[2] From the census of December 1926, "Statisticheskoye Obozreniye",
the organ of the Central Statistical Bureau, 1928, No. 5.

whole of the product of industry finds its way to the market, a considerable proportion of the product of agriculture is consumed by the agricultural producers directly, and does not get into the market at all. Of the total quantities of goods reaching the market, there belonged to large-scale and small-scale industry in the year 1913, 60·9 per cent, and to agriculture in the same year 39·1 per cent; in the year 1926–1927, the respective figures were 59·1 for industry, and 40·9 for agriculture. We see that, alike before the war and to-day, industry sends more goods to the market than agriculture. Down to the beginning of the last decade of the nineteenth century, Russia was a predominantly agricultural country, and one in which industry was poorly developed. By the time of the outbreak of the war, it had already become an industrial as well as an agricultural country, and we have learned in the first chapter that the increase in the share taken by industry was an extremely rapid one.

The Great War, the revolution, the civil war, and forcible nationalisation, combined to disorganise the industry of the Soviet Union so thoroughly, that at the beginning of the period of the Nep it had been almost completely destroyed. We have official figures to demonstrate this[1]:

Year.	Gross Production (Pre-War Prices).		Number of Workers.	
	Roubles.	Percentages as compared with 1913.	Absolute.	Percentages as compared with 1913.
1913	5,621,000,000	100	2,518,000	100
1916	6,831,000,000	121	2,926,000	113
1917	4,344,000,000	77	3,024,000	116
1920/21	981,000,000	17	1,480,000	57

In some of the branches of industry, production had been almost completely arrested. The smelting of copper had fallen

[1] [Jubilee Symposium of the Central Statistical Bureau], p. 168; data published by the State Planning Commission in "Planovoye Hozyaistvo", 1925, No. 6.

to 0·001 per cent, the mining of ores to 1·7 per cent, the production of cast iron to 2·4 per cent, the production of building materials to from 2 to 3 per cent, and so on.

The railway system was in a still more serious condition. There is good reason for saying that no other department of Russian economic life had suffered so severely from the effects of the war, and especially of the civil war. Overcrowding of the trains, lack of fuel, the badness of the quality of such fuel as there was, the putting-off of repairs to the rolling stock—all these things had gone almost beyond the bounds of the possible. The tracks were in a terrible condition. During the civil war more than 20,000 kilometres of track, 4500 railway bridges, 3000 points, 380 railway works, 176,000 kilometres of telegraph and telephone wires, 5000 railway buildings, and many thousands of hydrants and other technical appliances, had been destroyed or injured.[1] In the year 1920, a complete collapse of the railway system was already imminent. At the Congress of Economic Soviets in the year 1920, Professor Lomonosoff made a report upon the condition of the transport system, declaring it to be inevitable that the railway service would cease to function in the summer of 1920. A break-down in this department was only prevented by the introduction of the Nep. The reconstruction of industry did not advance in equal measure in all branches. Small-scale and domestic industry recovered more rapidly than large-scale industry. As far as the latter was concerned, more progress was made in the production of articles for general consumption than in the production of the means of production. A renewed impetus for small-scale industry and domestic industry was possible without any extensive supply of capital or of raw materials, fuel, and the necessaries of life; and it was to a great extent independent of a restoration of the integrity of the transport system and of the only now commencing reorganisation of large-scale industry. In this department, by the beginning of the second year of the Nep, production had already been

[1] [Statistics of the Means of Transport], 1921, p. 42.

increased by 30 per cent, and the share of small-scale industry and domestic industry in the total industrial production had risen to 40 per cent. By 1924–1925, when large-scale industry had forged ahead once more, the share of small-scale and domestic industry in the total production had fallen to 20 per cent; and by the year 1927–1928, to 15 per cent, this being the pre-war level.

Nearly 75 per cent of the production of handicraftsmen and of domestic workers is in private hands. Of the total production of small-scale industry, handicraft, and domestic industry, amounting in the year 1927–1928 to 1312 millions of roubles (estimated in pre-war prices), 2·1 per cent was produced by State enterprises, 24·1 per cent by cooperative enterprises, and 73·8 per cent by private enterprises. The policy of the Soviet government towards handicraft and small-scale industry is contradictory. The need for increasing industrial production compels the State to foster the development of small-scale industry and domestic industry to some extent. This is all the more necessary, seeing that in many regions the peasants derive as much as 20 per cent of their income from domestic industry; and also because the products of domestic industry and handicraft are very cheap. Furthermore, small-scale industry trains skilled workers for manufacturing industry in general. On the other hand, the Soviet government, being opposed on principle to the development of private enterprise, puts legal obstacles in the path of domestic workers and private handicraftsmen. The difficulty of obtaining a licence to practise a handicraft, high taxes, niggardliness in the supply of raw materials and half-manufactured goods, the classing with the kulaks of those peasants who practise a handicraft, the compulsory enrolment of handicraftsmen in cooperatives—all these things make the position of small-scale industry and domestic industry in contemporary Russia an extremely complicated one.[1] That is why, in many regions, the domestic

[1] Report of the Supreme Economic Council concerning the position of small-scale industry and domestic industry in "Ekonomicheskaya Zhizn", February 24, 1927.

industry of the peasants has not yet regained the pre-war level.

The reestablishment of large-scale and medium-scale industry grew proportionally with the growth of the demands of the market for industrial products. According to the reports of the Central Statistical Bureau, 98 per cent of the whole of what in Soviet Russia is called "census industry"[1] remains nationalised, that is to say under the direct control of the State.

The speediest recovery took place in "light" industry, that is to say in the production of textiles, boots and shoes, food-stuffs, matches, tobacco, and other products for general consumption. The supply of fuel was likewise set in order very quickly, since all the branches of industry and also the railway service were in crying need of coal, peat, and petroleum.

Much slower was the restoration of machine-building, for during the first years of the Nep the need for new machinery and industrial plant was very small. Even slower, for like reasons, was the recovery of ore-mining, smelting, and the metal industry generally.

Towards the end of the year 1924–1925, the cotton industry had recovered 67 per cent of the pre-war power of production; the woollen industry, 69 per cent; the matchmaking industry, 85 per cent; the salt industry, 68 per cent; the cigarette making industry, 96·7 per cent; the extraction of petroleum, 76·1 per cent; the extraction of coal, 55·4 per cent; machine-making, 43 per cent; the production of cast iron, 30·3 per cent; the production of steel, 44 per cent; the production of iron, 39·6 per cent; and the extraction of ores, 23·1 per cent. But as economic life in general revived, there was an increasing demand for metals and metallic products generally. This was already manifest in the year 1924–1925. Since then, there has been rapid progress towards the pre-war level in smelting,

[1] By "census industry" is meant enterprises that do not use mechanical power, provided they employ more than 30 workers, and enterprises with mechanical power, provided they employ more than 15 workers. The undertakings belonging to this group must furnish reports of their activities to the proper authorities.

machine construction, the electro-technical industry, and the production of building materials. The extraction of ore is likewise on the up grade, though here recovery has been slower.

The increase in the production of the means of production (group A) is now overtaking the development of the production of the means of consumption (group B). In the year 1925–1926, group A had increased by 42·6 per cent in comparison with the previous year, and group B by 41·9 per cent; in the year 1926–1927 the advance on the previous year was 24·5 per cent in the case of group A, and 13·8 per cent in the case of group B; in the year 1927–1928, the advance was 17·3 per cent in the case of group A, and 14·6 per cent in the case of group B.[1]

At the end of the first decade of Soviet rule, industrial production had in general regained the pre-war level, but not uniformly, for in some branches of industry the pre-war level had been excelled, while in other branches production still lagged behind the level of 1913. The following table shows the extent of the reconstruction of the various branches of industry as compared with 1913:

INDUSTRIAL PRODUCTION IN THE YEAR 1927–1928.

Branch of Industry.		Absolute Production.	Percentages as compared with 1913.
Coalmining	(Tons)	37,100,000	128·4
Petroleum	,,	10,130,000	110·6
Production of Iron Ores	,,	6,129,000	66·5
Cast Iron	,,	2,990,000	85·2
Martin Steel	,,	3,460,000	82·3
Rolling-Mill Products	,,	3,830,000	90·8
Cotton Goods	(Thousand Metres)	2,740,000	94·5
Woollen Goods	,, ,,	854,000	120·0
Sugar	(Tons)	1,593,000	69·0
Salt	,,	2,223,000	114·2

In the year 1927–1928, the value of the total production of "census industry" was 10,987 millions of chervonets roubles, of

[1] [Economic Reports] for 1927–1928, p. 499.

D

which 98·55 per cent had been produced in State enterprises, 0·81 per cent in private enterprises, and 0·64 per cent in concessionary enterprises.[1]

During the first years of the Nep, the managers of Soviet industry had a very difficult task to perform in restoring the balance between the various branches of industry. Elaborative industry suffered from the scarcity of half-manufactured goods. There was a scarcity of metal for machine-building enterprises. The textile industries could not get a sufficiency of raw wool and raw cotton. On the other hand, those industries which were not working to produce articles of general consumption had no demand for their products. Furthermore, the whole body of industry was gravely affected by the slowness with which the railway system was set in order. The locomotive-making works and the shipbuilding establishments were either idle, or, if they worked, they had no certainty of being able to get rid of their products. The managers of industrial enterprises did not know who their consumers would be or where their markets were to be found. All ordinary business ties had been broken. Years of complicated labour were required before the various branches of production could be brought into new harmonious relations. Not until a long time had elapsed could the lack of due proportion between the various departments of economic life be overcome.

No less complicated was the task of reorganising production within the individual enterprises, where the essential foundations of production had crumbled.

During the first two years of the Nep, the whole of Russian industry suffered acutely from the scarcity of fuel. The first use the State made of such capital as was available was to invest it in the production of fuel, to reorganise the technique of the extraction of petroleum and coal. Also, the State provision of timber for fuel and of peat was increased, and private producers were allowed to engage in these branches of industry.

[1] [Economic Reports] for 1927–1928, and "Finansy i Narodnoye Hozyaistvo", 1928, No. 32.

The upshot was that by 1924 the supply of fuel to industry was working normally, and there was no return of a fuel crisis until 1928. In that year, however, owing to the exhaustion of the old "reserves" in the coal mines and owing to the increasing export of petroleum, there was a renewed scarcity of fuel.

There has been much more difficulty about the supply of raw materials. A series of poor harvests, and the great decline (as compared with pre-war days) in the amount of agricultural produce finding its way to the market, have induced a permanent scarcity of raw materials. The U.S.S.R. is producing less than half of the cotton that was produced in pre-war days, and has every year to spend many millions of roubles in purchasing cotton abroad. There has also been a great decline in the crop of flax, and since, for the sake of the balance of trade, flax is exported in considerable quantities, the linen manufacturers suffer from a lack of raw material. During the years 1925–1926 and 1926–1927 for one month each, and during the year 1927–1928 for three months, the linen manufactories had to shut down. Wool has to be imported. Vegetable oil factories and soap factories are continually short of raw materials. The tanneries are not supplied with a sufficiency of the coarser kinds of hide. Owing to the scarcity of ores, whose extraction has not been restored to the old level, the metal works, the machine-building industry, and the railway repairing shops are continually in difficulties. The demand for building materials, such as tiles, cement, lime, timber, corrugated iron, etc., has greatly increased, owing to the widespread need for new houses and factory buildings and for the repair of the old ones. As a result of this, during the last few years the scarcity of building materials has been extremely acute.

A no less grave difficulty for Soviet industry was the scarcity of labour power. During the first years of the Nep, this scarcity was mainly due to the fact that a considerable proportion of the extant industrial workers had fled to the country in order to escape famine in the towns. The gradual reestablishment of industry has attracted them back to the urban centres, but there are not enough skilled workers to go round. Since 1924, in various branches of industry there has been a grievous lack of skilled labour power, side by side with increasingly widespread unemployment among unskilled workers.

During the first years of the Nep, the cost of industrial production was extraordinarily high. The enterprises were, for the most part, working only up to 20 or 30 per cent of their full productive power. The proportional expenditure upon fuel and raw materials was from twice to five times as great as usual, and the works were often idle for long periods at a time. In some factories, suspensions of work were an almost daily occurrence. The managerial staffs were unnecessarily large, and the costs of production were raised to a monstrous height in this way, and by the difficulty of disposing of the products. Thus running expenses were proportionally twice or thrice as large as in pre-war days.[1]

An extension of the scale of production, the carrying-out of the most essential repairs, a better managerial organisation, the regularisation of the supply of fuel and raw materials, an increase in the productivity of labour, cooperated, in the years 1923–1924 and 1924–1925, to reduce the cost of production, in the first-named year by 30 per cent, and in the second by 13·3 per cent. In the year 1925–1926, however, an increase in the price of raw materials, a rise in the charge for freight on the railways, the making of larger allowances for depreciation, and the rise in wages, led to an increase in the cost of production by from 2 to 3 per cent. During the following year, 1926–1927, there was a renewed lessening of the cost of production (by 1·8 per cent), but this was achieved mainly at the expense of wages and thanks to a decline in the price of raw materials and in the expenditure upon the marketing of products and upon administration; it did not result from the improving or cheapening of the technique of production. During the year 1927–1928, there has in several branches of industry been a fresh rise in

[1] S. Molchanoff [Costs of Production in the Industry of the U.S.S.R.], 1926, pp. 17 et seq.

the costs of production. The reason why these are still so high is no longer that the full productive capacity of the enterprises cannot be utilised. The trouble now is that production has to be carried on by enterprises with antiquated and worn machinery, so that there are frequent break-downs; there is still a scarcity of raw materials; the newly engaged workers lack skill; and there are manifold defects of management and organisation.

At the close of the year 1920, there were under the management of the central and local authorities (the Supreme Economic Council, the various industrial boards, and the local organs of the Supreme Economic Council) 37,000 enterprises. Each branch of industry was managed by a special board. The individual enterprises had no kind of independence, being under the orders both of the industrial board and of the local authorities. The transition to the Nep demanded a radical change in the organisation and management of nationalised industry.

The process of reorganisation began in 1921 and lasted until the middle of 1924. The management of nationalised industry has now been centralised, and is vested in the economic councils of the U.S.S.R., the various republics of the Union, and the different provinces. Groups of enterprises are combined in trusts, covering areas of varying sizes, some being comparatively local, others covering the territory of whole republics, or even the entire U.S.S.R. The smallest trusts are under the control of the provincial economic councils; those whose domain is a whole republic are managed by the supreme economic council of that republic; and the trusts whose operations cover the whole of the U.S.S.R. are managed by its Supreme Economic Council. These nation-wide trusts embrace all the enterprises which are of great economic or military importance. Most of the trusts are combinations of the enterprises in one branch of industry (such as the metal industry, the leather industry, the printing industry, etc.), including various accessory enterprises. But there are also "vertical" trusts, the so-called "industrial combines", in which enterprises of various kinds are amalgamated for the purposes of some particular production—the enterprises that provide the raw materials working hand in hand with those that provide half-manufactured goods, finished articles, and by-products, respectively. Vertical trusts of this order are the Chemical Combine, the Foodstuffs Combine, etc. In some of the lesser industrial centres, enterprises of the most diversified kinds, whose only common tie is one of locality, are assembled in trusts.

In the year 1925, there were in the U.S.S.R. 819 trusts, enrolling 2915 factories, workshops, and mines, and employing 1,470,852 workers. Of these trusts, 584 have only a local importance, 162 are trusts extending throughout the territory of individual republics, and 73 are nation-wide. Most of the trusts are combinations of comparatively small enterprises, many of whose workers are no more than handicraftsmen. Such organisations are not trusts in any sense comparable with the western European and American use of the term.

If we classify the trusts in groups according to the number of workers employed, we get the following figures for the year 1925:

	Number of Trusts.	Number of Workers.
Trusts employing—		
more than 30,000	6	349,588
from 20,000 to 30,000	8	193,818
from 10,000 to 20,000	17	237,846
from 3000 to 10,000	29	206,974
from 1000 to 5000	110	245,455
less than 1000	649	237,171
Total	819	1,470,852

Since 1925 there have not been extensive changes in the

number of trusts or in the scope of their operations. According to the official reports for the year 1927, 66 per cent of all the Russian trusts are organisations employing no more than 200 workers each, and only 8·6 per cent of the trusts employ more than 3000 workers each.

According to the most important of the decrees concerning the trusts (those of October 10, 1923, May 7, 1924, and May 14, 1924), a State trust has, legally considered, the rights of an individual, and constitutes a unified enterprise to which several subordinate units of production belong. The management of the trust has control of its property, but cannot alienate or pledge its capital without the approval of the Supreme Economic Council. Individual enterprises are managed by directors appointed by the trust. Their independence is limited as follows. The trust management controls production; it decides as to the purchase of the chief means of production and raw materials; it comes to terms with the trade unions as to wages and working conditions; and it decides as to the turnover of goods within the trust. The management is also responsible for the financing of the enterprise. But in all matters which concern a change in the capital of the undertaking, the building of new factories, the technical reorganisation of extant enterprises, the purchase of machinery and raw materials abroad, the formulation of plans of production, the provision of credit, etc.—the management of the trust is subject to the direction of the appropriate economic council, that of the U.S.S.R. of the republic, or the province, as the case may be.

The trusts work "upon a basis of commercial calculation, with a profit-making aim". Such is the wording of a decree of the All-Russian Central Executive Committee concerning the activity of the trusts. In 1927 it was declared that this formulation was not adequate to the needs of Soviet industry, and the trust legislation is being revised.

The profits made by the trusts are distributed as follows:

75 per cent go to the Supreme Economic Council; 20 per cent are placed in a reserve fund; and 5 per cent contribute to form a fund for the improvement of the condition of the workers and employees. Any losses made by the trusts are covered by State subsidies.

CHAPTER FIVE

INDUSTRIALISATION AND THE PROBLEM OF THE ACCUMULATION OF CAPITAL

THE utmost possible development of industry, and an increase in the share taken by industry in the economic life of the country, seemed to the Soviet government to be its main task.

According to official reports, the production of the nationalised industries had, on the average, reached the pre-war condition by the beginning of the year 1927–1928, that is to say at the opening of the second decade of the existence of the Soviet State. It must be said that there are serious grounds for doubting the accuracy of these reports. Above all, it is obvious that the values of the production of 1913, with which latter-day production is being compared, have been underestimated, for in pre-war days no comprehensive statistical statement of production as a whole in roubles was issued, and the value of the total production has to be calculated from a study of the reports issued by the individual branches of industry, and in accordance with the old lists of prices. The Soviet authorities themselves admit that this has been done in an extremely arbitrary fashion.[1] Furthermore, in a great many branches of Russian industry, productive and technical efficiency did not attain their climax until 1915 or 1916. The total production was at least 10 per cent higher in 1916 than it had been in 1913.

[1] Suffice it here to mention that the well-known Soviet economist V. Groman, a member of the Committee of the Central Statistical Bureau of the Soviet Union, in his report to the International Economic Conference of the League of Nations in May 1927, when comparing the level of present-day production in Russia with the pre-war level, declared that "the latest researches of the Central Statistical Bureau have shown that the value of the industrial production of 1913 (the usual year of comparison) has been under-estimated in the comparisons hitherto made to the extent of at least 10 per cent", so that all the percentages intended to represent a comparison between present production and pre-war production ought to be lowered to a corresponding amount.—Cf. V. Groman [The Economics of the U.S.S.R.], 1927, p. 47.

Nevertheless, when we study the economics of Soviet Russia, we shall do so on the basis of the official reports, for it makes no difference to the nature and the complications of the problems with which we are concerned whether present-day production does or does not exceed pre-war production by a few per cent more or less. We shall, then, start from the assumption that ten years after the overthrow of tsarism (an overthrow which was chiefly brought about owing to the restraints existing upon the forces of production and owing to the inadequate satisfaction of demand), the pre-war state of economic development has been regained. What really concerns us is to study the social and economic significance of this fact, which we take for granted.

The pre-war standard of production does not suffice to supply the needs of economic life, or to meet the wants of consumers in general. Indeed, even before the war, the supply of the country with the products of industry was altogether inadequate. The rapid advance in Russian industry that took place during the two decades before the war was due to the expansion of Russian agriculture and to the general increase in the demands of the Russian population.

Even under tsarism, although the forces of production were fettered by the political system which then prevailed, Russia could make headway in the process of industrialisation, and do something to catch up the more advanced industrial countries of Europe. Between 1894 and 1914, the increase in national income was greater in Russia than in Britain, France, or Austria-Hungary.

The overthrow of tsarism, the solution of the agrarian problem, the happy conjuncture of extensive sources of raw materials for industry with a potentially enormous market for industrial products—these were the factors favouring the rapid reconstruction of Russian industry. On the other hand, the military intervention of the foreign powers, the civil war, and the rigid enforcement of a utopian economic policy during the period of the "war communism", brought about an unprecedented collapse of industry, and account for the fact that the restoration of the pre-war standard of production was only effected, after many oscillations, in the beginning of the eleventh year of the Soviet regime.

During the fourteen years of war and revolution, Russia has lagged far behind the other countries of Europe. In respect of economic evolution, the difference between Russia and these countries (to say nothing of the United States) is much greater than it was before. None the less, the need for the products of industry has enormously expanded since the years of revolution and civil war. To heal the wounds resulting from the economic decay of the country, large-scale enterprise, transport, and peasant agriculture all need a huge quantity of industrial products. Besides, the revolution has raised the cultural level of the whole population, therewith raising the standard of life both in town and countryside. The scarcity of industrial products which has been persistent of late years shows that the peace level of industrial production does not suffice to supply the most elementary needs of the population of the Soviet Union. In the general interests of Russian economic life, there ought to be a much more rapid development of industry. But here the problem of industrialisation is intertwined with the necessity for the investment of large quantities of capital in industry.

Official reports show that in the year 1913 the total capital of Russian medium-scale and large-scale industry (leaving the value of the land out of account) was about 6 milliards of roubles, 4·3 milliards of roubles representing fixed capital. During the war, according to the reports of the joint-stock companies, 1256 millions of roubles of new capital were invested in industry, 920 millions being spent upon the provision of buildings, machinery, and plant. Strumilin, a member of the presidium of the State Planning Commission, has had to admit (though the communists in general are inclined to keep the fact to themselves) that, even making allowance for the wastage of capital during the war, and when the amount of fixed capital has been reduced in conformity with the extant area of the U.S.S.R., the productive capacity of Russian industrial enterprises was higher at the beginning of 1918 than in 1913. He estimates the increase at 40 per cent.[1] During the years of "war communism", part of the fixed capital was stolen or destroyed, another part remained unutilised, and the actually functioning portion of the fixed capital in the year 1920 was not more than 15 per cent of the pre-war capital. In the year 1922, after the introduction of the Nep, a reconstruction of industry began spontaneously, but was almost entirely limited to the setting to work of the factories and mines which the State had taken over from the former owners, but which had not previously been incorporated into the industrial process. Not until towards the end of 1927, in many branches of production, were these reserve enterprises in full working order, and it was not till then, therefore, that a further extension of productive capacity by the investment of fresh capital became possible.

But the technical condition of the enterprises which continue at work is no longer that of pre-war days. Most of them are of a venerable age, being already from twenty-five to thirty years old. Thus the trouble is, not merely that they are out of date in respect of technical equipment, but also that they are very much out of repair, seeing that in many of them no serious repair has been possible since 1913. Down to the year 1923, Soviet industry was carried on without any allowance for depreciation.[2] In 1923, indeed, allowances for depreciation began to be made, but without any regard for the wear and tear of the "lost" nine years; and besides, owing to the general scarcity of funds for the carrying on of enterprise, the money

---

[1] S. Strumilin [The Problem of Capital in the U.S.S.R.], in "Planovoye Hozyaistvo", 1925, No. 4.
[2] During the early days of Soviet rule, it was generally believed in communist circles that in nationalised industries no allowance need be made for depreciation, seeing that wear and tear, and the provision of new fixed capital, would be automatically effected under a generalised system of nationalisation. Time has dispelled these illusions.

assigned for depreciation had to be spent to defray current charges. According to the reports of the Supreme Economic Council for the year 1924–1925, during that year only 49·1 per cent of the assignments for depreciation were devoted to making good the results of wear and tear. Not until 1925, when the problem of the renovation of the fixed capital became extraordinarily acute, were there widespread endeavours to repair industrial plants, and to provide new ones. But the work was done in a chaotic and costly fashion. "Such mistakes as we are making in the carrying out of these plans to establish new plants, would be unthinkable in bourgeois countries," writes one of the leaders of industrial construction, the noted communist V. Sverdloff. In the next chapter I shall show in fuller detail how industrial reconstruction is being effected. Enough here to say that a number of investigations made by the Workers' and Peasants' Inspection in 1927–1928 showed that industrial reconstruction was being carried out in the absence of any unified plan, was failing to give the required result, and was costing far too much.

During the year 1924–1925, there was spent upon industrial reconstruction 339·5 millions of roubles; during 1925–1926, the sum was 779 millions of roubles; during 1926–1927, it was 1090 millions of roubles; and during the year 1927–1928, it was 1200 millions of roubles. According to the economic plan for the year 1928–1929, the sum to be invested is 1515 millions of roubles. According to the reports of the Supreme Economic Council, at the beginning of the year 1927–1928 new enterprises had been established or old ones reconstructed at a total cost of 219·3 millions of roubles, with an annual production of 470 millions of roubles. As yet, in the U.S.S.R., no calculations have been made to show whether the expenditure upon the reconstruction of industry and upon the installation of new industries has been a paying proposition. In the Russian economic periodicals, extremely pessimistic views are expressed concerning this matter. The most authoritative economists of the Union, when they estimated the total productive capacity of the fixed capital of Soviet industry after the investments of recent years and allowing for wear and tear, came to the conclusion that the fixed capital of industry at the close of the year 1927 was worth less than the fixed capital of Russian industry before the war.

The Five Year Plan instituted by the Supreme Economic Council[1] provides for the investment in industry during the next five years of 16·2 milliards of roubles,[2] with the proviso that simultaneously a further sum of from 15 to 20 milliards of roubles shall be invested in other economic fields (transport, electrification, housing, agriculture). Machinery and technical plant to the value of several milliards of roubles is also to be imported from abroad, seeing that before the war two-thirds of the technical equipment of Russian enterprises was obtained from foreign countries.

Since the introduction of the Nep, the Soviet government has tried various methods of solving the problem of financing industry. Down to 1923, this was effected by inflation, until the disastrous results of the crumbling of the main pillar of economic life made it necessary for the government to show a little moderation in the use of the note-printing presses. The next idea was to finance industry by charging very high prices for industrial products, but ere long this method too had to be abandoned, for the peasants naturally restricted their purchases more and more, and it was impossible for industry to market its products. Of late years, there has been a combination of

[1] In the year 1926 the Supreme Economic Council for the first time instituted a plan of industrial development for the ensuing five years. At the Fifth Soviet Congress, in June 1929, the sixth economic plan of the State Planning Commission (Gosplan) and the Supreme Economic Council was definitively adopted, and therewith acquired legal validity. According to this law, within five years, that is to say, by the year 1932–1933, the production of Russian industry is to be increased 2·5 times, that of agriculture 2·3 times, the housing fund is to be increased 2·4 times, the productivity of labour is to be doubled, and so on. Fuller details regarding these matters will be found in Chapter Sixteen below, "Purposive Economics and State Regulation".—See also [The Five Year Plan for the Economic Reconstruction of the U.S.S.R.], 1929, Vol. I, p. 152. Published by the Gosplan.
[2] The figures given in the text are in pre-war roubles.

various expedients. In the year 1927–1928, 48 per cent of the means required by industry for new plant and general repairs was obtained out of the actual capital of these industries, that is to say out of the depreciation funds and out of high profits; whilst 52 per cent was supplied in the form of State subsidies derived from taxation and from loans. According to the Five Year Plan recently instituted, the former source is to supply 55 per cent and the latter source 45 per cent of the required funds.

The first draft of the Five Year Plan counted upon an expansion of production to the extent of from 70 to 80 per cent by the year 1931. Later drafts contemplate a still more rapid advance. Whether in the first or in subsequent schemes, these variants of the Five Year Plan are less concerned with actual economic and financial conditions than with a compilation of statistics based upon the assumption that a regular yearly increase in industrial production can be reckoned on. In the latest version of the plan, this is reckoned at 18 per cent.[1]

Since the first draft of the Five Year Plan was elaborated, two years have passed, and the time has been amply long enough to show that the projected scheme for the expansion of industry finds itself in a blind alley. During the pre-war years, as I showed in the opening chapter, there was a notable expansion in Russian industry, the reason being that—despite adverse political influences—there was a rapid advance in general prosperity, so that the purchasing power of the population was growing, to the accompaniment of an increase in savings. Industry was able, through the foundation of joint-stock

[1] One of the few independent Russian economists, the sometime social democrat, V. Bazaroff, criticises the "statistical trend" of the schemes for industrial expansion, and shows that an 18 per cent steady annual increase in industrial production would make that production increase 2·4 times in five years, 5·4 times in ten years, 29·3 times in twenty years, and 160 times in thirty years. "In less than twenty years, our industrial development would have left that of the United States far behind (even if the advance of industry in that country should proceed at its present rate)."—"Ekonomicheskoye Obozreniye", 1928, No. 6.—Bazaroff describes such plans as "superficial industrial expansion", and insists that they have been drawn up regardless of actual financial, economic, technical, and cultural conditions.

enterprises, to draw upon the capital that was accumulating in the country, and, thanks to the increasing market, it could turn this capital to account usefully in production. At the same time, considerable quantities of foreign capital were flowing into industry, commerce, transport, and the banks.

Under existing conditions, in Soviet Russia, the prospects of being able to draw upon the two main financial sources, at home and abroad, are very unfavourable. Very little capital is being accumulated in the homeland, for the peasants, who form the great majority of the population, are recovering but slowly from the consequences of the years of economic decay, while the vacillations of Soviet policy (see below, under Agriculture) deprive them of any stimulus to the expansion of agricultural enterprise. For like reasons, the accumulation of capital on the part of private entrepreneurs in the towns is insignificant. Nor has the Soviet government free access to such scanty means as are accumulated, for people are afraid to show themselves to be well off. Those who can put any money by, will not deposit it in the savings bank or lend it to the authorities, but either hoard it secretly or use it for speculative purposes.

In his report upon the condition of industry, the chief of one of the departments of the Supreme Economic Council, A. Ginsburg, declares that "the attitude of the government towards private capital and the levelling of incomes tends to check the accumulation of capital in the country".[1] Another economist, A. Desen, uses similar terms regarding agriculture: "The general tendency of our economic life to consume all it produces is shown in a glaring light by the fact that the increase in wellbeing of the urban population results mainly in an increase in consumption. . . . The obstacles in the way of an increase in the wellbeing of the richer peasants, obstacles imposed by the policy of the Soviet government, have an inhibitive effect upon the accumulation of capital."[2]

[1] [Certain Presuppositions of the Five Year Plan for Industry], "Ekonomicheskoye Obozreniye", 1927, No. 4.
[2] [The Development of Industry and the National Accumulation of Capital], "Ekonomicheskoye Obozreniye", 1927, No. 5.

As far as accumulation of capital by the industries themselves is concerned, this cannot be effected to the extent looked for in the plan, for the experiences of 1923 have shown that high prices lead to a market crisis, so that the prices have to be reduced.

The burden of taxation has already reached the pre-war level, and Soviet economists are unanimous in declaring that it cannot be raised any further, so long as the national income remains no more than from 85 to 90 per cent of what it was in pre-war days. The attempt of the State to increase the subventions to industry by way of emission, has already, during the last three years, given rise to new manifestations of inflation, which have only failed to lead to catastrophes because the People's Commissariat for Finance has always been prompt to restrict the issue of notes at the first obvious signs of trouble. (In the year 1928, less caution was displayed in this matter, and in the latter half of that year a radical decline in the purchasing power of the chervonets began.) Attempts were also made to raise internal loans, but the possibilities of this means of providing capital are slender. Besides, since 1926–1927, a considerable proportion of the new loans has had to be devoted to paying off the earlier ones, which were issued for only short terms.

Nor has the Soviet government had much success in its endeavour to attract foreign capital for investment in the country. Many milliards are needed, and for long terms, but all it has been possible to secure is the purchase of goods on short credit, or loans for three or four years to be expended upon the purchase of machinery in the country from which the loan comes. When, three years ago, a credit of 300,000,000 marks was secured from Germany, this was hailed as a great success; but when, in the autumn of 1928, the first payments became due for the machinery which in most cases was not yet even mounted in the works, the most optimistic of the Soviet economists became aware that the industrialisation of their country would only be rendered possible by credits for a much longer term.

E

As I have already pointed out, the Soviet government considers this industrialisation of Russia to be the main object of
its economic policy. Sometimes the task of industrialisation is
regarded as consisting primarily in the development of those
means of production which are engaged in the making of other
means of production; but as a rule the industrialisation of
Soviet Russia is thought of rather as a general acceleration of
the development of Russian industry in conjunction with an
advance in agriculture. In neither sense has speedy industrialisation proved practicable. Despite the best endeavours, and
notwithstanding an appropriate assignment of State credits,
the production of the means of production in the year 1926–1927
had in medium-scale and small-scale industry attained to only
38 per cent of industrial production as a whole. If we include
the minor industrial enterprises under State management, the
ratio is still more unfavourable, for the share of the production
of the means of production in general industrial production
sinks to 27 per cent. In the year 1913, the share as regards
medium-scale and large-scale industry was 43 per cent. Even
for 1931, the Five Year Plan does not contemplate the attainment of the pre-war standard, and the most sanguine hope is
that in that year the production of the means of production in
medium-scale and large-scale industry will amount to 40 per
cent of industrial production as a whole.[1]

The mutual relationships between industrial production and
agricultural production are likewise unfavourable. Converting
the data of the "control figures"[2] and of the plans for industrial production into pre-war roubles, we find that the production
of large-scale industry in the year 1913 was 32 per cent of the
total production of the country, that in the year 1925–1926 it
was 30 per cent, and that in the year 1932 it is expected to
reach about 40 per cent of the total production of the country.

[1] A. Ginsburg [The Five Year Hypothesis of Industrial Development],
"Sotsialisticheskoye Hozyaistvo", 1926, No. 4.
[2] The "control figures" comprise the State estimates for the economics
of the ensuing year

Thus the speed of the process of industrialisation is not a remarkable one. When we turn to examine the figures showing the proportion of the population employed in industry and agriculture respectively, we find that these, likewise, are far from encouraging. Whereas in the year 1913, of 100 persons actively at work, 14 were engaged in industry, transport, building, or trade, and 77 in agriculture—in the year 1927–1928 the respective figures were 10 and 87.[1]

The part played by the urban operatives as compared with the agricultural workers is a smaller one than it used to be. Nor is this phenomenon a transient one; in the course of the year 1926–1927 the increase in the number of industrial operatives was only 110,000, and in the course of the year 1927–1928 it was only 164,000. Under these conditions, we can hardly speak of an intensive industrialisation, but must say that agriculture is gaining ground rather than industry.

Even during the most active years of industrial reconstruction, Soviet industry was unable to absorb the whole mass of urban unemployed and the superfluous rural population. As regards the future, the prospects in this respect are positively hopeless. In the year 1927, the number of unemployed was 1·7 millions; in the year 1928, it exceeded 2 millions; and, according to the calculations of the State Planning Commission, by 1931 it may have reached 3 millions. If the present policy is continued, it seems likely that for years and years the Soviet State will have no work to offer to many millions of its citizens.

The lack of capital, the consequent impossibility of rapidly expanding the technical process of production, the scarcity of raw materials, and the high cost of industrial production, have forced upon the managers of Soviet industry the rationalisation of production as an inevitable necessity. The Communist Party, the economic organisations, and the trade unions have all been mobilised on behalf of this rationalisation. In almost all branches of industry and in nearly all the great industrial

[1] The latter figures are deduced from the "control figures" for the last three years.

undertakings, central and local rationalisation committees have come into existence—nuclei for the propagation of Taylorism, Fordism, and the timing of work by the stop-watch. In the period from 1923 to 1928, reports have appeared in the Soviet press from time to time, recounting the "successes" of this work of rationalisation. Nevertheless, at the Rationalisation Conference summoned by the Workers' and Peasants' Inspection, sitting from August 30 to September 3, 1928, it was stated that the successes had been "quite insignificant". I shall return to the question of rationalisation in the chapters entitled "Labour" and "Purposive Economics and State Regulation". All I want to point out here is that the results of rationalisation (if by rationalisation we mean the introduction of an elementary working discipline and the overcoming of economic chaos) has been really remarkable as compared with what went on during the years of war communism and during the first years of the Nep. The irony of history has assigned to the communists, even after the introduction of the Nep, the role which usually has to be played by the representatives of the industrial bourgeoisie; they have had to compel the workers to emerge from revolutionary chaos. After scrapping the traditional methods of managing enterprise, they have had to return to a regime of steady work, to an enforcement of the authority of foremen and managers, to a realisation of working discipline. The Soviet State has been compelled to undertake no less strenuous efforts in order to overcome the perpetually recurring disproportions and "errors of calculation" that have arisen in connexion with the supply of raw materials and fuel, the furnishing of half-manufactured goods, and the organisation of transport.

Still, we can only speak of a success of rationalisation in Russia when we compare the present condition of affairs with the period of war communism, in which all orderly economy had been dissolved in a primal chaos of destruction, in which everything had been turned upside down. If when we speak of rationalisation we mean something less primitive than this, if we are not thinking merely of rendering some sort of production possible, but of increasing functional efficiency and the productivity of enterprises, of improving and cheapening the methods of production, of producing goods of better quality —then we shall have to admit that in the Soviet Union rationalisation has made little progress. Certainly it has been possible to reduce the consumption of fuel, to organise a more rational use of raw materials in the textile and the metal and the leather industries, to introduce better mechanical methods of internal transport in the coal industry and in smelting works and in the textile industry, to begin the practice of standardisation in a number of manufactures and to introduce both standardisation and specialisation to a considerable extent in machine-making and tool-making works. But in comparison with the general lack of proper economic management and organisation, these successes have been so trifling that in the opinion of most of those who participated in the before-mentioned Rationalisation Conference of the Workers' and Peasants' Inspection, they are hardly worth talking about.

Finally, we should waste our time if we were to try to estimate what proportion of the great mass of manufactured articles is made up by the 300 standardised articles mentioned by the Chief Rationalisation Board, or to ascertain how much saving has been achieved by the standardisation of production (seeing that, according to a report made to the above conference, the standardisation of these 300 products is as yet a matter of theory rather than practice). Can we speak of economy in the utilisation of raw materials and fuel when, for example, millions of metres of linen are used for making sacks, whereas elsewhere in Europe jute or hemp is always employed for this purpose? Can we seriously speak of advances in the mechanisation and specialisation of production when the costs of production in reorganised or newly-built establishments (coal mines, glass works, paper mills, etc.) are much higher than they were before reorganisation was begun? Besides, these "savings", which, thanks to rationalisation, have been made to the extent of a million or two roubles, are submerged in an ocean of losses which result from the spendthrift way in which money has been lavished upon the reconstruction of industry. According to the reports of the Rationalisation Conference, such losses amount to milliards!

The only domain of rationalisation in which considerable results have been achieved in the way of increasing productivity is that which concerns getting more intensive work out of the workers. Owing to the lack of raw material and its inferior quality, owing to technical backwardness, and owing to organisational incapacity, very little can really be done at present in the matter of rationalising technique and reorganising production. Consequently, as the communists themselves admit,[1] the practice of rationalisation follows the path of least resistance; that of forcing the Russian worker to produce more with the aid of rattletrap machinery and worn-out tools. But this method of rationalisation, to which the socialist labour movement is very strongly opposed, is not only antisocial, but gives very small results economically considered. Along such lines, the scope of production cannot be quickly extended, production cannot be cheapened, the industrialisation of the country cannot be achieved.

As soon as, in Soviet Russia, the fixed capital of industry as handed down from tsarist days was nearly all used up, and as soon as the "reconstruction period" was drawing to a close, the U.S.S.R. was confronted in full force with the nuclear problem of economic life, the problem of the accumulation of capital.

This problem is not simply one which concerns the further industrialisation of the country, for it also concerns the upkeep of the already functioning fixed capital of enterprise. For many years, in Russia, this fixed capital has been at work without the necessary repair, and it has to be saved from final destruction.

---

[1] See the proceedings of the plenary session of the Central Council of the Russian Trade Unions, as reported in "Pravda", March 6, 1928; and the proceedings of the plenary session of the Workers' and Peasants' Inspection, as reported in "Ekonomicheskaya Zhizn", September 1 and 2, 1928.

In the year 1927–1928, the Soviet government, having set a-going all the reserve enterprises, found it necessary, in order to increase industrial production, to have recourse to the expedient of a third shift. The utilisation of the extant technical equipment falls far short of technical possibilities. According to the calculations of the State Planning Commission, in the year 1928 Russian industrial plants were working on the average for 12·8 hours daily, this being 17 per cent less than the average working time of pre-war days. In some branches of industry, the possibilities of more extensive utilisation of productive capacity are greater than this, amounting in the metal industry to 25 per cent, in the foodstuffs industry to 40 per cent, and in the petroleum industry to 60 per cent more than the extant production.[1] Thus, since in the U.S.S.R. most industrial plants had hitherto been worked by only one or two shifts, it was now possible, by the introduction of two or of three shifts as the case might be, and by working seven days a week (the plants are to work seven days a week, the workers getting a weekly holiday on different days), it was possible to utilise the machinery more effectively, and to increase production without the investment of any serious amount of new capital.

The widespread introduction of the three-shift system accounts for the fact that in the year 1927–1928 there was a fairly rapid increase in production. This increase was achieved by the full utilisation of the productive capacity of those branches of industry in which, before the war, the three-shift system had not been practised, for technical reasons, or because it did not pay.

These are the last reserves of the heritage from pre-war days.

No doubt the adoption of a three-shift system and the introduction of a seven-day working week for the machinery does give an immediate result. Production is increased. But the increase is secured at the cost of the acceleration of the process

[1] A. Rabinovich [The Seven Hour Day], in "Ekonomicheskoye Obozreniye", 1928, No. 8.

of wearing out an already rickety plant, and it makes the problem of a renovation of the industrial capital more urgent even than before.

The lack of capital is the insuperable obstacle in the way of all attempts at speeding-up the process of industrialising Soviet Russia.

CHAPTER SIX

THE ADMINISTRATION AND ORGANISATION OF STATE INDUSTRY

ONE of the most difficult problems facing the Soviet government is that of the administration and organisation of State industry. The organisation of production, the administration of industrial finance, the supply of raw materials, the organisation of the disposal of all the products of medium-scale and large-scale industry in this gigantic country—these huge tasks seem almost beyond human power. The Soviet State has undertaken to perform them, and for the last ten years has been vainly endeavouring to do so in the most contradictory ways. Industry in the U.S.S.R. is in a condition of permanent reorganisation. At one time, individual enterprises or whole trusts are withdrawn from the control of the local soviets and confided to the care of the central authorities, or conversely. At another, the repairing works of the textile industry are taken out of the hands of the textile trusts, and the works for the elaboration of wood are removed from the control of the paper trusts, to be put under specialised management. Then, after a little while, there is a return to the plan of affiliating these accessory enterprises to the main branches of production. At the same time, within every trust there is going on a perpetual process of reorganisation, it may be as concerns the supply of raw materials, or as concerns book-keeping, or as concerns management.

Considering as a whole the history of industrial administration during the last ten years, we see that throughout this period two main conflicting tendencies have been at work, the tendency towards centralisation and that towards decentralisation. For brief periods, and at critical moments, decentralisation gets the upper hand; but always, ere long, there has been a return to centralisation, though this has assumed varying forms.

The year 1918 constitutes the first period of the nationalisation of industry. In that year, industry was conducted in a decentralised fashion by the local soviets, the management being entrusted to the workers' committees elected by the operatives in the various factories and workshops. The Supreme Economic Council issued plentiful instructions, but its supremacy existed only on paper.

Then came the years 1919 and 1920, the period of war communism. Chief administrative boards were formed for managing the various branches of industry, and the whole administration was centralised to an extreme in the hands of the Supreme Economic Council. All the officials and staff of each industry were appointed by the appropriate chief board, while the supply of raw materials and the disposal of the products was arranged by the Supreme Economic Council.

The years 1922 and 1923 were those of the transition to the Nep. Industry began to recover, and was being reorganised to pay on a commercial basis. The central authority appealed to the initiative and activity of the local organs. The administration of industry was mainly in the hands of the economic councils of the individual provinces. The local soviets appointed boards to manage economic activities, the chief boards were put out of action, and trusts came into being with the reservation of a great measure of independence for individual enterprises.

With the year 1924, the Supreme Economic Council began to centralise industrial administration once more. Central boards for the various industries were affiliated to the Supreme Economic Council, many of the trusts were withdrawn from the control of the local authorities and subordinated to the central authority. A decree concerning the trusts was issued, greatly restricting their powers, placing individual enterprises under the management of the appropriate trust, but that of the trust itself under the Supreme Economic Council.

Finally, in 1926, it became evident that undue centralisation was leading to bureaucracy, and that the endeavour to subordinate all the current activities of an enterprise to a supreme administration served only to disorganise economic life, and even to give a spurious character to the very necessary generalisation and centralisation of the supreme management.

Dzerzhinsky, who was then chairman of the Supreme Economic Council, in a report made only just before his death to the plenum of the central committee of the Communist Party of the Soviet Union, delivered himself as follows regarding the administration of industry: "Our industrial economy is being conducted in a terribly uneconomic fashion. . . . If you regard our whole apparatus, if you contemplate our administrative system, if you look at our incredible bureaucracy, if you consider the inconceivable way in which we tie ourselves up in coordinations,[1] you will be positively horrified."[2]

No less peculiar and complicated are the relations between the trust managements and the individual enterprises subordinated to these. At a conference concerning the reorganisation of industrial management, held in January 1927, Goltsman, representative of the People's Commissariat for Workers' and Peasants' Inspection, said: "The conditions under which the manager of an enterprise is placed make it impossible for him to manage it satisfactorily. The enterprises subordinated to a trust have ostensibly full responsibility, but in reality they have no responsibility at all. If you examine small-scale industry in the U.S.S.R., you will find that the productivity in small factories and workshops is often much higher than in the State enterprises of the same kind. Yet, in the State enterprises, we have better technical equipment and more capital, so that we ought to get better results. The cause of the difference is the peculiar relations between the State enterprises and the superposed managerial organisations. In our State enterprises, the actual managers do not know what their powers really are, whereas in foreign countries such concerns as the Allgemeine Elektrische Gesellschaft, which are at work all over the world,

[1] Dzerzhinsky was referring to the involved inter-coordination of the various departments of economic life.
[2] "Pravda", January 1, 1926.

have an independent balance sheet, their own general capital
and working capital, and are responsible to themselves alone.
In our case, a trust is at one and the same time a purveyor of
raw materials and an organ which has to find a market for
finished products, at one and the same time an institution
for financing an enterprise and an instrument for the regulation
of labour conditions. In foreign countries, no trusts of this
kind exist. Here in Soviet Russia, a trust is a sort of universal
institution, supposed to be omniscient and omnipotent, and
the manager of the individual enterprise is only the servant
of the trust. All our enterprises are under tutelage, in a
way which was quite unknown to pre-revolutionary industrial
enterprises." [1]

An acquaintance with the present trends in the administration
of Russian industry, as described by the Soviet press, suffices,
indeed, to inform us that the situation is far from satisfactory.
Bureaucracy, formalism, a lack of a sense of responsibility,
the dictation from above of programs which fail to take into
account the actual condition of the machinery of the enterprises and the nature of their technical equipment—these are
the characteristics of present-day management. The political,
technical, and financial proposals for production have to be
scrutinised by dozens of official bodies, and are held up by
each until the whole section of relevant business has been dealt
with. One revision of a scheme follows another, each of them
taking from three to five months. In practice, however, there
is a complete lack of proper supervision, so that funds are
extensively misapplied, and the most unheard-of defalcations
take place. There is a gigantic staff of clerks, book-keepers,
and statisticians, who compile tons upon tons of reports and
circulars, while all the time the trust management is without
the most elementary information concerning the work of the
individual enterprises, and the Supreme Economic Council
knows nothing about the activities of the individual trusts.
One committee sits to discuss the proceedings of another,

[1] "Ekonomicheskaya Zhizn", January 12, 1927.

and there is a continual going to and fro from each office to the next. Administrative expenditure is many times greater now than it was before the war. Periodically the managerial staffs are depleted by the discharge of supernumeraries, but after each of these purges the apparatus soon swells to its former size.

The most convincing demonstration of the defects of the present management of industry is given by the way in which, during the last few years, the inauguration of new industrial undertakings has been carried out. All the communist authorities are agreed in declaring that industrialisation is the supreme task of the State and the Party to-day. For this purpose, milliards have been assigned—to the detriment of the other needs of the country. The most active among the communist economists have been detailed to organise and supervise this work of industrialisation. The result, at the end of 1927, was that, after a succession of new beginnings, a complete collapse had occurred. The abundance of organisers and supervisors notwithstanding, factory buildings had frequently been erected without plans, without drawings, without any regard for the latest acquirements of technique, without any relevance to actual economic needs. What was built, was not what was needed; it was not built where it was wanted; and it was not built in the proper way. The building of a factory had taken three or four years, and the installation of the machinery needed from one and a half to two years more. The cost was twice or thrice as much as had been expected, and exceeded the cost of the old building. In many cases, within a few months the new factory buildings were in need of repair and rebuilding. The work had been done without method or plan. Sometimes there was no machinery to instal in the new factory when it was finished, and sometimes the machinery arrived without any factory to put it in. Sometimes the necessary machinery had never been ordered from abroad; and at other times, when new machinery did come from abroad, no one knew how to use it.

Let us consider a few examples from many hundreds, to substantiate the foregoing statements.

The building of the Volkhovstroy Electrical Works took six years, and cost four times the estimated sum. Then, in 1927, when the power plant came into use, it had only one-third of the requisite capacity; its working was frequently interrupted by defects; and during the first year a complete reconstruction of the works was required.

In the year 1927–1928, the extensive schemes for the utilisation of the energy of the Dnieper rapids were to be realised by the building of the Dnieperostroy Electrical Works. Warned by the poor results obtained in the previous case, the State was unwilling to entrust the construction to its own engineers, but, for protectionist reasons, it was unwilling to hand the work over to foreign firms, and therefore adopted a middle course. The construction was effected by Soviet engineers, with the advice and help of one American firm and one German firm. During the first year, 52·5 millions of roubles were spent. Machinery was ordered at home and abroad. Large areas were flooded, the population having been cleared out. Workers' dwellings were built. Dams were erected. Then, suddenly, it became apparent that in the plans no one had paid any attention to the question for what purposes the electrical power was to be used when the works were finished. There had been some thought of inaugurating aluminium works, but it was found that, after all, these could not be established in the Dnieper region. The necessary raw materials (bauxite ores) are found only in the north-west of Russia, where an electrical power station was already being built on the Svir, and would need a use for its electricity. It would be impossible to build smelting works and steel works near the Dnieper electrical works, for the ground was too marshy. Nor would it pay to carry the electric current to the Donetz basin, sixty kilometres away, for there it had already been decided to have another electrical power station, which was to be run by means of the poorer qualities of coal. There was talk, consequently, of stopping the construction of the Dnieper works, but in the end it was decided to go on with them, "in the interests of an accelerated industrialisation". The estimates were expanded from 120 millions to 200 million of roubles; [1] the expected cost of electricity increasing from 0·46 copecks to 1·7 copecks, a rise which will make it difficult to use the current economically.[2]

In Kerch, new smelting works were to be established. At the beginning of 1926, the cost of construction was reckoned at 20 millions of roubles; by May 1927, it had risen to 26 millions of roubles; by August of the same year, to 32 millions of roubles; by May 1928, to 39 millions of roubles; and by the following June, to 55 millions of roubles. It was originally supposed that the works would be ready by the end of 1928, but in the middle of that year it became plain that the best which could be hoped for would be to begin smelting in 1930.[3]

In Rostov-on-the-Don, the building of a factory for the production of agricultural machinery, farm carts, etc., was begun. This was to be "the largest of its kind in the world". After many millions had been spent, it transpired that in the whole of the Don area there was no possibility of procuring the timber which the economists of the Supreme Economic Council had authoritatively declared to be requisite.[4]

In Transcaucasia, a model factory ("The Fires of Daghestan") was to be set up for the making of glass and earthenware. As soon as the building was finished, it was found that the necessary raw materials were not obtainable locally, and that the sources of energy which had been counted on (local gas jets) were insufficient, so that it was necessary to procure a steam-engine.

At the newly constructed glassworks with power plant in Sergiyevsk, production costs six times as much as in the old

[1] "Ekonomicheskaya Zhizn", July 4, 1928.
[2] "Narodnoye Hozyaistvo i Finansy", 1928, No. 31.
[3] "Pravda", July 11, 1928.
[4] "Torgovo-Promyshlennaya Gazeta", August 25, 1928.

factories with hand power. Two-thirds of what is turned out by the enterprise is broken.[1]

Similar bureaucracy and muddle prevail in the other functions of industrial life, this applying equally to the provision of raw materials, to the supply of fuel, and to the marketing of the products. Towards the end of the year 1927, as the outcome of numerous conferences of factory managers, trust managers, and leading economists, it was decided that there must be a general overhaul of the conditions under which the reconstruction of industry was taking place. Rykoff, the chairman of the Council of People's Commissaries, in his report to the Fifteenth Conference of the Communist Party of the U.S.S.R., declared that "the main task of the Soviet government" was "to effect a radical reorganisation of industry".

But instead of this "radical reorganisation" of the whole management of industry, there has been nothing more than the usual pseudo-reorganisation. According to a resolution of the Central Executive Committee, adopted on June 29, 1927, the management of industry was to be remodelled as follows. The general conduct of industry in accordance with the needs of economic planning was to continue, and thenceforward, as previously, the direction was to be centralised, remaining in the hands of the departments of the Supreme Economic Council. At the same time, management was to be decentralised, being entrusted, partly to the supreme economic councils of the individual republics, and partly to the trust boards. The individual enterprises were to have a certain amount of freedom in the management of their own business affairs. The collaboration of the enterprises with the trusts to which they were subordinated was to be carried on "by way of agreement"; the trusts were no longer to issue commands to the individual factories, but were simply to ask for the supply of goods to an amount which would be decided by mutual arrangement; and these goods were to be delivered to the trust, no longer at a figure determined by arbitrary calculations, but

[1] "Pravda", March 4, 1928.

at prices decided by mutual agreement in advance. The enterprises were to be empowered to send part of their products independently to the market, to buy raw materials and half-manufactured goods or to make these without first obtaining the approval of the trusts, to draw bills of exchange upon the trusts, and to discount the bills of exchange of customers. Part of the savings resulting from the difference between the cost of production and the sale at agreed prices, together with a part of the profits, were to be left to the enterprise. The individual enterprise was to have the right of putting its own trade-mark on the goods as well as the trade-mark of the trust. Finally, the manager of the enterprise was to be appointed by the trust board for a specified period, and the board was not to interfere in the management of the enterprise. The manager of the enterprise was to have the right of appealing to the Supreme Economic Council against decisions of the trust board.

These reforms were fiercely opposed by the communist economists in the Supreme Economic Council and in the trust boards. By expatiating on the danger that the upshot of the changes would be to liberate nationalised industry from central control, they were able to ensure that the proposed reforms should get no further than the paper they were written on, and that in practice the reorganisation of industry should not be undertaken on these lines. For a whole year, the decree was ignored. Every one knew this, but no one said a word about it. Not until the mining scandal occurred, did people begin to ask why the law had not been put into effect.

"The excitement about the way in which the decree concerning the powers of the enterprises and trusts has been carried out, shows that even the minimal powers which the decision of the government has assigned to the enterprises and the trusts will only be actually given to these with great difficulty. The Supreme Economic Council finds it very hard to make any concessions to the trusts. Each trust finds it equally hard to make any concessions to the enterprises." Thus runs the report of the Workers' and Peasants' Inspection in March

F

1928, one year after the promulgation of the law concerning the "immediate" reorganisation of industrial management. In June 1928, the Workers' and Peasants' Inspection again drew attention to the fact that the larger trusts were ignoring the trust legislation, and that the Supreme Economic Council was failing to put it in application. The economic organism of Soviet Russia is seriously diseased, and the result is seen in a number of auditings and trials. The legal proceedings against the management of the irrigation works in central Asia, those against the Sovkino Trust, against the Textile Trust, and, finally, the mining trial, give an alarming picture of bureaucracy, lack of a sense of responsibility, and official delinquency.

Why is it that in ten years the Soviet State has been unable to discover a satisfactory method of administration and to ensure the normal functioning of nationalised industry?

It would be a mistake to attribute these troubles exclusively to the incapacity of the communists, or to defalcation and deliberate sabotage on the part of the technical experts. The real reason is to be found in the enormous extent of the task that has been undertaken, in the nature of the whole system of the organisation of nationalised industry, and in the general regime of dictatorship.

Bureaucracy, a lack of a sense of responsibility, chaos, and official delinquency flourish luxuriantly upon the soil that is prepared by depriving the general population of rights and by the complete lack of publicity and popular control.

The official newspapers refer often enough to the defects of the administrative system, especially as concerns the management of industry. They often use very strong terms. But they write in a way that leads the less well-informed among their readers to the conclusion that the trouble only takes the form of isolated defects, against which the government is taking strong measures. They blame these "little defects in the mechanism", instead of blaming the system that gives rise to them.

One of the oldest communists, Y. Yakovleff, has been bold

enough to allude to the main causes of these phenomena. In "Pravda" of March 4, 1928, he writes: "Every member of the Party and every intelligent citizen of the Soviet State has good ground for wondering that not one of the most important defects of our reconstruction of industry has been discovered soon enough by our press. The press still devotes far too much of its space to literary flourishes, to witticisms concerning the errors of the 'pointsmen', to censures of the minor Soviet officials. That is what leads their readers astray. I have asked a number of workers what they think of the accounts of malpractices given in the columns of our press. Their unanimous answer has been: 'That is not what we want. There is no use in making a parade of the "little defects". What we need is a frank disclosure of the great defects of the great machine which is at work'." Yakovleff's criticisms apply to the whole system of giving a press monopoly to the communist newspapers; to the regime of "self-criticism" which is not free criticism at all; to the refusal of political rights to the general population; and to the governmental lack of responsibility. But his voice has been a solitary one. The "Bolshevik" (1928, No. 10) speedily declared, with all the authority of the central organ of the Communist Party of the U.S.S.R., that any attempt "to generalise defects", or to discover "a philosophy of defects", ceased to be self-criticism, to become menshevism and counter-revolution.

But, quite apart from the regime of dictatorship (under which economic ineptitude and official delinquency flourish), there are other reasons why a purposive reorganisation of the management of nationalised industry is impossible. The abolition of the dictatorship would not put an end to the working of these causes. They are rooted in the objective conditions of Russian economic life, in the conditions under which nationalisation and the formation of the trusts occurred.

Most of the Russian trusts have suffered from rickets since the day of their birth. They did not come into existence by a process of organic growth on the part of the whole national economy, they did not arise because all the factors of economic life were ripe for the trustification of industry. Before the war, indeed, as we have learned, there had been a rapid process of concentration in certain branches of production, but only in the form of an increasing independence of industry as far as financial capital was concerned, and in the form of a syndicalisation of the means of distribution.

Besides, despite the before-mentioned changes, the organisation of production and of marketing was still of an extremely backward and primitive type. Professor V. Grinevetsky characterises as follows the backwardness of the organisation of pre-war industry in Russia: "The localisation of enterprises, and even of whole branches of industry, in Russia, was determined more by historical evolution than by the possibilities of marketing products and of obtaining raw materials. Production has been insufficiently specialised. . . . In many cases the larger enterprises, employing from five to ten thousand workers each, were merely agglomerations of several factories and workshops united rather by having a common administration than by any ties of technical organisation. Old enterprises, those developed historically, are quite out of date in respect alike of equipment and of buildings. . . . The buildings are old, confined, and dark, with the result that the costs of production are increased. . . . Worn-out and defective equipment, which may still suffice when labour power and fuel are cheap and when there is no need to turn out articles of really good quality (conditions characteristic of Russian industry in earlier days), will be disastrous for many undertakings if they persist in the future."[1]

Even in the branches of production in which the aforesaid rapid concentration had occurred, the requisites for a comprehensive trustification, for a complete amalgamation of the direction of the various enterprises, do not yet exist. The civil war and the communist experiments have disorganised the

[1] V. Grinevetsky [The Post-War Perspectives of Russian Industry], 1922, pp. 68 et seq.

market, and have destroyed the germs of syndicalisation and cartel-formation. Whereas in western countries trustification (the complete amalgamation of enterprises) is usually the last link in a long chain of intermediate stages of concentration; whereas trustification is there usually preceded by an allotment of markets, by a standardisation of prices and production, by the formation of syndicates, and so on—in the Soviet Union, trustification was effected by a mere decree of the Communist Party, and was not confined to those branches of production which were already fairly well concentrated in 1917 and had access to a tolerably well organised market, but was applied even to small and scattered enterprises. Experience in capitalist countries has shown that the most important condition of the viability of a trust is that there should be a reconstruction, a concentration within the trust itself, as an immediate result of the process of trustification. The enterprises which are best equipped technically speaking, those which work to the utmost capacity, and those which are antiquated and no longer pay, are put out of action. But in Russia, well equipped and huge enterprises were mechanically united with small workshops where the plant was technically obsolete. Attempts at rationalisation were, indeed, made in Soviet Russia; but, owing to the prevailing scarcity of goods, the lack of technical experience, and the want of capital, they only led as a rule to even greater disorganisation. In the majority of instances, therefore, this mechanical trustification did not bring about the formation of unified economic organisms, did not increase the technical level of production, did not reduce the costs of production—but merely created a cumbrous apparatus and led to a rapid rise in the price of the products.

This has been favoured, in addition, by the circumstance that the trusts in the Soviet Union, owing to their monopoly position and to the absolute governmental control of imports and exports, are protecte against competition more effectively than commercial undertakings have ever been protected before. In the west, trustification occurred after the attainment of a fairly high level of cultural and economic development. Russian industry, on the other hand, in the days of the revolution, was, as previously explained, still far from ripe for so comprehensive a trustification as occurred, or for trustification effected at such lightning speed and simultaneously all along the line. During the ten years of its existence, moreover, not merely has the Soviet government failed to promote the ripening of the conditions which would favour a purposive concentration of industry, but, by its mistakes and its utopian experiments, it has strengthened many of the factors that tend to hinder trustification.

One factor, which renders the management of State industry in the U.S.S.R. exceptionally complicated, must be discussed in detail. This is the lack of technical and organisational experts—a lack characteristic of Russia. The political and cultural atmosphere of tsarist Russia was not one fitted to produce a bountiful crop of persons competent to manage large-scale enterprises, or able to conduct them in a way which would make the work both accurate and frictionless. Still smaller, in Russia, was the number of noted technicians with a capacity for undertaking independent constructive work. It was not the outcome of mere chance that at the head of so many Russian industrial undertakings there were managers, engineers, and technicians who had been imported from abroad. During the ten years of Soviet rule, this thin stratum of highly-skilled managers of production, captains of industry, and engineers has become even thinner. Many of the Russian technicians vanished in the whirlpool of the civil war, died, or took refuge abroad; while the foreign technicians returned to their homes. Whereas, in the most advanced capitalist countries, on the average, the technical staff amounts to from 10 to 15 per cent of the whole working staff of undertakings, in the U.S.S.R. the ratio of technical experts to all those engaged in production is not more than 2 per cent. A census of technicians was undertaken by the Supreme Economic Council on October 1, 1927, and the figures speak for themselves. At that date, there were working in the nationalised industrial enterprises, 10,700 engineers, of whom more than half (5400) had a term of service which was less than 5 years—they were, that is to say, young engineers with a very brief experience, acquired only under the Soviet system. The number of highly qualified engineers is declining from day to day.

Meanwhile, the task of managing industry has become far more complicated. It no longer concerns individual factories, but whole trusts. The reconstruction of industry is being carried out at the cost of many milliards of roubles, and concurrently the nationalised industry has to be administered upon a new and unfamiliar basis. The need is not merely for skilled economists and engineers, but for economists and engineers who can look at their work socialistically.

During the early days of Soviet rule, an attempt was made to manage industrial enterprises by workers' committees. This was a complete failure. The manual workers had neither the necessary knowledge nor the requisite experience. On the other hand, the sometime leaders of industrial enterprise, together with the engineers and the chief employees, were hostile in their attitude towards the Soviet State (which, indeed, regarded them merely as prisoners released on probation), so that they would neither help the communists in the management of production nor undertake this function themselves. But the experience of the last six years, the period that has elapsed since the introduction of the Nep, has shown that the second method, that of getting technical experts and communist commissaries to undertake the management of trusts and enterprises, is also a failure.

No doubt a few able, and even talented, economists and managers of enterprise have risen from the ranks of the workers in the course of these years, but they must be counted by tens, whereas the State needs them by thousands. Y. Yakovleff, the previously quoted member of the committee of the Workers' and Peasants' Inspection, describes very plainly how the administration of enterprise by communists works out. He says: "Most of our managers are workers. It will be self-evident that they cannot be distinguished by an especially high level of intellectual culture, or by the possession of wide knowledge. Where would such culture and such knowledge come from, seeing that the typical history of one of our managers is that, he was a worker to begin with (and generally at the same time a revolutionist burrowing underground), and then, after the revolution, became a war commissary, a chekist, or something of the kind, and after that a factory manager or trust manager. He has never had a chance to cultivate his mind! Yet the lack of culture and skilled knowledge was never so acutely felt as it is to-day, was never so dangerous politically as it is to-day, when milliards of roubles are being spent upon the reconstruction of industry." [1]

We have instructive numerical data throwing light on this problem. On January 1, 1928, the Registration and Distribution Department of the Supreme Economic Council collected data for a report concerning the personal composition of the management of industry. As regards membership of the Communist Party, the "political qualification" is fully secured. In the managing boards of the trusts, 71·4 per cent of the members are communists; in those of the syndicates, 84·4 per cent; in those of the individual enterprises, 89·3 per cent. But the "Bolshevik", the organ of the Central Committee of the Communist Party of the U.S.S.R., when publishing these figures, remarks with concern: "As regards general culture and scientific and technical training, which are so urgently needed in the present period of the reorganisation of industry, the position is very much worse".[2] Among the members of the trust boards, 45·6 per cent have had only an elementary school education; among those of the syndicate boards, only 50 per cent. Among the managers of the 770 enterprises concerning which figures were quoted, 3·5 per cent had had no schooling at all; 71·6 per cent had been at elementary

[1] "Pravda", March 4, 1928.
[2] "Bolshevik", 1928, No. 8.

schools; 16 per cent had had a high-school education; and 8·9 per cent had been at a university.

The reader will have no difficulty in picturing for himself how difficult must be the management of whole branches of industry for a proletarian who has had neither general nor technical training for the task.

But whereas the defective education of the communist workers is a direct consequence of the conditions under which the Russian proletarians had to live before the revolution, the frequent changes in the personnel of the industrial managers are solely due to the decisions of the supreme leaders of Soviet enterprise. The managers, most of whom were originally manual workers (in the trusts, 43·1 per cent, and in the management of individual enterprises, 63 per cent) have no chance of making up for the lack of technical training by prolonged experience such as can only be acquired by those who stick to the same job for a considerable time. The before-mentioned enquiry showed that from 30 to 35 per cent of the managers of enterprise did not remain in the same situation longer than one year, 32 to 33 per cent not longer than 2 years, and only 13 to 20 per cent more than 3 years.

Under stress of political considerations, or thanks to the whims of the local and central authorities, the communist managers (even when they are devoted adherents of the Party) are continually being shifted from post to post, so that they cannot possibly become well informed concerning the duties entrusted to them. Such a man will either become a mere pawn in the hands of the experts, or else, under the stimulus of an impulse towards self-preservation, he will fanatically ignore "bourgeois science". Many a communist manager inclines to regard any reference to the importance of technical knowledge as a personal insult. "When I played my part in the revolution I was cultured enough, and now I am to be told that I am lacking in this respect!" Such, according to Yakovleff, is the usual objection raised by these communists.

On the other hand, among the technical and commercial managers, the experts, the engineers, and so on, many are hostile to the Soviet government; many find it impossible to accommodate themselves to the continually changing demands of that government, and do their work formally, bureaucratically, with a minimal sense of responsibility, and also with the least possible amount of initiative. A few, only, of the technical experts, engineers, etc., are of that peculiar type who have a passion for their work, and do it zealously, to the utmost of their skill and capacity. Even then, most of the initiative and activity that are displayed run to waste, owing to the prevalence of bureaucracy and of the peculiar mistrust of experts. Suffice it, in this connexion, to refer to the suicide of Oldenberg, the engineer of the Moscow Waterworks, who saved the enterprise from ruin during the years of war communism, and was afterwards hounded to his death by the communist nucleus; to the death of the engineer Klasson, the manager of the Moscow Electrical Works, one of the few engineers who hastened to put their services at the disposal of the Soviet State and devoted themselves to carrying out their difficult technical tasks (Klasson died of a broken heart, after an unmerited public reproof); and to an engineer's cry for help, in a letter to Rykoff, to the effect that the "bureaucracy and bungling" by which he was surrounded had deprived him of his power to work.

The mining trial has made it especially clear that even at the beginning of the eleventh year of Soviet rule the problem of industrial management has not been solved by setting the technical expert and the communist commissary to work side by side. Let us pay no heed now to those elements in the affair which were the outcome of politics or were attributable to the spy system. Let us ignore "conspiracies" and denunciations. Apart from all these things, the trial has disclosed a picture of chaotic and uneconomic management on a colossal scale.

The Donugol (Donetz Coal) is the largest trust in the

U.S.S.R. In this key position of Soviet Russian industry, the communist commissaries were not merely unable to prevent corruption from flourishing for years, not only did they neither know nor suspect what was going on in this way, but in the press they actually had written of the trust as a model undertaking, and had approved of describing as "heroes of labour" the very engineers who were subsequently to be condemned in the mining trial.

At the head of Donugol were prominent communists; first of all Ruhimovich, now deputy chairman of the Supreme Economic Council; and subsequently Lomoff, one of the participators in the November revolution of 1917. Both are men of a very energetic type, but lacking in the culture, in the knowledge and experience, indispensable for the managers of the entire coal industry of a great country. They were as helpless as children when important technical and economic questions came up for solution. The experts were accused of having "maliciously restricted the extraction of coal, upon the orders of the sometime owners", whereas the order to "restrict the extraction of coal because of the great accumulation of supplies and the standing danger of fire" was signed by Ruhimovich, the communist chairman of the trust. The decision to cease work for a time in a number of the pits was also taken by the trust management. Let us consider another item in the indictment, the stopping of work on big anthracite seams. The order to "stop the working of big seams as obsolete", was issued by Lomoff, the chairman of the trust. It transpired during the trial that orders had been placed abroad for coal-cutting machines of a type which could not possibly be used in the Donetz coal mines. The present writer does not know whether the machines would really have been unsuitable; but at any rate the order was made at the instance of the technical advisers, and was confirmed by the management of the trust. Nay more, these same technical advisers, only a few months before the mining trial, were stated by the Supreme Economic Council to constitute a most authoritative body of persons.

which had made well grounded and carefully thought-out plans for the reorganisation of the mining industry.[1]

Here we have a sort of magic circle, in which the technical incapacity of the communist commissaries becomes amalgamated with the misdeeds and the indifference of the official experts! In this way the mining trial becomes an indictment of the extant system of administering Russian industry through the instrumentality of technically incompetent communist commissaries.

Neither in the Donugol nor in the other industrial enterprises has any improvement in working conditions been achieved, or an atmosphere of public control of industrial activity been created, by the methods of trade-union and workers'-committee control, which the Russian communists have not dared to abolish, but have realised bureaucratically, and in a dead-alive sort of way.

After the foregoing description of the objective conditions which stand in the way of a rational organisation of the management of industry, it will easily be understood that the everlasting swing of the pendulum between centralisation and decentralisation is as fruitless as the search for the philosopher's stone.

The main cause of muddle and ineffectiveness is not to be found in the external forms of administration. The economic and social conditions, the cultural and moral environment, are in conflict with the utopian experiments.

If, under a system of centralisation, the program of production, the financial schemes, the plans for building, and the regulation of the circulation of commodities, are nullified by the tacit and open resistance of the hundreds of trusts, we cannot but see that in a system of decentralisation this phenomenon will inevitably be intensified by the resistance of the thousands of individual enterprises. The spontaneous power of market conditions, self-seeking, speculation, and

[1] See [Data for the Five Year Plan], issued by the Supreme Economic Council.

malversations, cannot fail to bring the whole extant system of a "purposive economic" direction to naught. As has been shown, centralisation creates bureaucracy, leads to high prices, engenders chaos. Decentralisation threatens to make trustification and nationalisation a mere pretence.

Neither by their own powers nor with the aid of technical experts, have the communists been able, during the last ten years, to ensure the normal working of a system of industrial management. The causes of their failure are rooted, as we have seen, in the very foundations of Soviet policy and Soviet economics: in the regime of dictatorship by which the population at large is deprived of political rights; in the lack of public control; in the artificial promotion of a trustified form of industry; and in the inapplicability of the nationalisation of industry on the present scale to a country so backward as contemporary Russia.

CHAPTER SEVEN

NATIONALISATION OF INDUSTRY

No one interested in social problems can fail to ponder the question whether the policy of the thoroughgoing nationalisation of industry, which has been stubbornly pursued for ten years by the Soviet government, has been justified from the outlook of the Russian national economy, and from that of the interests of the Russian working class. Now that the Soviet State has lasted for a decade, it is already possible to draw some valid conclusions upon this matter.

At the outset of the eleventh year of Soviet rule, there is a fresh and severe crisis in Russian economic life. Developing industry finds itself in a blind alley, owing to the lack of capital. The bureaucratic system of industrial management, which is at the same time an uneconomic one, presses heavily upon the shoulders of the population. The retarded tempo of industrial advance results in a permanent famine of commodities.

The adversaries of socialism emphatically declare that the nationalisation of industry, the breach with the system of privately owned capital, is the essential cause of the crisis in Soviet economy. They point out that in Russia the main demand of all socialists, namely the socialisation of the means of production, has been carried out in the purest possible form; and they declare that the failure of nationalisation in Russia is tantamount to the failure of socialism. They contend that the root of all the evil is to be found in the infringement of the "sacred institution of private property", and that no rational method of conducting economic life can be found outside the domain of free economic initiative and the independent management of production by private property owners. They consider that the Russian experiment provides them with a powerful weapon of defence against the struggle of the working class on behalf of socialism. Nevertheless, an attentive study of the Russian experience of nationalisation shows that the difficulties and crises that have occurred in Soviet Russia have not been the outcome of nationalisation as a new way of organising industry, but are simply due to the conditions under which and the methods by which nationalisation has been realised by means of the communist dictatorship.

Nationalisation is an item in the program of a great number of socialist parties. But the question when nationalisation is to take place, how much is to be nationalised, and in what way, cannot be answered by socialists on abstract principles. It must be considered concretely.[1] Whereas in countries where industrial development is far advanced and where there is a strong and well organised working class, that is to say in countries where the objective pre-requisites of nationalisation already exist, even the program of the extreme left (including that of the communists, as shown by the new program of the Communist International, adopted at the Sixth Congress in the summer of 1928) contemplates a process of nationalisation which shall take place by a series of stages—in Russia, a backward country both culturally and economically, nationalisation was effected suddenly, comprehensively, and at one blow. Thereby, not merely were the deficiencies of Russian economic life accentuated and the pace of economic reconstruction slowed down, but, further, the way was opened into that impasse in which the U.S.S.R. now finds itself.

The communists tell us, indeed, that nationalisation has been a great success, adducing in support of this assertion data showing that the pre-war level of production has been regained. The argument is unconvincing. After a report had been made by Buharin, a member of the audience handed up the following question: "You say that the tsarist government was in crass conflict with the whole development of the country. How,

---

[1] If, in any country, the government should be one hostile to the working class, the nationalisation of industry would serve only to strengthen the reaction. Should, for instance, the counter-revolution triumph in Russia, the attitude of the working class toward the nationalisation of industry would change considerably, and nationalisation might cease to be one of the immediate demands of the labour parties.

then, can you explain that in the last years before the war Russia made such rapid economic advances?" To this query Buharin replied, with good reason: "The development took place in spite of the tsarist autocracy."[1]

The mere fact that the reconstruction of Russian industry has taken place with fair speed (although there have been distressing checks and relapses), does not by itself justify either the scope or the methods of nationalisation in Soviet Russia. The communists are satisfied to simplify the problem and to fend it off by asking whether things would have gone any better under private capitalism. The problem at issue is not comprised within these limits. The experience of western European countries has shown that wherever a system of private capitalism not subject to State regulation persists, the reconstruction of industry can only be effected at the cost of the workers' standard of life, and must be paid for by extensive sacrifices on the part of the working poulation. One may be very strongly opposed to private capitalist profit and to a speculative economy, without, for that reason, ceasing to believe that the method and scope of Soviet nationalisation have been utopian and uneconomic.

To a socialist, the nationalisation of industry seems so eminently desirable from the outlook of national economy and for the promotion of the interests of the proletariat, that he will not without very strong reasons repudiate nationalisation or try to limit its scope. But he must do this when it becomes urgently necessary in the interests alike of the Russian national economy and of the working class.

Up till now, the Russian national economy has been in course of reconstruction, though not without crises and relapses. The overthrow of tsarism, the partition of the estates of the sometime great landlords, the existence of a huge home market, and the country's wealth in natural resources, have not merely supplied the conditions requisite for a rapid process of development, but have strengthened the integrity of the

[1] "Pravda", March 10, 1927.

complicated economic national organism and have enabled it to resist the disastrous after-effects of the war and war communism.

Up till now, however, the reconstruction of the national economy has been effected by the using-up of the heritage from the old days of capitalism, and thanks to this alone has it been possible to reconstruct at such speed. But now, when all the fixed capital of the old industry has been used up or has got worn out, new investments to the tune of milliards are required, not simply for a step forward, but merely to maintain the present achievements. In the fifth chapter I showed that the extension of industrial production during the first years of the Nep was effected by using up all the working capital of industry. Subsequently, from 1923 onwards, the State tried to secure the necessary means by inflationist measures or by fixing high prices for the products of industry while the prices for grain and other agricultural produce were kept low. The result was that, again and again, the country was convulsed by market crises and crises due to the scarcity of commodities, that the process of intensifying peasant agriculture and of reestablishing peasant production for the market was slackened. Still, these methods enabled the State to supply nationalised industry with a round sum of three milliards of roubles. Now the way towards such expedients is barred. The State cannot risk having further recourse to inflation, for this would have a disastrous effect upon all branches of the national economy- Nor can the prices of industrial products be raised; and the screw-press of taxation has been used to the utmost limit. Nevertheless, the exhaustion of the reserves of fixed capital makes it necessary that capital to a multiple of the previous amount should be invested in industry forthwith, if even a moderate advance in industrialisation is to be rendered possible. The seizures of goods and the repressive measures taken against private enterprise in town and countryside, have reduced the accumulation of capital in Russia to a minimum. At the same time, the policy of monopoly and nationalisation has made it impossible to attract capital from abroad to the necessary

amount. Yet, under the existing system of universal nationalisation, all the capital needed by Russian industrial enterprise,
whether of the first grade of importance or of the second,
and whether the enterprise is one which will pay or will not
pay, must be provided by the State.

Nationalisation to the extent which is now being maintained,
exceeds the powers of the country. It is quite out of
correspondence with the financial resources of the State.
It has become a fetter, a hindrance to the development of
the productive energies of the country. The extent and the
forms of nationalisation being, as they are, unsuitable to
Russia, stand in the way of the positive developmental possibilities which, if realised, would make nationalisation practicable
upon scientific instead of upon utopian lines.

To socialists, the nationalisation of industry seems desirable
when it will establish the requisites for a purposive economy,
will secure for the democratic State the profits that usually
go to entrepreneurs, will safeguard industrial democracy for
the workers, and will provide the population at large with
cheap commodities.

But what are the realities in Soviet Russia to-day?

After the disorganisation caused by the Great War and the
civil war, Russian economy was in need of an active and
purposive guidance by the State. But the communists, for the
sake of a pseudo-simplification of this task, nationalised the
whole of industry, the whole of foreign commerce, and nearly
all the internal trade of the country. By this "maximalism"
they degraded the purposive conduct and management of
economic life to a mere semblance.[1] There can be no doubt
that better results would have been achieved had the State
restricted its attempts at purposive guidance to the most
important departments of the national economy, without
attempting wholesale nationalisation.

---

[1] The question of economic planning and that of the influence of spontaneous
economic factors will be discussed in fuller detail in Chapter Sixteen,
entitled "Purposive Economics and State Regulation".

In actual fact, the Soviet process of nationalisation, working in the most radical fashion, excluded from production thousands upon thousands of private owners, the aim being to relieve the workers and peasants from the need for paying millions of roubles to non-working members of society. Ere long, however, it became plain that, owing to the unduly comprehensive scope of nationalisation, the State was unable to organise the administration of industry purposively. The thousands upon thousands of private property owners were replaced by new hosts of "red" bureaucrats, trust managers, and commissaries, who gobbled up all the savings which might otherwise have been made by the expropriation of the expropriators. A. Vainshtein, a government official, writing about the problem of the accumulation of capital, says: "The apparatus of our nationalised enterprises is more cumbrous and has a larger personnel than had the apparatus of private enterprises in pre-war days. The lower salaries of our industrial managers are in part compensated by 'invisible' payments made in the form of allowances at the cost of the enterprise for the satisfaction of the personal needs of the managerial staff. ... From the point of view which interests us at the moment, that of the accumulation of capital, we find that the 'personal consumption' of the responsible administrators is perhaps but very little less than was that of the managers of capitalist large-scale enterprise in pre-war days." [1]

The nationalisation of industry in the U.S.S.R. during the last ten years, and the resulting abolition of the unproductive individual consumption of the old property owners, have not resulted in supplying the country with cheap goods of a high quality. Not only do we find that the products of Soviet industry are twice or thrice as dear as foreign goods. This might be attributed to the difficulty of overtaking the industrial countries of western Europe, with their more rapid march of development. But we also find that the products of contemporary Soviet industry are from one-and-a-half times to twice as dear as the

[1] "Sotsialisticheskoye Hozyaistvo", 1926, No. 4.

products of Russian pre-war industry—and very much worse than these in respect of quality. And when we come to study the determinants of price, we find that the dearness of latter-day industrial products in Russia is not due to any great rise in the prices of raw materials (for the peasants are not paid anything like the full value of their produce), and that they are not mainly due to an increase in wages, but that the trouble arises chiefly from an enormous increase in the costs of management and other current expenses.

Nor has the nationalisation of industry been able to bring about any exceptionally good working conditions for the operatives. Real wages to-day are somewhere near the pre-war level,[1] but every one knows that the Russian worker of pre-war days was condemned to an exceedingly low standard of life, and that this was the main cause of the frequent and widespread strikes of that epoch. In its endeavours to expand the scope of production, the Soviet government has followed the line of least resistance, and work has been speeded-up to the limit by piece-work, overtime, and the forcing down of piece-work rates. Furthermore, the sluggish tempo of the development of nationalised industry of late years, and the exclusion of private initiative in industry, have made the problem of unemployment extremely acute. According to official data, the number of unemployed trade unionists reached two million at the beginning of 1928, and unemployment continues to increase at an accelerating speed.

The participation of the workers in the management of industry, of which the communists were so proud during the first years after the revolution, has for some time past been restricted to a mere semblance, taking the form of "conferences of production", in which trifling problems and difficulties of the enterprise are discussed. The real management is in the hands of the "red" directors and of the engineers. No doubt the members of the communist nuclei, and those non-Party workers who are in close touch with the communists, form a

[1] "Ekonomicheskoye Obozrenive", 1927, No. 8.

privileged group in each enterprise, but the great mass of the workers have been reduced once more to the status of mere sellers of the commodity labour power.

It cannot be denied that the Soviet State honestly desires to improve the working conditions of the proletariat, but strict limitations are imposed upon the realisation of these good wishes by the difficulties entailed on industry through the scarcity of capital and the comprehensiveness of the process of nationalisation. Far be it from me to attribute to nationalisation per se the comparative failure of Soviet rule to improve the condition of the workers, for even the best machinery may do immeasurable harm when set to work clumsily and at the wrong time. But there is even less ground for acclaiming such very modest improvement as has taken place in the working conditions of the Russian operatives, as a positive achievement of nationalisation.

It is quite possible to carry on a struggle against the belief now growing in Russia that private property and the initiative of free enterprise have a saving power, and that industry and commerce ought to be completely denationalised, while simultaneously repudiating the Soviet method of an all-embracing and indiscriminate nationalisation.

During the phase of transition to the Nep, there was a moment when the leaders of communist policy were themselves prepared to go a long way in the direction of denationalising industry. In an ordinance concerning the carrying-out of the principles of the new economic policy, issued by the Council of People's Commissaries, under date August 9, 1921, we read:

"§ 4. In order to prevent a further retrogression of the national economy, a change must take place along the following lines:

"*a*. The State, in the form of the Supreme Economic Council and its local instruments, should concentrate in its hands certain branches of industry and a definite number of large-scale enterprises, of or such enterprises as for one reason or another are of importance to the State, as well as accessory enterprises which mutually reinforce one another.

"*b*. Enterprises will remain in the official domain of the Supreme Economic Council and its local instruments only in so far as this is accordant with a general national plan for providing these enterprises with materials, means of subsistence, and monetary resources, both through recourse to the general nationalised organs and to other sources—such as self-provision, a free market, etc."

The ordinance continues:

"The Soviet instruments must energetically and persistently carry out the decree as to the leasing of those enterprises which cannot be set a-going, and must thus contribute to the disburdening of the State apparatus."

Unfortunately, in the leading circles of the Communist Party, other trends got the upper hand within a few days. Already on October 27, 1921, a decree was issued amplifying the extent of nationalisation, and declaring that the enterprises which could not be set a-going were to remain in the hands of the State in a condition of "conservation". This decree was reinforced by appropriate action on the part of the Supreme Economic Council and its instruments.

Nay more, not only was it decided to continue the unduly comprehensive nationalisation of industrial enterprises already effected, but the conditions that would maintain a monopoly of State industry in the future were laid down. New large-scale industrial enterprises were only to be established in Russia by private persons on the basis of special concessions.

Thus enterprise remained wholly dependent upon the State for raw materials, technical equipment, transport, import, taxation, credit, and the marketing of products. Above all, the property of private entrepreneurs was still exposed to the risk of confiscations and new nationalisations whenever governmental policy should take a fresh turn to the left; while the private entrepreneurs were always in peril of arrest or deportation. And yet, under such conditions, during the first year of the Nep not one single large-scale enterprise that had been private could be set to work under the auspices of the Russian State authorities. Even the foreigners who enjoyed the protection of their own governments preferred to put their capital into trading concerns and not into industrial enterprises; or they invested in industrial concessions for the exploitation of already existing enterprises, instead of founding new ones.

The nationalisation of all Russian industry as it existed in the year 1917 was regarded by the Soviet government as an exclusive monopolisation of State industry. But in view of the State's lack of capital and the continued scarcity of goods, the effects of this monopolisation were practically nullified.

In the before-mentioned ordinance of the Council of People's Commissaries under date August 9, 1921, the principles that should guide a decision as to the amount of industry to remain in the hands of the State, were correctly specified. Not merely did the ordinance renounce the idea of an exclusive monopoly of nationalised industry, but it envisaged nationalisation of industry upon such a scope only as would have made it possible for State enterprise to work economically. But this document has long since been forgotten by the communists, and any advocacy of similar ideas is now regarded as manifestly counter-revolutionary.[1]

In the economic, social, and cultural conditions that prevail in contemporary Russia, State economy can only be one of the forms of national economy. "Where the State will not organise an enterprise any worse than a private entrepreneur, nationalisation and State management must persist," wrote L. Martoff at the end of the year 1922, in support of the program of action of the Russian Social Democratic Labour Party.[2] If nothing more than the banks, the railways, the petroleum industry, the coal mines, the metal industry, the

[1] The ordinance has been reprinted in V. Sarabyanoff's [Economics and Applied Economics in the U.S.S.R.], State Printing House, 1926, p. 271.
[2] Published by the Wiener Volksbuchhandlung, Vienna, 1925.

main sources of water power, and particular large-scale enterprises in other branches of industry, remain under State management, this will be enough to give the State a decisive influence in the economic life of the country.

If the State selects the best equipped enterprises, if it puts them under the management of captains of industry who combine high technical capacity with a sense of social responsibility, and if it provides these enterprises with adequate financial resources, it will be able to organise such foci of production in an exemplary fashion, to furnish cheap goods of the best quality, and to ensure that the workers in the State enterprises shall have the best possible labour conditions and shall be able to participate actively in the management of production. That will be the best, the most convincing, the most effective agitation on behalf of nationalisation.

In the general interest of the national economy, all other enterprises than those which come under the before-mentioned categories must be denationalised. Furthermore, the starting of new industrial enterprises must be allowed, and conditions must be provided which will admit of their functioning normally. Obviously, denationalisation must not be carried out in the same hurried and wholesale fashion as nationalisation. Nothing must be done that will disorganise the working of industry. Nor is there any reason, when denationalisation of an enterprise occurs, why it should be given back to its former owner. After the many years of civil war, after the reorganisation, and after the technical transformation and reconstruction of industry, it would no longer be possible to discover the sometime actual owners, or to ascertain the extent of their former possessions. Besides, many of the ex-owners no longer possess the capital which is needed for the successful conduct of their aforetime enterprises. In the process of denationalisation, the government must bear in mind the general interest of the State, and may therefore, in suitable cases, restore enterprises to the old possessors, in so far as these can guarantee normal functioning; whereas in other instances it must sell enterprises to new owners, Russian or foreign; or, finally, it must lease them for long terms.

The large sums which would accrue to the State through the denationalisation of a part of industry could be used to amplify the working capital of those parts of industry which would remain nationalised. I have already insisted that there is no need to fear lest partial denationalisation should deprive the State of its dominant influence in economic life, or involve the risk that State enterprise would be submerged in an ocean of private enterprise. Any one who is timid in this respect shows that he is not convinced that the socialist methods of production, nationalisation and communalisation, are superior economic forms to private enterprise.

On the other hand, in order to safeguard the satisfaction of the needs of the national economy, and in order to ensure the protection of the workers, the State must retain the purposive control of the nationalised industry, while at the same time inaugurating the most extensive regulation of private enterprise. I am referring, of course, to a regulation that shall be prescribed in all its details by law, and not to administrative pressure or arbitrary interference on the part of the authorities. The legislative regulation of economic life by the State will be assisted and strengthened by the fact that the State will retain the most important branches of industry in its own hands, and will conduct them independently.

While for every socialist the need for the socialisation of the means of production is axiomatic, this proceeding can only be defended against all its enemies and against the doubts of the pusillanimous by one who is prepared to denounce the scope and the methods of Soviet nationalisation.

The blind alley into which the economy of the U.S.S.R. has been led by the Soviet policy, is the blind alley of utopism. When we find that in a backward country, in one economically immature, an all-embracing nationalisation of industry carried out in a barbarous fashion has been a failure, we cannot but recognise in this an additional confirmation of the accuracy of the main propositions of Marxism.

CHAPTER EIGHT

PRESENT CONDITION OF RUSSIAN AGRICULTURE

IN pre-revolutionary days, Russian agriculture suffered, above all, from the scarcity of available land. At the beginning of the war, there were in Russia (in round figures) 11 million landless peasants, and more than 6 million peasants who were land-poor, this meaning that they had not enough land to provide food for themselves and their families by agricultural labour alone. The major proportion of the cultivable land of the country belonged to the great landlords, the treasury, the monasteries, etc. In the year 1905, of all the cultivable land in the country, 34·1 per cent belonged to the peasants as their share of what had been allotted to them when the serfs were freed, and an additional 7 per cent represented what had been bought by them; 34·7 per cent belonged to the treasury, to the crown, and to public institutions; 22 per cent was in the hands of private individuals other than peasants; and 2·2 per cent belonged to the monasteries and the churches. The amount of land actually tilled by the peasants was considerably larger, for a notable proportion (about 40 per cent) of the land of the great landlords, and a somewhat smaller proportion of the land belonging to the treasury was leased to the peasants. But about 97 per cent of the land owned by the State consisted of forests and swamps, and in northern Russia was very thinly populated. After the revolution of 1905, and especially after Stolypin's reforms, the comparatively well-to-do peasants, aided by the Peasants' Bank, began to buy land from the great landlords. At this time, too, the renting of land by the peasants assumed larger proportions. According to the calculations of Professor N. Oganoffsky,[1] just before the February revolution of 1917 the land used agriculturally by the peasants belonged to the following categories:

[1] [Sketches of the Economic Geography of Russia], pp. 105–109.

	Desyatines.[1]
Land allotted when the serfs were freed ..	138,700,000
Land bought	27,000,000
Land rented	35,600,000
Total	201,300,000

Apart from the land owned by the treasury, the land cultivated at this date by non-peasant owners amounted to 56 millions of desyatines, this being approximately 28 per cent of the land cultivated by the peasants.

The revolution made an end of land ownership by the great landlords, the treasury, the monasteries, etc. According to the reports of the Central Statistical Bureau, after the revolution there was farmed by peasants 96·8 per cent of all the land previously under cultivation; farmed by the Soviet authorities, 2·7 per cent; and farmed collectively, 0·5 per cent.[2] During the revolutionary redistribution of the land, there were divided up, not only the estates of the great landlords, the treasury, the capitalists, etc., but also, in most districts, land which had been owned by the peasants but had not usually been kept under cultivation by them. The area in question was considerable. According to official statistics, in the year 1905, in the fifty provinces of European Russia, there were 800,000 peasant farms which were more than 25 desyatines in size. In many regions, through the "equalisation of land ownership," the farms of the peasants who had cut adrift from the village communes were completely absorbed. Unfortunately, we have no trustworthy data, as far the whole extent of the U.S.S.R. is concerned, relating to the changes in the utilisation of the land by the peasants. Some idea as to the extent of these changes is given by the results of an enquiry made by the Central Statistical Bureau in twenty-nine of the provinces of European Russia. It appears than in 53 per cent of the village areas, there had been no considerable increase in the amount

[1] A desyatine is 2·7 acres.
[2] Soviet farms ("sovhoz") are State-owned large-scale farms which have been made out of the estates of the great landlords. Collective farms ("kolhoz") are amalgamations of peasant farms run on a more or less developed collective plan. See below, Chapter Ten.

of land under cultivation; in 47 per cent there had been an increase to the average extent of 24 per cent, the increase ranging between 7·3 per cent and 58 per cent. In these provinces, before the revolution, there had been on the average 1·87 desyatines of land per head of the peasant population; after the revolution, there were 2·6 desyatines, this signifying an average increase of 21 per cent.[1] The redistribution of the land led to far-reaching changes in the relative amount of land cultivated in various peasant farms. The general upshot was an equalisation of the size of the farms.

Study, for example, the figures for this matter in the respective years 1917 and 1919 given on the opposite page.[2]

There has been a reduction in the extremes at both ends of the scale, in the very small and the very large farms. There has been an extraordinarily large increase in the number of small farms with a cultivated area of less than 4 desyatines, and in the number of those worked with only 1 horse. The proportion of these groups has, as judged by the cultivated area, increased from 57·6 to 72·1 per cent; and as judged by the number of horses worked, from 47·6 to 60·1 per cent. It has become the dominant type, whereas the large peasant farms, worked by 4 horses and more, and having a cultivated area of more than 16 desyatines, have almost disappeared.

This process of the equalisation of peasant farms continued until the beginning of the Nep period.

The hopes of the Russian peasants that after the partition of the large estates there would be a superfluity of land had been disappointed. In the first place, before the partition, as much as 40 per cent of the cultivable land owned by the great landlords and the treasury had already been leased to peasant farmers. In the second place, the reserve of land (consisting mainly of what used to be State domains, and comprising an area nearly as great as that of the land already cultivated)

[1] See the collective work [The Land], No. 1, 1921.
[2] [Economic Stratification of the Peasantry in the years 1917 and 1919], published by the Central Statistical Bureau, 1922.

could only be brought under cultivation after the expenditure of large amounts of capital upon various improvements—irrigation, the making of roads, surveying, etc.

CLASSIFICATION OF PEASANT FARMS IN ACCORDANCE WITH THE AREA UNDER CULTIVATION

(In percentages of the total number of farms)

	1917.	1919.
No cultivated area	11·6	6·6
A cultivated area of less than 2 desyatines	28·7	42·8
A cultivated area of from 2 to 4 desyatines	28·9	29·3
A cultivated area of from 4 to 6 desyatines	14·6	12·4
A cultivated area of from 6 to 10 desyatines	11·2	7·3
A cultivated area of from 10 to 16 desyatines	3·8	1·4
A cultivated area of from 16 to 25 desyatines	0·9	0·2
A cultivated area of more than 25 desyatines	0·3	0·01
Total	100·0	100·0

CLASSIFICATION OF PEASANT FARMS ACCORDING TO THE NUMBER OF HORSES WORKED

(In percentages of the total number of farms)

	1917.	1919.
No horses	28·9	25·1
With 1 horse	47·6	60·1
With 2 horses	17·6	12·3
With 3 horses	3·9	1·8
With 4 horses	1·2	0·5
With 5 horses or more	0·8	0·2
Total	100·0	100·0

The results of the revolutionary redistribution of the land showed that the Russian social democrats (both mensheviks and bolsheviks) had been right when, before the revolution, they declared, as against the socialist "populists" (the socialist revolutionaries, or essers), that even the most radical redistribution of the land would not suffice to satisfy the land hunger of the peasants. If the social democrats advocated the confiscation of the estates of the great landlords and the handing-over of the land to be administered by local self-governing authorities, this was because they regarded such a step as the most radical way of getting rid of the vestiges of feudalism and of freeing the peasants from the remnants of the servile state; and because they considered it essential that rents should be reduced and that supplementary land should be distributed to the needier peasants out of the reserve of land that would then be in the hands of the local self-governing bodies. But the social democrats never proposed the dividing-up of rationally managed large-scale farms, for they knew that this would result in a reduction of the amount of agricultural produce, thus having an injurious effect upon the welfare of the population as a whole, without adequately satisfying the land hunger of the peasants.

The social-democratic view was that the problem of land scarcity must be solved, not by a radical redistribution and subdivision of the land as a whole, but by reforming agriculture itself. Whereas it was primitive, uneconomic, and extensive, it must be modernised, become comparatively intensive, and must be conducted in such a way as to make the application of labour more effective. At the Fourth Congress of the Russian Social Democratic Labour Party held in April 1906 (before the cleavage between the bolsheviks and the mensheviks) there was general agreement as to the need for supporting "the revolutionary activities of the peasants up to the point of confiscating privately owned land". This decision was based on political considerations. Nevertheless, the congress rejected the proposal of one group of delegates to include in the agrarian program of the Party a universal redistribution of the land. It is interesting to note that Lenin at this time described the demand as "erroneous but harmless".

During the November revolution of 1917 the bolsheviks abandoned their former position. In his speeches and writings, Lenin declared on several occasions that after the November revolution the communists, when they demanded the general equalisation of the size of farms and a universal redistribution of the land, did so, not because they regarded these measures as good in themselves, but only because it was necessary to conform to the wishes of the peasant masses.

If, however, the revolution was not successful, in all districts and in respect of all strata of the peasantry, in satisfying the peasants' long-standing desire for a notable enlargement of their farms, nevertheless it delivered all categories of the peasants from the burden of high rents,[1] land taxes, and interest on mortgages. The revolution gave the peasants rights as a class, and freed them from their semi-feudal dependence upon the great landlords. Thus did the revolution fulfil its main historical task, and therein must be discerned its greatest achievement.

One of the first decrees of the Soviet government was the Decree concerning the Land, under date November 8, 1917. The legislative measures enacted at various times in order to carry out this basic decree were elaborated and incorporated in the general Land Code of October 30, 1922. The Land Code declares that "the right of private property in land, in natural resources, rivers, lakes, and forests, within the area of the U.S.S.R., is abolished once for all" (§1). "All the land in the country, to whomsoever it may have belonged, and however it may be used, is henceforward State property" (§ 2). The State allots land gratuitously for the use of actual cultivators and cattle breeders, and to combinations of these, as well as to settlers from the towns and to State organisations. "The right to the use of land kept under cultivation is not terminable" (§ 11). "The purchase, sale, testamentary disposition, or giving away of land, and the mortgaging of it, are prohibited" (§ 27). The Land Code leaves it open to land cooperatives and individual holders to cultivate the land in any one of the following ways: a. communal cultivation, in which the land is managed by a land cooperative, and is

[1] At the beginning of the twentieth century, the peasants were paying about 150 millions of roubles annually as rent.

allotted among the members (usually in accordance with the number of members of a family) after the lapse of three sowing periods (9 to 12 years); b. partially individual cultivation, in which all the arable of the individual farmer is compacted into an independent farming enterprise, while the peasant farmstead remains within the village settlement; c. exclusively individual cultivation, in which the farm is cut completely adrift from the village community; d. collective cultivation, in which the land is tilled (either wholly or in part) collectively by the peasants.

According to the reports of the Central Statistical Bureau, on January 1, 1927, the land cultivated by the working agricultural population could be classified as follows: 95 per cent was worked by the rural communes (agricultural cooperatives); 3 per cent was under partially individual cultivation; 1.2 per cent under exclusively individual cultivation; and 0·8 per cent under collective cultivation. In addition, with the aid of the State land reserve, Soviet farms working for the market had been formed out of the estates of the sometime great landlords.

According to the data issued by the Central Statistical Bureau,[1] the rural area of the U.S.S.R. was distributed as follows in the year 1927:

	Millions of Desyatines.	Percentages.
Farmsteads	8	0·5
Arable	162	10·8
Hayfields	36	2·4
Pasturage	34	2·4
Forests and Woodland	397	26·6
Used in other ways	35	2·4
Total utilisable	662	45·1
Unutilisable	180	12·6
Total investigated	852	57·7
Additional area not investigated	640	42·3
Grand total	1492	100·0

[1] [Statistical Year Book of the U.S.S.R. for 1927], pp. 51–52.

Obviously these figures must be very inaccurate, but they suffice to show that more than half of the whole agricultural area is either uninvestigated or unutilised. Only 10 to 15 per cent of the area is used more or less satisfactorily. Especially inadequate has been the study of the forest and woodland regions; and no attention at all has been paid to the tundras, the swamps, and the vast marshy forest lands of Siberia.

The area under forest has been very inaccurately determined, but is estimated at round about 397 millions of desyatines, of which only 180 millions are actually used for economic purposes or have been improved in any way. All the forests, including those at one time held by the peasants, belong to the State and are subject to the supervision of the State forestry department, but since 1924, 21 millions of desyatines of forest land have been handed over to the peasants for exploitation.

The most important branches of Russian agriculture are arable, which accounts for 57 per cent of the total income of the peasant population; cattle breeding, which accounts for 21 per cent; and forestry, which accounts for 8·9 per cent. Of the whole arable area, 87·2 per cent is planted with grain; with potatoes and other crops, 10·6 per cent; while 2·2 per cent is used for market gardening and horticulture.

In the year 1921, the total cultivated area had fallen to 73 per cent of the pre-war area, but by the year 1927-1928 the extent of pre-war cultivation had been nearly regained (96 per cent). The area under intensive culture and producing raw materials for industry, has increased by 11·8 per cent as compared with pre-war days. Inasmuch as the yield per unit of land remains lower than before the war (from 85 to 88 per cent), the aggregate yield of pre-war days has not been fully regained.

As regards farm stock and draught beasts, at the beginning of the year 1927 the number of head of horned cattle had exceeded the pre-war number by 5 per cent, but the number of draught beasts was only 85·7 per cent of the pre-war figure. The number of swine and sheep is now equal to the pre-war figure. The number of draught horses has increased more slowly. In Russia the percentage of peasant farms without horses has always been a very high one, but now it is even higher than of old. In the year 1927, in the whole area of the U.S.S.R., there were 8 millions of peasant farms (more than 30 per cent of the whole number) on which there were no horses. In Ukraine, the proportion of peasant farms without horses is even larger, being here 45 per cent.

YIELD OF GRAIN

Year.	Per Desyatine in Poods.	Gross Yield in Millions of Poods.
1913	62·2	5896
1921	29·5	3160
1923	45·6	3364
1927	51·7	4525
1928[1]	49·5	4200

In contemporary Russia, the poorness of the harvests is one of the most painful aspects of agricultural development. The subjoined table enables us to compare the yield in various countries for the year 1925 reckoned in double hundredweights per desyatine:[2]

	Rye.	Wheat.	Potatoes.	Sugar-beet.	Flax.
Great Britain and Ireland	17·1	22·9	170·9	205·8	3·9
U.S.A.	7·5	8·6	70·4	254·4	4·6
Denmark	16·3	33·1	173·9	320·9	7·8
Belgium	23·8	26·7	193·8	300·4	10·1
Germany	17·1	20·7	148·5	256·2	5·6
France	12·8	16·0	103·8	245·7	8·2
Poland	13·3	14·4	123·4	214·3	5·9
Latvia	11·8	12·2	94·9	—	3·9
Lithuania	12·2	12·8	97·0	—	5·1
U.S.S.R.	6·0	6·1	73·0	128·0	2·4

Although the reserves of unoccupied cultivable land have

[1] Temporary data, "Pravda", November 3, 1928.
[2] Statistisches Jahrbuch für das Deutsche Reich, 1927, and [Collective Volume issued by the Central Statistical Bureau of the U.S.S.R.], 1927.

long since become extremely slender, and although the natural fertility of the cultivated area has long since been exhausted, while the density of population is increasing year by year— Russian agriculture, being petrified as it were in an extensive system, has long ceased to be a paying proposition.

Owing to the extensive character of Russian peasant agriculture, to its backwardness, and to its lack of proper technical equipment, failures of the harvests are frequent, rising from time to time to the proportions of veritable famine. During the first half of the nineteenth century, from 1800 to 1854, there were 35 years in which there was a more or less serious failure of the crops. In the twenty-year period from 1891 to 1911, there were 13 poor harvests, 4 good harvests, and 3 famine years. During the ten years of Soviet rule, there have been 2 famine years, 5 years with poor harvests, and only 3 years with good harvests. No doubt in other European countries, agriculture is not wholly independent of nature. But whereas, elsewhere in Europe, the gross yield in years with a bad harvest only falls behind the average by the amount of from 7 to 10 per cent, the falling-off in Russia is from 20 to 30 per cent in years of bad harvest, and as much as 50 per cent in famine years.

In Europe and the United States of America[1], the risks of a failure of the crops are minimised by a suitable system of rotation, by careful ploughing, and by the use of the best possible fertilisers. Whereas in Germany before the war, 166 kilograms of manure were used per hectare [2] of ploughland, in Russia only 6·9 kilograms were used. By the year 1926, the quantity of manure per hectare had been doubled in Russia, whereas in Germany the increase in the same period amounted to only 0·6 kilograms.

[1] In the United States of America, where there are an abundance of arable land and a plentiful supply of machinery, we find also that the use of mineral manures is steadily increasing. For instance, the production of phosphatic manures in the year 1922 was double that of 1910.—Die Wirtschaft des Auslandes, 1900–1927, Berlin, 1928.
[2] The hectare is approximately 2¾ acres, and for rough comparisons may be considered identical with the desyatine.

The production of mineral manures in the U.S.S.R. is only one twenty-fifth of the quantity actually needed. The import of manure has fallen to one twenty-sixth of the pre-war figure. Nevertheless, experience in the use of fertilisers in Russian agriculture has shown that the effect is remarkable, the increase in the crop being so great that all expenditure upon manure is repaid within the first year. For instance, in the year 1925–1926, mineral manures were used on the arable land of peasant farms in the Vladimir province, with the result that the yield increased from 880 kilograms to 1470, that is to say by 70 per cent.

The supply of agricultural machinery and farming implements in Russia is just as defective as the supply of manures. In this matter, Russia was in a very bad position even before the war To-day (1927), the supply of agricultural machinery is only 70 per cent of the pre-war supply. According to the results of an enquiry made by the People's Commissariat for Agriculture, for 24 million farms there were only 9 million ploughs and 8 million harrows, so that there were 7 million farms without either a plough or a harrow. Still worse is the position as regards complicated agricultural machinery. A sowing machine, which normally should serve 50 desyatines, must to-day, on the average, serve an area of 470 desyatines; for a reaping machine, the figures are respectively 75 desyatines and 153; for a threshing machine, they are 60 and 197 respectively. The demand for tractors is enormous, but they can only be imported in very small numbers, and their use must therefore be reserved mainly for the collective farms and the Soviet farms. In round figures there are to-day in the U.S.S.R. 25,000 tractors. There is an extremely vigorous demand from the peasants for agricultural machinery, milk separators, and other modern appliances, but this demand cannot be satisfied because the home production lags so far behind what is wanted (even before the war, 50 per cent of the agricultural machines used in Russia were imported), and the State will only permit of import in small quantities. The peasants are acutely aware of the need for machinery, fertilisers, and seed of better quality. The impossibility of supplying what they want in sufficient quantities and at moderate prices, arouses widespread discontent.

In the Russian countryside to-day, 9 millions of able-bodied peasants can find no employment for their productive activities, and according to the calculations of the Soviet authorities this number is likely to increase year by year by 0·75 to 1 million. The effects of the radical redistribution of the land after the revolution have shown that a fresh redistribution will not solve the problem of the scarcity of land. No doubt, in the north and in the south-east of European Russia, in Siberia, and in central Asia, there are still extensive regions which can be brought under the plough, but to bring them under cultivation will demand the investment of large amounts of capital. Before the war, in the course of twenty years, through the activities of the Settlement Board (between 1896 and 1915), 2·5 millions of peasants were given new homes and provided with land. This was in an epoch when the best land was still unoccupied![1] Since the introduction of the Nep, comparatively little has been done in the way of settlement. According to the reports of the Central Statistical Bureau, no more than 6500 peasants are newly settled on the land every year.

According to the plans of the Settlement Board, in the course of the next ten years 5 millions of persons are to be newly settled on the land, but this would need funds to the amount of 1 milliard of roubles. In actual practice, in the year 1926, the Soviet government was able to devote only 26·4 millions of roubles to this purpose; in 1927, only 15·1 millions; and in 1928, only 17·5 millions[2]. None the less, this settlement scheme gives a certain amount of help towards the solution of the problem of over-population in the countryside. It would,

[1] Collective Volume [Agriculture in the Twentieth Century] edited by Professor Kondratieff, pp. 44-45.
[2] [Control Figures], 1927-1928, p. 131.

however, be utopian to expect this problem of over-population to be fully solved by any such settlement policy. There is no present prospect of removing from 25 to 30 millions of peasants to a distance ranging from 8000 to 11,000 kilometres, and of providing them with the requisites for carrying on agriculture in their new homes. Besides, the settling of peasants in steppe areas comes into conflict with the need for maintaining cattle breeding in these regions.

The only effective, the only realist way of solving the problem of land scarcity and over-population in the rural areas is to bring about the rapid industrialisation of Russia and to make Russian agriculture intensive. A rapid increase in industry and trade would doubtless provide employment for the extant surplus population of the countryside; but nothing short of an industrial and commercial advance at a truly American pace could absorb the huge annual increase of the Russian rural population. The essential thing, therefore, is that there should be a prompt industrialisation and intensification of Russian agriculture itself.

At present the three-field system is dominant, with the result that year by year one-third of the whole area of cultivated land remains unplanted. In the European area of the U.S.S.R. alone, the fallows amount every year to from 28 to 30 millions of desyatines. By a transition to a more intensive system (such as the ten-field system), the fallows would be reduced to from 9 to 10 millions of desyatines, and the peasants would acquire a new actually planted area of from 18 to 20 millions of desyatines.[1] Again, by reducing to the utmost the trackways between the fields, the cultivable area might—so say the experts—be increased by no less than 4 millions of desyatines.[2] These and other measures could be adopted during the transition to better methods of cultivation. That the amount thus gained would be considerable will be realised when we remember that during thirty years of new agricultural settle-

[1] A. Aihenvald [Soviet Agriculture], p. 145.
[2] P. Guroff, an article in "Na Agrarnom ronte", 1925, No. 10.

ment in Siberia only 9 millions of desyatines have there been brought under the plough.

But the intensive exploitation of the soil implies that the land should be more carefully and effectively ploughed and harrowed, and also that fodder plants, tubers, oil-bearing plants, and various other useful plants and vegetables, should form a more considerable portion of the crops. This would not only make peasant farming pay much better, but it would need a greater expenditure of labour upon the land, and would thus give productive occupation to many millions of peasants.

The industrialisation of agriculture might well be of even greater importance. The elaboration of agricultural products; the making of different kinds of meal, meal products, and vegetable oils; market gardening; horticulture; bee-keeping; the primary elaboration of flax; dairy farming; poultry farming; cattle breeding; the canning of meat, fruit and vegetables; the building of repairing shops; home industry; the growth of rural trade—all these things would provide occupation and a means of livelihood for the population which is superfluous to-day.

In countries where peasant agriculture has attained a higher cultural level, the land hunger of the peasants is less acute, although there the peasant farms are smaller. In Germany, for instance, peasant farms of a size ranging from 1·8 to 4·5 hectares are regarded as small ones, although they can still be made to pay; but farms ranging from 6 to 8 hectares are considered to be of a fair size, grow crops for the market, and employ agricultural labourers. Similar conditions prevail in Denmark, where peasant farmers whose holdings range from 5 to 7 hectares are quite well-to-do.

The poverty of the Russian peasants will be done away with, not so much by enlarging the size of their farms, as by promoting a more intensive culture of the farms they have. A noteworthy general advance in Russian agriculture can only be expected along these lines. On the other hand, if Russian agriculture is to be intensified and industrialised, it is essential that there should be a simultaneous advance in Russian industry, trade, and transport, for only in this way can the market be provided and the technical and political conditions be created which are indispensable to an advance in agriculture.

CHAPTER NINE

AGRICULTURE AND THE MARKET

SINCE the introduction of the New Economic Policy, that is to say since the time when agriculture was enabled to take economic advantage of the most important achievements of the revolution (the abolition of large-scale landed proprietorship and of the semi-feudal subordination of the peasantry), there has been a rapid reestablishment of the circulation of commodities, and the peasants have been able to resume working for the market.

Market conditions, at the outset of this period, were extremely favourable for the peasants. On the one hand, there was a steadily increasing demand for grain, both for home consumption and for export; and, on the other hand, there was an increasing demand for raw materials on the part of the industry that was now in course of reconstruction, and this gave a stimulus to the increased cultivation of the various plants that provided raw materials to industry, and a stimulus also to cattle breeding.

The revolution, having made a clean sweep of the patriarchal conditions that had prevailed in rural life for centuries, removed the psychological hindrances to the transformation of agricultural methods, giving a vigorous impetus to the replacement of the three-field system by a many-field system, to the adoption of modern ploughs, to the use of chemical manures in place of cattle dung, and to the consultation of agricultural experts instead of relying upon traditional knowledge. Professor Gogol-Yanoffsky describes the mood in the villages as follows: "Never was there a situation more favourable for the introduction of improved technical methods. The rural population shows itself extremely receptive, and the advice of experts is readily followed, for there have now returned to the villages numerous peasants who had been war prisoners in Germany and Austria, and had there learned of the existence of more advanced agricultural methods."[1]

In addition, the revolution had tended to raise the general cultural level of the peasants, enlarging their horizons and arousing in them new needs, whose satisfaction could only be secured by transcending the limits of a natural economy. The result was that peasant agriculture now required a larger supply of industrial products, and they became more closely connected with the market. In fact, during the first years of the Nep, the damage Russian agriculture had sustained during the civil war and owing to the compulsory levies of grain, was made good with extraordinary speed, and the peasants' demand for industrial products increased so rapidly that industry was unable to satisfy them.

Since 1923, however, the speed of the reconstruction of agriculture has slackened, and in many respects the advance has been arrested—at a rather low level. Especially does this remark apply to the development of a monetary economy in agriculture instead of a natural economy; and, furthermore, there has been a falling-off in the quantity of agricultural products offered for sale in the home market and the foreign market. Although the area under cultivation is now as large as it was before the war, and although the total agricultural production has regained the pre-war level, the amount of agricultural produce sold in the market is much smaller than it used to be. If, for instance, we compare the year 1913 with the year 1926–1927, we find that in the former year 28 per cent of the whole grain harvest was sent to the market, whereas in the year 1926–1927, only 14·5 per cent was sold in the market. In like manner, the sale of agricultural products for industrial use has been restricted, and cattle breeding has declined. In the year 1926–1927, the sale of flax was 66 per cent of the pre-war amount; of hemp, 54 per cent; of hides, 82 per cent; of poultry and eggs, 58 per cent; of wool, 46 per cent.[2] We find a similar

[1] Introduction to a Report to the Eighth Soviet Congress.
[2] "Ekonomicheskaya Zhizn", May 3, 1927.

decline in the export of grain, as is shown by the following table:

					Millions of Poods.
1913 ..	..	..	..	..	636·0
1924/25 ..	..	..	..	..	182·0
1925/26 ..	..	..	..	..	124·9
1926/27 ..	..	..	..	..	120·6
1927/28[1]	..	..	..	..	25·0

Although the harvests were good during the years 1924–1925, 1925–1926, and 1926–1927, there was no increase in the export of grain, but a decline. Moreover, the average level of the "stabilisation" of export is much lower than the level of "stabilisation" in other branches of Russian economic life.

How are we to account for the failure of the agricultural producers in Russia to enter into closer relations with the market?

One of the reasons why a comparatively small amount of agricultural produce finds its way to the market is that the peasants' own consumption of their produce has increased since the war. In pre-war days, although Russia was accounted one of the principal granaries of Europe, the actual producers of Russian grain, the peasants who form the majority of the Russian population, used to go hungry. Before the war, the government did its utmost to promote the export of grain. The saying of Vyshnegradsky, the minister of State, has often been quoted: "Though hungry, we shall continue to export grain." But it is not generally known that at the very time when Russia was exporting grain she was producing so little that she ought rather to have imported it than exported it. According to the calculations of Professor D. Pryanishnikoff,[2] during the five-year period 1908–1913, the total production of grain per head of population in various countries was as follows:

[1] In the year 1928/29, during the early months, 20 millions of poods of grain were exported, but when the harvest proved a bad one grain to the amount of 15 millions of poods was imported from Argentina. Reports of the People's Commissariat for Trade, "Ekonomicheskaya Zhizn", July 28, 1929.
[2] "Pravda", July 1, 1928.

In Grain-exporting Countries.			In Grain-importing Countries.		
Canada	..	.. 111 poods	Denmark	..	.. 41 poods
U.S.A.	..	.. 62 ,,	Sweden	..	.. 31 ,,
Argentina	..	60 ,,	Germany	..	.. 28 ,,
Rumania ..	..	46 ,,	France	..	.. 26 ,,

During this same period, Russia produced per head of population only 24·9 poods of grain, so that, as a comparison with other countries shows, it should have been an importing country and not an exporting one. Comparing Germany and Russia, and adding to the grain figures an equivalent for the production of potatoes, we find for the five-year period 1908–1913, in Germany 38 poods of agricultural produce per head of population, and in Russia 28 poods. After the revolution, when there had been a relief from the heavy burden of taxation and the vestiges of feudalism, and when there had ensued a general levelling of the size of agricultural holdings, there was an improvement in the nutritive conditions of the peasant population.

Precise data are lacking as regards the amount of agricultural produce consumed by the peasant population, but according to the data published by the Central Statistical Bureau, the consumption per head of the agricultural population is as shown in the table opposite.

According to the reports of the Central Statistical Bureau, as summarised by S. Brike,[1] during the years 1926 and 1927 there prevailed among the peasantry a tendency to a rapid decrease in the consumption of grain and to a rapid increase in the consumption of meat, eggs, and butter.

The table shows that the consumption of milk, eggs, and meat per head of population has greatly increased as compared with pre-war conditions; but we see that the consumption of grain has only just regained that of pre-war days.

If, however, there has been a certain decline in the consumption of grain per head of peasant population, the aggregate grain consumption of the peasant population has greatly increased, if only because the rural population increased by 7·5 per cent between 1913 and 1917.[2]

[1] [Problems of the Home Market], in "Ekonomicheskoye Obozreniye", 1928, No. 9.

[2] Russian economists and statisticians have tried to tabulate a grain

Products.	Pre-war.	1921.	1922.	1923.	1924.	1925.
1. Grain per head per annum:						
(a) Areas producing an excess of grain, poods	17·0	8·2	16·8	17·4	15·3	16·7
Percentages of pre-war condition	100	48	99	102	90	98
(b) Areas producing a deficiency of grain, poods	14·7	11·4	14·5	15·7	14·5	15·0
Percentages of pre-war condition	100	77	98	106	99	102
2. Meat in poods	1·03	—	—	0·75	0·86	1·18
Percentages of pre-war condition	100	—	—	73	84	1·15
3. Butter in poods	0·10	—	—	0·10	0·10	0·10
Percentages of pre-war condition	100	—	—	100	100	100
4. Milk in poods	6·18	—	—	7·95	8·33	8·81
Percentages of pre-war condition	100	—	—	129	135	143
5. Eggs in the piece	36	—	—	36	37	45
Percentages of pre-war condition	100	—	—	100	103	125

(No figures are available regarding meat, butter, milk, and eggs for the years 1921 and 1922.)

Of even greater importance is the fact that the Russian peasants have for various reasons abandoned their "compulsory vegetarianism". Before the war, the consumption of meat per head of rural population was approximately 1·03 poods, but in 1926 and 1927 there had been a considerable advance upon this figure. An enquiry into the standard of life of the rural population instituted by the Central Statistical Bureau showed that the consumption of meat per head of the rural population

balance for Russia. The practical value of the table is not very great. For instance, the consumption of the rural population in the years 1925–26 and 1926–27, is shown to be smaller than in the year 1913, although the consumption of the countryside had increased greatly owing to the increase in population. Besides, the table fails to take into account the increased consumption of fodder. Nevertheless, the figures are of some interest as giving a general indication. I quote them from the periodicals "Ekonomicheskoye Obozreniye", 1926, No. 9, and "Statisticheskoye Obozreniye", 1927, No. 4.

GRAIN BALANCE OF THE U.S.S.R. (*In Millions of Poods.*)

	1913.	1925/26.	1926/27.
A. Income.			
Gross Harvest ..	5896·1	4368·8	4658·2
B. Expenditure.			
1. Consumption by the rural population:			
(a) for sowing	871·0	701·9	739·6
(b) Personal consumption	2008·9	1680·2	1756·6
(c) Food for cattle and poultry	1002·5	963·2	1050·6
(d) Various (including grain used for making vodka)	—	148·8	139·1
	3882·4	3530·1	3685·9
2. Consumption by the urban population:			
(a) Personal consumption	397·8	267·6	288·7
(b) Food for cattle and poultry	109·8	70·6	74·6
(c) Various	—	14·0	15·2
	507·6	352·2	378·5
3. Army and industry	76·5	60·0	70·0
4. Annual reserves	} 1429·6	301·5	246·9
5. Exported and stored	}	125·0	276·9
	5896·1	4368·8	4658·2

(Owing to the defects and inaccuracies of the Soviet statistics, the foregoing data are not wholly accordant with the official data found in the Table I published in Chapter Eight.)

in the year 1926 was 38 kilograms (2·34 poods) in areas producing a surplus of grain, and 37 kilograms in areas producing
a deficiency of grain.[1] S. Brike gives identical figures for the
consumption of meat in the rural areas.[2] I think these figures
are somewhat exaggerated. Still, even if the consumption of
meat per head of rural population was only from 18 to 20
kilograms in the year 1926, as a special enquiry into the
meat consumption of the U.S.S.R. instituted by the Central
Statistical Bureau indicates[3] (this signifying that the peasant
nowadays eats meat about once a week), the amount of grain
(or its equivalent) which the peasant devotes to the feeding of
his horses, cattle, and poultry, has a great effect in reducing
the amount of produce, and especially the amount of
grain, sent to market. Such increase in agricultural produce
as there is, finds its way to market much more in the
form of meat, butter, and milk, than in the form of grain.
In the absence of a special investigation, it is not easy to
ascertain how large a part is played in this matter by
the natural increase in the consumption of the rural population (whose demands are most easily satisfied at the
expense of their own natural economy) and how much
of it depends upon unfavourable conditions in the matter
of price.

Of great importance, too, is the fact that, whereas the total
production of grain has, on the average, nearly regained the
pre-war level (80 to 85 per cent), cultivation for the peasants'
own consumption has attained a much higher than the pre-war
level, whilst there has been a corresponding decline in production for the home and foreign market. The gross harvest of
the year 1927 is, in the following table, compared with the
average harvests of the five-year period 1909 to 1913, as
recorded in official statistics:

[1] "Pravda", July 1, 1928.
[2] Op. cit., and "Ekonomicheskoye Obozreniye", 1928, No. 9.
[3] B. Nifonoff [The Meat Market of the U.S.S.R.], "Statisticheskoye
Obozreniye", 1928, No. 9.

Gross Harvests.	1909–13. Millions of Poods.	1927. Millions of Poods.
Rye	1411	1500
Maize	96	230
Wheat	1508	1250
Barley	667	286

Of late years, both in the town and in the countryside, there has been a general inclination to eat wheaten bread in place of rye bread. According to data published by A. Lozitsky, in the four years from 1922 to 1925–1926, when the total consumption of grain was practically unchanged, the consumption of wheat on the part of the rural population increased by 39 per cent, and on the part of the urban population by 72 per cent, whereas the consumption of rye fell by 15 per cent in the countryside and by 49 per cent in the towns.[1] In the year 1926–1927 there was on the average an increase of from 7 to 8 per cent in the consumption of white bread.

One of the reasons why there are difficulties about the export of grain from Russia, and why there are frequent disharmonies between supply and demand in the home grain market of the U.S.S.R., is that there is a comparatively small production of grain for the market whilst the peasants' own consumption of grain has increased.

The sale of agricultural produce was, of course, likewise diminished by the circumstance that large-scale agricultural production for the market was destroyed by the revolution. Before the war, the percentage sales of the various kinds of grain from the estates of the great landlords and from the peasant farms were as stated in the table on page 129.

According to the calculations of Professor Kondratieff,[2] the well-known agricultural expert, 15 to 20 per cent of all the agricultural produce brought to the market came from the estates of the great landlords, and the breaking-up of these

[1] "Ekonomicheskoye Obozreniye", 1928, No. 1.
[2] [The Grain Market], p. 14.

large estates led to a notable restriction in the amount of grain sent to the market. The larger peasant farms that produced for the market were also parcelled out. According to the statement

	Peasant Farms.	Estates of Great Landlords.
Wheat	51·3%	81·1%
Rye..	21·5%	42·0%
Oats and Barley	28·8%	65·8%

of Lyashchenko,[1] 70 per cent of all the grain marketed before the war came from the estates of the great landlords and from the larger peasant farms.[2]

[1] [Russian Grain Production], 1927, Chap. 16.
[2] In order to show the importance of the estates of the great landlords and of the larger peasant farms in the matter of sending grain to the market and to facilitate a comparison of the agriculture of pre-war days with contemporary agriculture, Nemchinoff, a member of the committee of the Central Statistical Bureau, has compiled the following interesting table ("Pravda", June 2, 1928), in which the figures must not be regarded as perfectly accurate:

	Gross Production of Grain.		Grain Brought to Market.		Sales in Percentages of the Production.
	In Millions of Poods.	Per Cent.	In Millions of Poods.	Per Cent.	
Pre-War:					
Estates of great landlords	600·0	12·0	281·6	21·6	47·0
Larger peasant farms	1900·0	38·0	650·0	50·0	34·0
Middle-sized and small peasant farms ..	2500·0	50·0	369·0	28·4	14·7
	5,000·0	100·0	1300·6	100·0	26·0
1926/27:					
Soviet farms and collective farms ..	80·0	1·7	37·8	6·0	47·2
Larger peasant farms	617·0	13·0	126·0	20·0	20·0
Middle-sized and small peasant farms ..	4052·0	85·3	466·2	74·0	11·2
	4749·0	100·0	630·0	100·0	13·3

The dividing-up of the peasant farms, which went on at a great pace after the revolution, had a similar effect. Before the revolution, only about 1·7 per cent of the peasant farms were on the average divided-up each year for family reasons, but after the revolution the percentage reached from 2·3 to 3·5. In many districts, the falling-off in the marketing of agricultural produce that resulted from the splitting-up of the peasant farms amounted to 15 per cent, and in some even to 20 per cent. It was impossible for the collective farms and the Soviet farms to counteract this to any considerable extent, seeing that, according to the calculations of the Central Statistical Bureau, the total area cultivated by these amounts to only $1\frac{1}{2}$ millions of desyatines, so that they supply no more than 6 per cent of all the grain which comes to market.

But the most important cause of the decline in the amount of grain sent to market is not to be found either in the increased personal consumption of the peasants, or in the splitting-up of the farms, but in the fact that there is no adequate stimulus to induce the peasants to increase the amount of grain marketed. As an indirect proof of this, it may be pointed out that at the beginning of the year 1928 the peasants had very large quantities of grain stored in their granaries. According to the statistics published by the Central Statistical Bureau, these stores amounted to 600 millions of poods,[1] whilst according to a calculation made by the communist opposition the amount was 900 millions of poods. Very likely even the lower figure is a great exaggeration, but there can be no question that large quantities of grain are actually hoarded by the peasants. Since the export of grain is now almost completely in abeyance, millions of poods of grain that used to be exported are kept in the country.

There are two main reasons why so little agricultural produce finds its way to the market, the first being that the prices of agricultural products are so low, and the second that there is a scarcity of industrial products in the market.

[1] "Statisticheskoye Obozreniye", 1927, No. 4.

Although since the introduction of the Nep the preparation and sale of agricultural produce in the Soviet Union has nominally been free, in reality the State (which supervises the food supply of the population and the provision of agricultural raw materials to industry, controls export, and has concentrated into its own hands all the machinery of transport and of credit) has a monopolist's power to fix prices. During the Nep period, the prices the peasants could obtain by the sale of agricultural produce to the State have, indeed, varied; but even when the figure was higher it was scarcely high enough to repay the peasant farmer for the cost of production. In any case, the prices paid by the State were considerably lower than those obtainable by the peasants in the open market. The extent of the difference is seen in the following official data for the years 1927 and 1928[1]:

	Wheat.	Rye.	Oats.	Barley.
1927 (July)—				
State purchase price[2]	6·29	4·64	3·54	4·03
Market retail price[2]	8·18	6·17	6·59	6·65
1928 (July)—				
State purchase price[2]	6·77	4·56	4·35	5·67
Market retail price[2]	11·54	11·11	12·09	9·28

In the year 1929, the difference between the State purchase prices and the market prices has increased yet further, so that in the open market the peasant receives three or four times as much for his produce as he receives from the State.[3]

As a result of the various legislative and economic measures which make it difficult for the peasant to sell his grain to private traders or in the urban market, and compel him to sell it at a loss to the State or the cooperatives, he naturally tends

[1] The figures are taken from a survey published in "Finansy i Narodnoye Hozyaistvo", 1928, No. 36.
[2] The figures in the table are averages for the whole of the U.S.S.R. in roubles per hundredweight.
[3] "Bolshevik", 1929, No. 7.

to restrict his sales to the minimum which will provide him with the money needed to pay taxes and outstanding liabilities. The peasants, in fact, have declared a sort of sellers' strike as against the State (whose integrity is thereby imperilled), and in so far as they dispose of their produce in the towns they incline to do so by underground and illegal channels, through the instrumentality of private hucksters.

Even more important than the influence of the price at which State purchases of agricultural produce are made, is the effect upon peasant agriculture of the mutual relationship between the prices of industrial and of agricultural products respectively. At no time during the prevalence of the Nep has the exchange of agricultural and industrial products been effected upon the basis of equivalent values. The result has been the appearance in Russia of the phenomenon known as the "scissors". Of course, these "scissors" are not peculiar to Russia. Since the war, owing to the disturbance of the balance between the supply of industrial commodities and the supply of agricultural produce, the same condition of affairs has been manifest in various other countries. But nowhere has it developed to the same intensity as in the U.S.S.R.

The divergence between the prices of industrial commodities and agricultural products reached its climax in the year 1923, but was still very great down to the year 1927. The table on page 133, in which due allowance has been made for fluctuations in the currency, makes this divergence very plain.

After a study of the value ratios shown in this table, V. Groman, a member of the committee of the Central Statistical Bureau, comes to the conclusion that "the purchasing power of grain for industrial products in Northern Caucasia and in Ukraine is less than a third, and in the Volga region and in Siberia less than a half, of the pre-war purchasing power".[1]

Apart from this undue enhancement of the prices of industrial products when compared with the prices of agricultural products, it has often been difficult and sometimes impossible

[1] "Ekonomicheskaya Zhizn", September 3, 1927.

for the peasant to get the industrial products he needs at any price whatever. In the State shops and the cooperative stores, it often happens that the articles most urgently needed by the peasant, such as textiles, boots and shoes, nails, hardware, agricultural machinery, etc., are not on sale at all. In view of the general scarcity of industrial products in the home market, the villages can secure only minimal quantities of the things they want, and there is a complete lack of many articles of ordinary consumption in the rural areas.

RATIO OF VALUES IN EXCHANGE.[1]

For one hundredweight of rye could be obtained:

	In the 5-year Period 1909/1913 (Autumn).		1927/1928 (Autumn).	
	Cooperative Stores.	Private Dealers.	Cooperative Stores.	Private Dealers.
Cotton .. .. (metres)	—	23·72	12·42	10·35
Sugar .. .. (kilograms)	—	14·60	7·23	7·02
Salt .. .. (kilograms)	—	182·5	125·2	83·2
Vegetable oil .. (kilograms)	—	12·60	8·42	5·05
Petroleum .. (kilograms)	—	41·53	41·16	36·25
Soap .. .. (kilograms)	—	16·17	9·18	7·95
Nails .. .. (kilograms)	—	24·36	15·59	12·94
Wheat (State prices) (cwts)	0·78		0·71	

Peasant agriculture is also seriously injured by the policy of the government in the matter of foreign trade. In Russia to-day, the State is the only exporter of agricultural produce, and it is at the same time the only importer of goods (including those needed by agriculture). Since so small an amount of the grain required for export finds its way to the market, the export of wheat and barley diminishes year by year, with the result that the balance of trade is unfavourable, and the whole national economy of Russia is subject to recurrent crises.

Despite its best endeavours to promote export, the Soviet

[1] "Ekonomicheskoye Obozreniye", 1928, No. 6.

government is not able to make the export of grain a paying business. In the chapter on "Foreign Commerce", we shall enquire whether a State monopoly of foreign trade in the U.S.S.R. has been maintained, and what forms it has assumed. Meanwhile, suffice it to point out that the State, in its function as exporter of grain, has been a very unsuccessful agent for the peasants. Before the war, the peasant was able to secure for the grain he sold from 65 to 75 per cent of the sale price in the world market; but to-day, under the system of the State monopoly of foreign trade, he gets no more than from 40 to 50 per cent.[1] On the other hand, only from 50 to 60 per cent of the peasant demand for agricultural implements and machinery is satisfied, for the program of imports is based upon the principle of promoting industrialisation, whilst the home production of agricultural machinery (though it has considerably increased) is still far from adequate. Besides, when the peasant buys imported agricultural machinery, he has to pay the State three or four times as much as the latter has itself paid for the articles. Thus, as far as peasant farmers are concerned, the State has become a barrier intervening between their product, the grain for which there is an effective demand in the foreign market, and the agricultural machinery, the manures, etc., which they need, and which are purchasable in that foreign market at reasonable prices and in sufficient quantities. The position in which the peasant is placed as between the home market and the foreign market, is the basic cause of the decline in the amount of agricultural produce sent to market. At present, the Russian agriculturist has very little motive for selling grain and for making the most of the land he cultivates. Consequently, he restricts purchases and sales to the utmost, produces very little, and stores any surplus there may be. The State policy towards the "kulaks", the comparatively well-to-do peasants, has a similar effect on peasant agriculture. From the fear of being classed as "kulaks" the peasants are careful to hide their successes, incline towards speculative

[1] "Vestnik Finansoff", 1927, No. 9.

affairs, increase their unproductive consumption, take to drink, and so on.

To sum up, the peasants have very little interest in extending the scale of their farming, and have practically nothing to gain from the establishment of stable and extensive relations with the market. During the early years of the Nep period, there was a rapid transition from the three-field system to the many-field system, but the rate of this transition has now perceptibly declined. In the Soviet Union during the year 1927, only from 8 to 9 per cent of all agricultural operations were conducted on the many-field system. It is no chance matter that between the years 1923–1924 and 1926–1927, the area of land under cultivation increased annually by 3·5 per cent, whereas in the year 1927–1928 there was a decline of 3 per cent.[1] Before the war, there was in progress an annual increase of from 8 to 10 per cent in the area under cultivation.

The scarcity of commodities and the unhappy ratio between industrial and agricultural prices (the "scissors") hamper the development of Russian agriculture and hinder advance towards a more intensive method of cultivation. Still more unfortunate is the circumstance that the five-year plan of economic development does not justify any hopes of an improvement in the position. Even if we suppose that the projected expansion of industrial production will occur, the supply of commodities in the year 1931 will still be lower than the effective demand of the countryside. More important still, industrial prices will not be reduced by more than 15 or 20 per cent. Bazaroff, the well-known economist, writes: "Before the war, the ratio of prices in Russia was unfavourable to the peasants. On the tenth anniversary of the revolution, this ratio is still more unfavourable, having changed for the worse (from the peasant point of view) to the extent of 30 per cent as regards wholesale prices and to the extent of 100 per cent as regards retail prices."[2] The expectation that within five years, should

---

[1] "Ekonomicheskaya Zhizn", October 3, 1928.
[2] [Economic Perspectives], in "Ekonomicheskoye Obozreniye", 1927, No. 4.

all work out for the best, there will be a decline in industrial prices to the extent of 20 per cent, is, as Bazaroff aptly remarks, no more than a drop of water upon a hot iron plate.

The expected tempo of industrial development is not one that will allow of the satisfaction of the most elementary needs of peasant agriculture, not one which can promote the reconstruction of rural life. But if this be so, industry will continue to lack indispensable raw materials, and will not secure the requisite market for its products.

The problem of the mutual economic relations between industry and agriculture is crucial for the whole economic life of the country. The recently deceased Hermann Gorter, a left-wing Dutch communist, when visiting Russia, obtained a clear insight into this complicated problem. In a letter to Pannekoek he wrote: "As soon as the Russian peasants come to understand that they can get agricultural implements and machinery, manures, etc., cheaper and of better quality from foreign capitalists than from the Soviet State, and that they can sell their own produce to these capitalists more profitably than to the Soviet State, they will promptly take action against the Soviet government."

No doubt Hermann Gorter overestimated the energy of the Russian peasants, and failed to understand their fighting tactics, but he was perfectly right in thinking that the main interests of the peasants run counter to the extant governmental policy of the Soviet State.

CHAPTER TEN

DEVELOPMENTAL TRENDS IN RUSSIAN AGRICULTURE

1. State Policy towards the Peasants, and the Economic Evolution of the Rural Districts

During the first years of the Nep, the reconstruction of agriculture went on at a far more rapid pace than the reconstruction of industry. The explanation of this is that, in the first place, agricultural production (even in the most difficult years) never fell below 60 per cent of the pre-war level; and that, in the second place, since Russian agriculture is still in so primitive a condition, less capital was requisite than for the reconstruction of industry. On the other hand, whereas industry was assisted by an uninterrupted stream of State subventions, agriculture received no help whatever from the State—and, indeed, every important step towards the reconstruction of agriculture was taken in incessant conflict with the utopian and contradictory policy of the Soviet government.

Down to the present day, two tendencies continue to wrestle each with the other within the policy of the communist government of Russia. In the interest of the general economy of the country, there is a demand for an advance in peasant agriculture, for "the unrestricted development of the productive forces of the countryside, a development that shall be free from needless obstacles", although this necessarily signifies an accentuation of the "omnipotence of private economy".[1]

The representatives of the other trend are afraid that the well-to-do peasants, the "kulaks", if their economic position were further improved, would increase their predominance, and that in the ocean of that predominance "socialised industry" would be drowned. Those who take this view, therefore, demand for the countryside a policy

[1] "Na Agrarnom Fronte", 1926, No. 9.

"aiming at the speediest possible development of a socialised agriculture".[1]

The practical upshot has been that the policy of the Soviet government has been persistently under the influence of both these tendencies. When the economic crises grow more serious, when agriculture is gravely affected by them, and when the export of grain declines, there is an inclination to favour agriculture, laws to this effect are passed, articles appear in the newspapers concerning the alliance between the proletariat and the peasantry (the so-called "smychka", or "leash"), the local authorities issue instructions that peasants who improve their farms and own two horses are not to be regarded as "kulaks" or treated as pariahs, declare that the individualistic husbandry of the middle peasants will for a long time to come be the foundation of the general reconstruction of the national economy, and so on, and so on. But as soon as there is any improvement in the economic situation, "Pravda", the central organ of the Communist Party, fills its columns with articles declaring that the main object of Soviet policy in the country-side must be to fight the "kulak".—"The sheep's wool is growing once more, and the beast must be shorn."

In the beginning of the year 1928, the policy of the Soviet government took an especially radical turn. Under stress of the beginnings of inflation, decrees were issued concerning the "supplementary self-taxation" of the peasants,[2] and the richer peasants were burdened with a new tax of 80 millions of roubles. At the same time, the "committees of the poorer peasants", which had been in abeyance since the introduction of the Nep, were revived. The peasants were ordered to subscribe to a compulsory loan of 200 millions of roubles. Finally, owing to the failure of the campaign to secure larger supplies of grain, the government decided upon a reinstitution

[1] "Bolshevik", 1927, No. 10.
[2] Apart from the taxes ordinarily fixed by law, the rural communes can impose "supplementary self-taxation" in order to finance local needs. Decisions to impose "self-taxation" are to be taken by the general assembly of the villages, and must be confirmed by the village soviet.

of compulsory levies. Posses moved from farm to farm, making domiciliary searches in order to discover stores of grain. Peasants who refused to sell their grain were arrested and deported by thousands; those who were found to have large stores of grain were prosecuted and the grain was confiscated. As in the days of war communism, barriers were established at the entrances to the towns, and the village markets at which the peasants were accustomed to sell their grain were closed by the militia.[1]

Ostensibly this campaign was directed against the "kulaks" only, but the line drawn between a "kulak" and a middle peasant is so hazy that the repressive measures everywhere affected the peasants as a whole. According to the reports of the People's Commissariat for Justice, among the peasants who were arrested and tried for refusing to sell grain to the State authorities at the officially fixed prices, there were only 66 per cent of "kulaks". In one of the Siberian districts, of those sentenced under clause 107 of the Penal Code (the clause concerns confiscation of grain because of the owner's speculative activities), only 7 per cent were "kulaks", whilst 64 per cent were middle peasants, and 25·5 per cent were actually poor peasants.[2]

Not until a report that the Nep had been abandoned had spread throughout the country, not until the disastrous effects of this "swing to the left" had become obvious, not until the food crisis had begun to become acute, did the plenum of the Central Committee of the Communist Party of the Soviet Union decide "to abandon extraordinary measures".[3]

But apart from these unduly accentuated vacillations, the policy of the Soviet government in the countryside is essentially determined by hostility to the well-to-do peasants, and in the conduct of this campaign the government does not shrink from measures which conflict with the primary needs of the national economy as a whole. The well-to-do peasant has no right to vote in elections to the village soviet; the taxes he has to pay

[1] Russian police.   [2] Speech by Rykoff, July 13, 1928.
[3] "Pravda", July 14, 1928.

amount to 30 per cent of his income;[1] he is the last to receive agricultural machinery and implements from the State sources of supply; he is refused credit; and in the assignment of land he is given the worst and the most inaccessible plots. The penalisation of a peasant who puts a galvanized iron roof on his cottage, on one who starts dairy farming or buys a horse, the cautious and suspicious attitude which is assumed towards one who owns a threshing machine—these things cannot fail to hinder the development of the productive forces of the countryside. No matter which branch of peasant agriculture you contemplate, you will find that any advance can only be effected after a prolonged and arduous struggle against the dominant mood of governmental circles.

Above all, the peasant is uneasy because of the insecurity of his legal tenure of the land he farms. His mentality is through and through possessive. To-day, having acquired his land in a revolutionary epoch when all rights of property were suspended, he is eager to have his ownership of the land he tills legally endorsed. The Soviet legislation concerning the land is beyond his understanding, is opposed to his traditional attitude, and is calculated to arouse his fears. Of course, on general

[1] In the year 1927–1928, a new clause (No. 28) was added to the law concerning the taxation of the peasantry (the Agricultural Taxation Law). By this clause the local tax authorities were empowered to tax well-to-do peasants individually,—quite apart from the taxes specified in the general body of legislation. This system of individual taxation was applied in various parts of the U.S.S.R. as a means for "ridding the villages of kulaks", and of contributing to the ruin of the well-to-do peasants. In an address to the Moscow Soviet on September 18, 1928, M. Kalinin, the chairman of the Central Executive Committee of the U.S.S.R., declared that he considered "the way in which the system of individual taxation had been carried out to be unjust". He went on to say: "Certain provinces, certain persons, have been taxed twice or three times as heavily as last year; and some of the peasants have actually been taxed five or six times as heavily." Kalinin gave a number of instances in which "individual taxation" had been applied to peasants who lived exclusively by their own labour. "The poor peasants and middle peasants see that the comparatively well-to-do peasants are taxed in such a way as to ruin them. What sort of a class line is that? Is it not a class line which will involve the destruction of agriculture?" Such were the words of the veteran communist Kalinin, who in 1928 was suspected of a deviation to the right.—"Pravda", September 23, 1928.

principles he could accommodate himself to the nationalisation of the land and to the prohibition of the sale of land, seeing that before the revolution he was not entitled to sell or mortgage his land. Except for the comparatively small stratum of well-to-do peasants (those who dream of becoming large-scale landowners) the peasant would, in general, be readily satisfied with a practical working ownership of the land, with the right to enjoy the usufruct of the land in the absence of any express title to ownership—provided only he were granted a permanent right to use some particular portion of the land. No doubt the uncertainty of tenure in the Russian countryside is due to historical and social causes, but that uncertainty has been intensified by the policy of the Soviet government.

During the years of the radical redistribution of the land (1918–1920), not only was there, as previously explained, a confiscation of the estates of the great landlords, the treasury, the monasteries, etc., but there was also an "equalisation" of land ownership within the rural communes. By 1927, about two-thirds of all the cultivated land in European Russia had been redistributed. During the first years of this process, the attitude of the government towards redistribution was a vacillating one. The law concerning the nationalisation of the land established a limit to the amount of land which could be used and worked by one person, and excluded the farms of the poor peasants and the middle peasants from redistribution. But the endeavour towards the equalisation of the land holdings during the early years of the revolution was a mass phenomenon. After the confiscation of the estates of the great landlords, the whole of the land (including that of the peasants) was thrown, as it were, into the melting pot, and was then redistributed to the individual peasants. In some districts this took place in accordance with the number of agricultural workers, and in others according to the number of members of the families. During the years of the civil war and the corn levies, the aim of the Soviet government was to secure the support of the lower strata of the rural population. With this end in view, it established "committees of poor peasants" in every village, and with the aid of these committees undertook frequent and demagogic redistribution of the land.

Again, the soldiers returning from the Red Army after the close of the civil war, were many of them in favour of a fresh redistribution of the land. In many districts, redistribution took place every two or three years, with the result that the peasant had no inclination to pass from a three-field system to a many-field system, and was even disinclined to do anything in the way of improving the land he tilled. At length, the need for promoting the export of grain compelled the Soviet government to dissolve the committees of poor peasants; and in the year 1923 a decree was issued to the effect that the periodical redistribution of the land should only take place once in every nine or twelve years (this period being thrice or four times the period of rotation in the three-field system). Nevertheless, as a part of the campaign against the "kulaks", in many districts redistribution at much shorter intervals has continued down to the present day, with the approval of the authorities. The draft law concerning the land elaborated in the year 1927 by the Committee for Legislative Initiative, was designed to put an end to the insecurity of tenure which was interfering with the proper use of the land. By Clause 48 of the draft it was specified that "the individual peasant is to be secure in the tenure of the land he farms, and the farm is not to be subject to a further process of equalisation by redistribution". But this conflicted so strongly with the equalising spirit of the fundamental land legislation of the country, that a campaign against the proposed reform was at once begun in the communist press, and the draft law has never been enacted.

Nor, indeed, can there be any security of tenure until there has been a radical land reform, both as regards the organisation of redistribution and also as regards improvements in the land. During the revolutionary epoch, the peasants took over the land in a quite unorganised way, the general practice being for each man to occupy the nearest parts of the estates of the great landlords and the monasteries. Most of the redistribution occurred within the domain of particular districts (volosts), and less often within the domain of whole circles (uyezds). In some districts, the area of appropriated land was large, and the population scanty; in other districts, population was thick on the ground and the amount of land available was very small. As far as the individual villages were concerned, the redistribution was effected by rule of thumb, without any preliminary surveying.

The upshot has been that the extreme complexity of the circumstances of land tenure, the unequal distribution of the land, the splitting-up of the land belonging to particular communes among various villages (these things having been the curse of Russian agriculture already before the revolution), have become greatly accentuated. This is the chief obstacle to the adoption of a more intensive system of cultivation, to the transition from a three-field system to a many-field system, to rotation of the crops, etc.

According to the reports of the People's Commissariat for Agriculture, an average peasant farm consists of about sixteen separate plots of land, while in some districts (in northern and south-western Russia) it may consist of as many as a hundred plots of land. The fields of the various farms are inextricably mixed up, and are situated at very great distances from the villages. In southern and south-western Russia, in 94 per cent of the peasant farms, the usual distance of the fields from the villages is more than 5 kilometres, in one direction or another. The result is that, according to the calculations of the Workers' and Peasants' Inspection, a peasant has on an average, going to and from his work, to walk 1898 versts per annum, whereas if the farms were consolidated this distance could be reduced to 474 versts.

How slowly the process of land reform and land surveying goes on is shown by the following official figures. Down to the year 1928, surveying of the land within the rural communes had been achieved to the extent of only 15 per cent, and that of the land between the rural communes to the extent of only 7 per cent. On an average, surveying is effected each year in an area of from 15 to 20 millions of desyatines. Now, in European Russia alone, there are 200 millions of desyatines needing to be surveyed, so that it will be a good many years, at this rate of progress, before the surveying of all will have been effected. According to data published by the People's Commissariat for Agriculture, in the year 1924, only 64 per cent of the projected amount of surveying was achieved; in the year 1925, only 49 per cent; in the year 1926, only 45 per cent; and in the year 1927, only 44 per cent. The slowness with which the work is being done is attributable, above all, to the insufficiency of the means available to the State for this purpose. In the year 1924–1925, there was voted for the work of surveying a total sum of 2·04 millions of roubles; in the year 1925–1926, a sum of 9·2 millions of roubles; in the year 1926–1927, a sum of 14·8 millions of roubles; and in the year 1927–1928, a sum of 23·1 millions of roubles.

Such slow progress arouses acute dissatisfaction among the peasants, for as long as his farm has not been surveyed, the peasant does not regard it as his own property, and is unwilling to invest the capital needed for its improvement. But another reason for the slow progress made in this work of land surveying is that there is not a sufficiency of expert surveyors. In the whole of the U.S.S.R. there are only 8,000 persons engaged in the work of surveying. Before the revolution, the peasants did everything they could to avoid having their land surveyed, for they considered that surveying was likely to disturb the patriarchal relationships of rural life. To-day, however, they suffer so much from the defective organisation of agriculture, that as soon as a land surveyor makes his appearance in a village, the village assembly is unwilling to let him go away until all the area has been surveyed. "Prompt surveying" is the peasant's main demand.[1]

Discontent among the peasantry is promoted, not only by

[1] "Ekonomicheskaya Zhizn", October 18, 1927.

the delay in the work of land surveying, but also by the policy pursued by the land authorities in this matter of land surveying. The Russian communists themselves describe their land surveying as a "class policy". This does not merely mean that the work of land surveying is done gratuitously on the land farmed by the poor peasants. Likewise, and above all, it means that, as the outcome of a land survey, the best land is to be reserved for the poor peasants and the collective farms, even when before the survey it was farmed by one of the well-to-do peasants. This leads to endless squabbles and abuses. Furthermore, since 1926, the detachment of a farm from the rural commune for the purposes of individual farming has been entirely prohibited, the Soviet authorities having come to the conclusion that this individual method of cultivation is what principally tends "to increase the 'kulak' element".

An important hindrance to the improvement of agriculture is also to be found in the partition of the farms among the members of a family. According to the law, any member of a family, of either sex, can on demand detach for his own use a share of the family land, cattle, and farm utensils. However desirable it may have been to accord this right, in actual practice in the Soviet villages it has acquired a peculiar significance. The Soviet policy of hampering the activities of the well-to-do peasants is furthered by frequent divisions of the farms, and these are disastrous to farming. Sometimes, again, there are pretended divisions which are undertaken to conceal the growing prosperity of a peasant family. The net result has been that division and subdivision proceed apace. According to official figures, at the present time such partitions are from 150 to 200 per cent more frequent than they were before the revolution. That is why, in the area now comprised within the U.S.S.R., there were in the year 1916 only 16 millions of peasant farms, whereas in the year 1925, the number was 24 millions, and in the year 1927, 25·3 millions.

No less important is the hindrance to the development of peasant farming which arises from the prohibition of leasing

K

and of the hiring of labour. During the first years of the Nep neither the one nor the other was tolerated, for the State regarded them as forms of exploitation. Subsequently, however, the Soviet government, constrained to base the reconstruction of Russian economic life upon increasing the prosperity of the peasants as producers and consumers, and acting "in the interest of the further development of capitalist principles in the village", made certain concessions, and in the year 1924 passed a decree permitting land to be leased and allowing the well-to-do farmers to employ wage labour. At first the term of such a lease was not to exceed twelve years. In the year 1928, during the period of the "swing to the left", the presidium of the Central Executive Committee reduced this term, deciding that the maximum period of a lease of land was to be six years. Before the war, 35 millions of desyatines were leased; at the beginning of the year 1927, the extent of land under lease was only 15 millions of desyatines, but, according to the results of an enquiry made at the instigation of the Workers' and Peasants' Inspection, "the leasing of land was a very general phenomenon in all the districts of Russia". The great majority of the leaseholders were middle peasants, but the larger areas of leased land (ranging up to 45 desyatines) were in the hands of the rich peasants. As a result of the before-mentioned enquiry, it appeared that 13 per cent of the peasants, who must be reckoned as rich peasants, enjoyed the usufruct of 30·5 per cent of all the land that was leased.[1] In pre-revolutionary Russia, a considerable amount of land was leased by the poor peasants, Russia being in this respect very different from western European countries; and the extent to which land is leased by poor peasants has considerably increased in Russia since the revolution. As leaseholders to-day we find in Russia many more poor peasants than rich ones—peasants who have neither horses nor ploughs of their own, and who have no right either

[1] The communist opposition declares that these figures have been toned down, and that in reality 16 per cent of the peasants (kulaks) have the usufruct of 75 per cent of all the land that is leased.

to mortgage or to alienate the land they farm. Still, in the main, a leaseholder is not a land-hungry peasant, but a peasant who is improving his economic position, for the leasing of land masks the process of primary accumulation.

The employment of wage labour is now widely generalised in the Russian countryside. Before the war, there were 2·7 millions of agricultural labourers in Russia, and by now that figure has been nearly regained, for there are 2·5 millions. The number of agricultural labourers is increasing with especial rapidity on peasant farms where intensive culture is practised, and on farms exceeding 10 desyatines in size. Not less than 50 per cent of all agricultural labourers are employed on such farms.

Despite the general equalisation of the size of farms effected only a few years ago, the process of economic differentiation among the peasantry is advancing with rapid strides. No data have been published relating to the U.S.S.R. as a whole. But on the tenth anniversary of the bolshevik revolution, the Central Statistical Bureau published data relating to the separate republics and areas of the Soviet Union, and from these samples can be selected.[1] From a study of the classification of farms, in accordance with their respective areas, and with the amount of live stock, in various characteristic districts (Ukraine and Northern Caucasia as regions producing a surplus of grain, north-western Russia and the Moscow area as industrial regions producing an insufficiency of grain), we secure the composite picture shown on pages 148–149.

The official press considers itself entitled to deduce from these figures the conclusion that the process of economic differentiation of the countryside in the U.S.S.R. has characteristics very different from those of the analogous process in capitalistic countries. The number of farms without horses and without cultivated land has not only not increased, but has declined; the middle groups are not dwindling; and there is

[1] [The Balance of Ten Years of Soviet Rule], published by the Central Statistical Bureau, pp. 136–141.

CLASSIFICATION OF PEASANT FARMS IN ACCORDANCE WITH THE NUMBER OF FARM BEASTS, IN PERCENTAGES OF THE TOTAL NUMBER OF FARMS

	Year.	No Beasts.	One Beast.	Two Beasts.	Three Beasts.	Four Beasts and more.
Ukraine	1922	42·0	35·2	20·7	1·6	0·5
	1925	40·6	38·1	18·7	1·9	0·7
	1926	38·6	36·8	22·0	2·0	0·6
Northern Caucasia	1922	45·7	25·3	19·0	5·2	3·8
	1925	49·0	25·3	17·8	4·5	3·4
	1926	43·6	24·4	20·8	6·1	5·1
Moscow Industrial District	1922	36·8	61·9	1·6	0·0	0·0
	1925	35·0	61·7	3·1	0·2	0·0
	1926	36·1	60·6	3·2	0·1	0·0
North-West	1922	26·8	65·9	7·1	0·2	0·0
	1925	25·4	66·2	8·0	0·4	0·0
	1926	25·7	66·2	8·3	0·4	0·0

CLASSIFICATION OF PEASANT FARMS IN ACCORDANCE WITH THE AREA UNDER CULTIVATION, IN PERCENTAGES OF THE TOTAL NUMBER OF FARMS

	Year.	No Cultivated Area.	Under 2 Desyatines.	2–4 Desyatines.	4–6 Desyatines.	6–10 Desyatines.	10–16 Desyatines.	More than 16 Desyatines.
Ukraine	1922	5·8	32·8	35·1	15·3	8·9	1·8	0·3
	1925	3·0	22·6	37·0	18·1	13·4	4·5	1·4
	1926	3·7	19·1	33·3	19·2	16·0	6·5	2·2
Northern Caucasia	1922	20·8	29·4	22·1	13·2	10·1	3·4	1·0
	1925	10·4	16·9	22·1	17·5	19·5	9·0	4·6
	1926	11·3	14·7	17·5	15·5	20·4	13·0	7·4
Moscow Industrial District	1922	5·4	62·0	26·8	4·6	1·1	0·1	0·0
	1925	4·7	50·2	35·0	7·9	2·0	0·1	1·0
	1926	5·1	48·5	35·0	8·8	2·5	0·1	0·0
North-West	1922	6·2	62·8	25·0	4·8	1·1	0·1	0·0
	1925	6·3	56·3	29·1	6·2	1·7	0·2	0·0
	1926	4·2	53·5	31·7	7·9	2·6	0·1	0·0

a gradually accelerating movement of the poorer enterprises into the region of the comparatively well-to-do enterprises.

But let us look a little more closely at the material out of which the foregoing table is compiled. The sample figures relate to from 1 to 2 per cent of the farms in each district. There is nothing to show how large this or that group of farms was. These defects notwithstanding, the tables certainly give a fairly exact impression of the main trends of the process of differentiation. Still, on closer examination, we cannot fail to note the following fact, that between 1922 and 1926 the proportion of farms with a cultivable area of less than 2 desyatines declined very considerably in the areas producing a surplus of grain, while the proportion of the adjoining groups, that of the farms with no cultivated area, and that of the farms with a cultivated area of 2 to 4 desyatines, likewise diminished, though not so much. What has become of the enterprises belonging to the classes which have thus undergone diminution, for we cannot suppose that in so short a time they could have moved into remotely situated classes?

Here is the explanation of this remarkable phenomenon. The second part of the table does not show the distribution of farms in accordance with the total area of land, but in accordance with the area of land under cultivation. Since the introduction of the Nep there has been going on a general reconstruction of peasant agriculture, on farms of all sizes, sometimes accompanied by an extension in the area under cultivation; but the peasant has not been expanding the area under cultivation at the expense of the farms belonging to the class next above or the class next below; he has been doing it by bringing under cultivation land he already owned, but had not previously tilled. That is the explanation of what at first seemed inexplicable, the upward movement in the farms of all sizes down to the year 1925. Not until the year 1926, when the reserve of cultivable land had been exhausted, did the dynamic of the movement of growth assume a different character.

If we draw our conclusions from official data (which all

sections of the communist opposition regard as deliberately toned down), we arrive at the following result:[1] the fundamental trend of evolution is taking the form of a comparatively rapid growth of the larger farms. To-day, as before the war, this process is especially plain in the areas producing an excess of grain. In Ukraine and in Northern Caucasia, the number of large farms, those comprising more than 16 desyatines, has increased sevenfold within four years. The result has been, not an equable ascent in all the classes, but a disproportionate growth in the class of rich peasants. Since 1925, the decline in the number of landless peasants has been arrested, and an increase has set in. Since 1925, likewise, the number of farms on which there are no horses has begun to increase in the areas producing a deficiency of grain. The process of social stratification characteristic of Russian village life before the war, namely proletarianisation at one pole and an increase in wealth at the other, has again become a marked feature of the Russian countryside.

We have no statistical data of our own to contrast with the official figures, but the disputes among the communists suffice to illustrate the fact that the before-mentioned differentiation is going on. There is a slow increase of wellbeing among the mass of the peasant population, to the degree to which the achievements of the agrarian revolution make this possible. Simultaneously, however, there is a growth in the number of the poor peasants and of the rich peasants. Furthermore, all enquiries into agricultural development in Russia combine to show that the increasing wealth of the comparatively well-to-do peasants is mainly secured by an increase in the area of leased land and by the use of the agricultural machinery and implements owned by the richest peasants. This last circumstance is of great importance to Russian rural life. An increase in peasant

---

[1] It is interesting to compare the material here utilised with the data adduced in the eighth chapter to show the movement of peasant agriculture in the period 1917–1919. The process of the general equalisation of the size of farms has been replaced by an equally obvious process of social differentiation.

wellbeing through an expansion of the area under cultivation (be it only on leased land) is a very difficult matter owing to the present policy of the Soviet government. On the other hand, the rich peasant who buys agricultural machinery acquires, not only an important aid to his own farming enterprise, but also capital which he can turn to useful account in other ways. The hiring-out of agricultural machinery is, in contemporary Russia, a widely practised method of exploitation, a means whereby the rich peasants can enrich themselves yet further at the expense of their poorer brethren, and it has thus become one of the most important factors of social differentiation in the countryside. The urgent need for agricultural machinery in the rural districts gives extensive opportunities for this kind of exploitation. An enquiry made in the year 1925 yielded the following information as to the amount of agricultural machinery owned on farms of various sizes[1]:

	Per 100 Farms there were	
	Ploughs.	Sowing and Reaping Machines.
No cultivated area	2·1	—
Cultivated area—		
under 2 desyatines	29·2	1·8
from 2–4 desyatines	49·7	6·8
from 4–6 desyatines	52·4	17·3
from 6–10 desyatines	70·2	39·0
from 10–16 desyatines	104·1	94·4
from 16–25 desyatines	137·0	161·3
exceeding 25 desyatines	193·1	241·7

According to subsequent calculations made by A. Gaister, we find, in like manner, that in Ukraine, in the year 1927, 40·8 per cent of all the agricultural machinery and implements belonged to the well-to-do peasants; in Northern Caucasia,

[1] A. Anisimoff [Developmental Trends in Peasant Farming and in the Use of Agricultural Machinery], "Bolshevik", 1928, No. 15.

58·3 per cent; in the Ural region, 58·2 per cent; and in Siberia, 42·3 per cent.[1] According to the 1927–1928 report of the State Planning Commission, 30 per cent of all agricultural machinery is in the hands of 6 per cent of the rural population. Payment for the use of such machinery is made in kind (sometimes in grain, and sometimes in labour), a method which renders crass exploitation possible.

On the other hand, it is enough to study the reports of the People's Commissariat for Agriculture concerning over-population in the countryside in order to learn how large a proportion of the peasant population is no longer able to make a livelihood there. In the year 1927, there were ten million peasants whose farms were less than what is regarded as the necessary minimum (1 desyatine per head), and who lacked farm beasts and the necessary implements. The yearly increase of those belonging to this category is not less than one million.

As regards the U.S.S.R. as a whole, there have been no trustworthy investigations into the social stratification of the peasant population.[2] In the disputes between the "Stalinists" and the "Trotzkyists", each side declares that the figures adduced by the other have been cooked. To give some sort of general idea as to social stratification in contemporary Russian rural life, I adduce figures based upon the reports of the Central Statistical Bureau. Of the 120 millions of the rural population there are:

	Millions.
Rural proletarians	3·4
Poor peasants	34·0
Middle peasants	52·0
Well-to-do peasants	11·0
Rich peasants	5·0
Rural population not working on the land	14·0

Assignment to the various groups was made summarily in

[1] [Stratification in Soviet Villages], published by the Communist Academy, 1928, p. 111.
[2] The Soviet economist, A. Vainshtein writes with good reason: "An experienced statistician may well despair when he contemplates the chaos that prevails in the statistics of peasant agriculture." "Ekonomicheskove Obozreniye", 1927, No. 7.

accordance with the area of land under cultivation, the number of beasts owned, the amount of machinery and tools on the farm, etc.

To the rural proletariat belong the workers upon the State farms and in the State forests, shepherds and cattlemen, the workers employed by the cooperatives, those employed by the local authorities, and the agricultural labourers hired by the rich peasant farmers.—The second group, that of the poor peasants, comprises those whose farms are less than 2 desyatines in size, and who have no horses and no agricultural implements. The income from such a farm will not suffice to nourish a family, and these peasants, therefore, must either sell their labour power to be used on the land, or must make a living in some other way than by agriculture. The peasants belonging to this category usually cultivate their own land with the aid of hired beasts and implements; but many of them lease their land to other peasants.—The third group, the most numerous in the countryside, consists of the middle peasants. To this category belong the peasants who are able to make a livelihood on the land by strenuous labour on their own part and on that of the other members of their families; and also those peasants who own enough land, farm beasts, and agricultural implements to make a moderate profit out of their farming enterprise. Some of these middle peasants rent land in addition to what they regard as their own, but only enough to provide full occupation for their own and their families' labour power, and they only engage agricultural labourers for harvest work.— The fourth group comprises that of the well-to-do peasants with farms ranging from 6 to 10 desyatines in size. They own a sufficiency of farm beasts and implements.—The fifth group consists of the rich peasants, whose farms range from 10 desyatines upwards. They are accustomed to hire out their surplus stock of beasts and their surplus agricultural machinery. The peasants belonging to the two last-mentioned groups rent considerable quantities of land, employ wage labour, and in addition, as a rule, undertake trade in agricultural produce.—

As for the sixth group, that of persons living in the country who are not engaged in agricultural occupations, it comprises factory workers, handicraftsmen, home workers, school teachers, doctors, agricultural experts, etc.

However sketchy the foregoing picture of social stratification in the Russian countryside, it at least gives us a general impression of the present state of affairs. We see plainly enough that the main body of the rural population consists of poor peasants and middle peasants. This is the stratum which gives village life its prevailing characteristics. The stratum of the well-to-do peasants and of the rich peasants is still very small. Consequently, the campaign against the "kulaks" is directed almost exclusively against those peasants who have attained economic independence. The stratum of the rural proletariat has increased very rapidly, and has nearly regained pre-war proportions. The number of agricultural labourers employed on peasant farms already exceeds that of pre-war days.

2. COLLECTIVE FARMING AND STATE FARMING

In the early summer of 1928, when the general economic crisis became intensified, when the failure of the State to secure adequate supplies of grain had become manifest, and when it was obviously necessary to discontinue the export of grain, the Soviet government became animated with a new utopian idea which was promulgated simultaneously with a fresh "swing to the left". It was decided to intervene actively in the process of grain production. The old utopian idea of the Russian communists, the idea of transforming peasant farming from an individualist enterprise into a collective enterprise by State intervention, was revived, and practical attempts were made to realise it. Writing in "Pravda" under date June 2, 1928, Stalin formulated the communist plan as follows: "The main cause of all our difficulties as concerns the supply of grain is that the production of grain for the market does not keep pace with the increase in the demand for grain. . . . The production

of grain for the market proceeds at a hopelessly slow pace."
The way out, he said, was to be sought in a transition from the
individual enterprise of the small peasant farms to collective
enterprise. The collective farms would be compelled by the
State, "under threat of the withdrawal of subventions
and privileges", to hand over grain at fixed prices. There
was also to be an expansion of the extant State agricultural
enterprises, the Soviet farms; and additional ones were to be
founded.

Stalin's expectation was that within three or four years these
two measures would result in the marketing of from 120 to
150 millions of poods of grain, one-third of which would come
from the collective farms, and two-thirds from the Soviet farms.
In order to carry out the decision of the Communist Party, the
government issued a number of decrees favouring collective
farms, and the organisation of Soviet farms was taken in hand.
Of course there can be no doubt that, other things being equal,
the transition from small-scale farming to large-scale farming
marks a step forward, and is economically advantageous.[1] It is
equally indubitable that an important step would be taken if
the Soviet government were to organise large-scale collective
or State enterprises—provided, of course, that these were not
inaugurated to the detriment of individual peasant farming
enterprises. But is the scheme realisable? What is likely to be
the effect of such an attempt upon private peasant farming?
Let us look into the matter more closely, basing our investigations upon officially published material.

To-day, the Soviet farms and collective farms send, per
annum, 37 millions of poods of grain to the market. This figure
must certainly be accepted with some reserve, for the official
estimates of the share of the collective farms in the production
is somewhat exaggerated. But even supposing the official
statement to be correct, the marketing of 150 millions of poods
of grain would only be practicable if the area under cultivation

[1] Prof. Lauer, Die Oekonomie der Landwirtschaft, p. 175; and Prof.
J. Hirsch, Der Erfolg der Organisation der amerikanischen Landwirtschaft.

were to be increased from three to three-and-a-half times. Can we expect anything of the kind?

The collective farms, despite all the privileges they receive, are declining enterprises, and the area of land cultivated by them fell off throughout the period 1922–1927. It is true that in the year 1927–1928, when a campaign on behalf of collective farming was begun, there was a great increase in such enterprises, so that between October 1, 1927, and July 1, 1928, the formation of 18,000 new collective farms was reported.

According to the statement of the People's Commissariat for Agriculture, in the whole of the U.S.S.R. on October 1, 1928, there were 35,000 collective farms cultivating in round figures 1·7 millions of desyatines,[1] and providing occupation for about half a million persons. In the middle of September, 1928,[2] the Workers' and Peasants' Inspection announced: "The reason why there has been so phenomenal an advance in collective farming is that during the current year strong pressure has been exercised on the capitalist elements in our agriculture." The actual fact is that the collective character of many of these enterprises is fictional, for the peasants have in numerous instances merely adopted a collective label in order to secure privileges for the supply of seed, machinery, credit, and other advantages. Often enough, the well-to-do sections of the villagers hang out a collective sign, just as in former days petty employers who worked on the sweating system used to pretend that they were cooperative producers. That was how it was in the Balashov circle of Saratov province, where, in the year 1928, the number of collective farms increased by 70 per cent within a few months. An enquiry showed that at least 20 per cent of these collective farms must be regarded as "dead souls" and as purely fictitious. Again, some of these "collective farms" are very peculiar enterprises indeed, constructed upon the joint-stock principle, and for practical purposes owned by rich peasants, each of whom has twenty-five

[1] "Pravda", November 21, 1928.
[2] "Ekonomicheskaya Zhizn", October 15, 1928.

shares, while poor peasants have only one or two shares each. The product of the collective activities is divided in proportion to the shares held. The collective farm Hodok, which was an amalgamation of eight separate farms, gave employment to 8 permanent and 30 temporary workers. Since it professed to be a collective enterprise, there were hired out to it a steam-mill, an oil-mill, a hulling-mill, an orchard, more than 300 desyatines of State land over and above the amount of land legally assignable, two threshing machines, six sowers, four reapers, etc. The Agricultural Credit Cooperative gave credit to Hodok, and the local tax authorities reduced its land taxes.[1]

The characteristic feature of this movement is that there is no formation of real cooperative farms, in which the individual possession of the separate farms is replaced by collective ownership—in which the land, the agricultural implements, and the live stock become collective property. All that happens is that the most primitive and most easily dissolved cooperatives are formed, organisations in which only a part of the larger machines and part of the land is held collectively.

Thanks to the special advantages granted to collective farms, the registering of land holdings as held cooperatively (75 per cent of all "collective farms" are nothing more than this) makes it possible for peasants who have very little land and a very small supply of agricultural implements at their disposal, to put their undertakings on a better footing. But it is extremely doubtful whether this sort of cooperation implies any real advance towards true cooperative farming, an advance towards a system of more intensive culture and towards one in which producers join hands effectively.

Furthermore, the problem of the marketing of the crops seems insoluble for these enterprises. If the State is going to compel the collective farms to hand over grain at the official "directive" prices, which are below the market prices, they will speedily be ruined—as happened in the early days of the propaganda for collective farming. Besides, these collective enter-

[1] "Ekonomicheskaya Zhizn", December 25, 1928.

prises, formed with undue haste, are economically unsound. Most of them are dwarf undertakings cultivating an area ranging from 30 to 60 desyatines. They differ very little from individual peasant farms, are less able to pay their way than these, and soon get into hopeless difficulties. After having secured the privileges granted to "collective farms", and after having protected themselves during the evil days of the "swing to the left" by hanging out a "collective sign", the peasants quietly revert to their customary methods of individual small-scale farming.

To prevent this, a hopelessly utopian idea has been conceived in the offices of the People's Commissariat for Agriculture. It has been decided to pass a law to the effect that the capital of the collective farms (money, land, live stock, and implements) is to be secured to the enterprises as property, and is not to be subject to division or to liquidation. The individual peasants who withdraw from the collective farms will then have no claim upon the indivisible funds of the enterprises.[1] Thus in the form of "collective farming" there is to be revived the old rural commune based upon the principle of the enslavement of the individual. Now, as in tsarist days, the individual peasant is only to be able to withdraw from the joint organisation under pain of forfeiting his property.

Even in communist circles the view is gaining ground that the extant collective farms, far from realising the principle of socialised labour "do not even achieve a paying application of funds and labour". That no doubt is why the government is now transferring its hopes to the Soviet farms, the "State corn factories". By a decree dated March 16, 1928, it is proposed to establish, in rural districts where the land is not all divided up among the peasants, huge State farms, each of them cultivating an area ranging from 10,000 to 30,000 desyatines. These large-scale State agricultural enterprises are to provide, within three or four years, grain to the amount of 100 millions of poods. This, however, will necessitate the cultivation of

[1] "Ekonomicheskaya Zhizn", June 26, 1928.

from $4\frac{1}{2}$ to 5 millions of hectares of land not now assigned to any one.

If the State farms are to pay, it will likewise be essential that their lands shall be near railways or navigable waterways, shall be fertile, shall be adequately watered, and so on. But the State does not possess such lands to the requisite amount, except what has already been reserved for settlements or else leased. This was repeatedly ascertained when in the famine years the question of the resettling of the peasants now inhabiting arid regions came up for consideration. The scheme proposes the use of certain areas in Northern Caucasia, on the lower and middle Volga, in Siberia, in the Ural region, in the Bashkir republic, in the district of Orenburg, and in the Kazak republic. But all this will not suffice. A. Muraloff, one of the leaders of agrarian policy in the Soviet State, writes[1]: "We have not a sufficiency of fertile land for Soviet farms in order to be able to produce grain to the amount of 100 millions of poods. We must therefore reconsider the use of all the land which has been set aside for other purposes. In addition, the land to be devoted to colonisation and settlement must be reexamined, so that we can have a sufficiency for the new grain production."

The foundation of the first large-scale State agricultural enterprise, which took place in the district of Salsk in the Don basin, in July 1928, has justified the belief that the new utopian policy of the Soviet government will be extremely detrimental to agriculture in general. The district of Salsk is one of the few remaining areas in European Russia reserved for horse breeding and sheep farming. Hitherto, in the interest of such old-established enterprises, new settlers have not been admitted to this district. The allocation for State farming of large areas of well-watered pasture land hitherto used by the local population for their own purposes, has aroused great dissatisfaction, and has seriously restricted the possibilities of horse breeding and sheep farming.[2]

[1] [The Soviet Corn Farms], "Ekonomicheskaya Zhizn", June 17, 1928.
[2] In the middle of 1928, in order to provide land for the proposed State

If, in the end, it proves possible to get the use of the necessary amount of land, the organisation of Soviet farms on the proposed scale will need the investment of amounts of capital which are far beyond the competence of the State. Agricultural machinery at a cost of several hundreds of millions will be needed (12,000 tractors, for instance); the area to be used in the Soviet farms must be properly surveyed; the peasants who are now farming the land taken over for the Soviet enterprises must be resettled elsewhere; housing accommodation must be supplied for hundreds of thousands of agricultural labourers; the new farms must be stocked with cattle and horses, must be provided with means of transport, must be irrigated, etc. All this will demand an expenditure out of proportion to the financial resources of the country. According to the calculations of the People's Commissariat for Agriculture, the primary organisation of Soviet farms will need a sum of 335 millions of roubles.[1]

Where, finally, is the State to discover the managerial staff requisite for these extensive agricultural enterprises, in which land to the amount of tens of thousands of desyatines is to be used. Under the prevailing conditions of agriculture in Russia, where farming has for the most part been on a very small scale, there are very few persons with the experience necessary for conducting large-scale agricultural enterprises.

Experience in the management of the industrial trusts and in the reconstruction of industry has shown that the Soviet State, even when it has the necessary capital and skilled personnel, is not able to effect the purposive organisation of centralised industrial production. An attempt to undertake a

farms in the Kazak area, the land hitherto occupied by sheep farms on a large scale was taken over by the government. Hitherto, seeing that the production of wool had fallen to one-fifth of the pre-war production, the Soviet government, recognising the need for the reestablishment of sheep farming, had tolerated the existence of great sheep farms, but now the policy of "down with the kulaks" was applied to this region.—In like manner, as regards Ukraine, Kossior, secretary of the Central Committee of the Communist Party of Soviet Ukraine, reports numerous instances of the expropriation of peasant land for the purposes of the Soviet farms.

[1] "Ekonomicheskaya Zhizn", August 1, 1928.

L

new enterprise of the kind above sketched, in Russia, which has always been a land of petty farms—the attempt to bring into being, within three or four years, in response to a resolution of the Communist Party, gigantic "corn factories"—is foredoomed to failure.

The organisation of large-scale farms needs an abundance of capital, ample knowledge, and wide experience. As many people know, in the year 1923 the great German industrialist Krupp was fascinated with the idea of establishing huge grain-growing farms in southern Russia. He was granted, under very favourable conditions, a concession comprising an area of tens of thousands of desyatines; he invested millions of roubles, imported agricultural machinery of the most up-to-date kinds, and entrusted the management of his "corn factories" to German agricultural experts. After three years, when he had lost a great deal of money, he decided to abandon corn growing, and to use his concession for sheep farming, which in this region has for centuries been conducted on a large scale. He had learned that "corn factories" could not be made to pay in these arid steppes, far from railway communications, thinly populated, in districts where civilisation was backward and where labour power was dear.

It is noteworthy, too, that Professor Lyashchenko, one of the most loyal of the Soviet economists, has issued a warning to the effect that the production of grain on the proposed Soviet farms cannot fail to be somewhat more costly than on individual peasant farms.[1] According to the calculations of P. Grekoff,[2] the cost of production of grain on the State farms, even if the enterprises are set a-going exactly in accordance with the plan, and if there is an average crop of 46 poods per desyatine, will amount to 1·07 roubles per pood, this being from 20 to 25 per cent more than the cost of production on individual peasant farms.

[1] [The Perspectives of Corn Growing, and the State Corn Factories], "Ekonomicheskoye Obozreniye", 1928, No. 6.
[2] [The Scheme for the Organisation of Great Soviet Farms], "Ekonomicheskoye Obozreniye", 1928, No. 9.

The governmental farms have intensified the discontent of the peasant masses. Whereas before the inauguration of these schemes, it could at any rate be said that the middle peasants and the poor peasants were granted a preferential position, and that only the "kulaks" were treated as pariahs, now, since the initiation of the new policy, individual peasant farming is regarded with disfavour in governmental circles. Privileges are to be reserved for collective farms and State farms. They are to receive special advantages in the matter of taxation; they are to have the first claim when credits are assigned. Agricultural machinery, pedigree stock, good seed, manures, industrial products, when these are scarce, are to be assigned first of all to collective farms and Soviet farms. Land surveying and land improvement are to be carried out first and under the best conditions upon these enterprises. Finally, according to the latest decisions, in the case of peasants who have failed to till all the land at their disposal, the "superfluous" areas of land are to be annexed for use by the collective undertakings.

The upshot of this new turn of governmental policy is that even such means as the State can dispose of for use in agriculture (and we have seen how scanty these are) are not to be used for the advantage of the great mass of the peasant population, but are to be squandered upon a utopian endeavour to conjure up out of the ground collective farms and State farms on the largest scale imaginable.

CHAPTER ELEVEN

INTERNAL TRADE

1. Internal Trade since the Introduction of the Nep

During the period of war communism there was no unified or continuously enforced system of internal trade either on paper or in practice. It is true that the decree concerning workers' control issued on November 14, 1917, which represented the first step towards the nationalisation of production, contemplated also the supply of enterprises with raw materials and fuel and the marketing of the products. In actual practice, as a rule, nationalisation set out from the department of trade rather than from that of production. War communism, coming into existence under war conditions and in circumstances of grinding poverty, was mainly a "consumers' communism". The main task of the State was the supply of the necessaries of life to the army and to the population in general, with the result that the first economic monopoly established by the Soviet State was a monopoly in the supply of the population with the means of subsistence. Hence the first confiscations of private property were confiscations of goods actually to be found in the shops and warehouses. The local Soviet authorities in town and countryside took a similar course in their first acts of expropriation.

The nationalisation of production and the organisation of labour upon the new basis were complicated undertakings. It was much easier to nationalise or communalise the shops and warehouses, and to distribute the commodities found in them, in order in this way to satisfy the most urgent needs of the impoverished population. That is why the nationalisation, or, to be more precise, the communalisation of trade, both wholesale and retail, was effected in the very earliest days of war communism, and was effected to an almost unrestricted extent. On April 2, 1918, the first step towards the nationalisation of trade was taken. A decree was issued according to which "the People's Commissariat for Food Supply" was "to take over the stores of textiles, boots and shoes, matches, soap, and agricultural machinery, in order to effect exchanges of commodities with the country districts". The People's Commissariat for Food Supply was to organise the supply and distribution of goods throughout the country. Four months later, by the decree of August 8, 1918, it was decided that industrial products were only to be supplied to the peasants by way of exchange, that is, only in return for agricultural produce. Finally, on November 21, 1918, there was issued a decree "for the complete nationalisation of trade". In order to effect the replacement of the apparatus of private trade, and in order to promote the supply of the population with all products in accordance with a generalised plan, the People's Commissariat for Food Supply was instructed to produce and to distribute all the products necessary for personal and household consumption. The production and distribution of the means of production was assigned to the Supreme Economic Council. In March 1919, private trade of any kind was prohibited. On March 20, 1919, there was issued a decree concerning consumers' communes, whereby the whole cooperative system was made compulsory instead of voluntary, and it was obligatory upon all citizens to become enrolled at one of the distribution stations. Trade was completely abolished, and was replaced by a system of rationing.

In the chapter on "Russian Economics during the period of War Communism", we studied the results of the complete nationalisation of trade. With the introduction of the Nep, freedom of trade was restored, at first under the modest formula of "Freedom of the Local Markets"; but subsequently the right of State organisations, cooperative societies, and private persons to trade throughout the country was established. No doubt it is only with considerable reservations that we can denote as freedom of trade the system which developed in Russia after the introduction of the Nep and which persists at the present day. Above all, no private individual has any right to trade across the frontier, whether by buying or by selling. Furthermore, the State retains in its own hands almost the entire production of industrial commodities, and withdraws various other commodities from the domain of private enterprise whenever such withdrawal is considered desirable on behalf of the political or economic interests of the government. According to law, the organisations which carry on State production must primarily dispose of their products to the State and cooperative trading organisations, and only in the last resort can they sell to private traders. Finally, the greatest possible difficulties are imposed upon private trade in the matter of credit, taxation, and the use of the means of transport. Nor do even the State trading organs possess the right of free trading in the ordinary sense of the term. As far as wholesale disposal of goods is concerned, these are mainly distributed in accordance with the decisions of the economic planning authorities, and not by way of trade.

At the present time the commercial system of the U.S.S.R. assumes the following aspect. From the State productive trusts, industrial commodities find their way, either to the wholesale trading departments of the trusts, or else to the warehouses of the syndicates which exist in almost all important branches of industry. The syndicates are the instruments for disposing of the goods manufactured by the State trusts. In some branches of industry it is incumbent upon them to dispose of the greater part of the products of the respective trusts: in the case of the Petroleum Syndicate, to the extent of 100 per cent; in the case of the Textile Syndicate, to the extent of from 85 to 90 per cent; in the case of the Leather Syndicate, to the extent of 55 per cent; in the case of the Metal Syndicate, to the extent of 33 per cent; and so on. Thus the goods find their way into the second stage of wholesale trade, the specialised departments of the syndicates, or the specialised organisations for State trade (Gostorgs), or ultimately to the cooperative centrals (Centrosoyus; for Ukraine, Vukopspilka). Thence the

goods are despatched to the selling stores of the various organisations in the different provinces, circles, towns, and villages;
and at length, to a certain extent; they pass into the channels of
private trade. Retail trade is carried on in shops and markets,
and by hawkers. As a general principle, however, it is held that
retail trade should be in the hands of the cooperatives, and
these are instructed to compete with private traders so as to
cut the ground from under their feet in the matter of retail
trade. In practice, the State trusts and syndicates have their
own selling stores in the towns and village markets; or even
organised cooperatives of hawkers to which the disposal of
goods is entrusted. For these reasons, there is no end to the
friction that results from rivalry between the cooperative
organisations and the State organisations. At each stage through
which a commodity has to pass between the hands of the pro-
ducer and those of the consumer, an addition to the price is
made to cover the cost of transit, so that in the end this price
is notably increased. The purchase and sale of grain, agricultural raw material, and other agrarian products, are in the
hands of special State organs (Hleboprodukt for grain, the
Sugar Trust, Sherst for wool, the Cotton Committee, and so
on), of cooperative organisations for purchase and sale, and of
private persons. Besides this, agricultural produce is sold at
the nearest town market by the peasants, the actual producers.
All business relationships between the various State trading
organisations and between these and the consumers are upon
a monetary basis. Buyers pay for goods in cash or in bills of
exchange. Sellers try to secure a traders' profit. There is fierce
competition among the various State organisations, so that
violent disputes and acrimonious lawsuits are of everyday
occurrence in connexion with Soviet trade. The principle of
exchange in the market and an endeavour to secure trading
profits determine the activities, not only of private traders, but
in the last analysis of State trade and cooperative trade.

To promote the development of trade, there are in the
U.S.S.R. (in Moscow and in other great towns), goods

exchanges (formerly 70, now 14), whose business it is to register the main transactions between the trading organisations, and to bring them to a formal conclusion.

The whole regulation of the exchange of commodities throughout the country is in the hands of the United Commissariat for Home and Foreign Trade (Narkomtorg). As far as home trade is concerned, the main tasks of this commissariat are to manage the business relations of the State trading organisations, to supervise the cooperatives, and to enforce the State policy towards private trade.

COMMODITY PRODUCTION[1]

(*In Millions of Pre-War Roubles*)

	Industry.		Agriculture.		Jointly.	
	Absolute.	Per cent Increase.	Absolute.	Per cent Increase.	Absolute.	Per cent Increase.
1921/22	1710	100·0	1740	100·0	3450	100·0
1922/23	2220	129·8	2550	146·5	4770	138·3
1923/24	3030	136·5	2720	106·7	5750	120·5
1924/25	4460	147·2	3810	140·1	8270	143·8
1925/26	5930	132·9	4260	111·8	10,190	123·2
1926/27	6800	114·7	4610	108·2	11,410	111·9
1927/28[2]	7990	117·5	4868	105·6	12,858	112·7

During the years of war communism, there was a catastrophic decline in the circulation of commodities. In the year of the greatest falling-off in this respect, 1920–1921, according to the calculations of the State Planning Commission, the total Russian production (as far as commodities which found their way into circulation were concerned) was only 25 per cent of the pre-war circulation of commodities. In the countryside, and to a considerable extent in the towns as well, economic life had returned to the methods of a natural economy. The following table, in which the value of the commodities put into

[1] The table has been compiled upon the basis of the "control figures" and of materials published by the Central Statistical Bureau.
[2] Provisional estimate.

circulation has been reduced to pre-war prices, shows the rate of the growth of that part of the national production which entered into the circulation of commodities.

Coming to consider the turnover of goods, the most exact data are obtainable as regards the turnover of wholesale trade, and above all, the turnover of State trading and cooperative trading. The reports of the goods exchanges in Moscow and the provinces, those of the syndicates, the cooperatives, and of private traders—reports published by the State Planning Commission—have been used in the compilation of the following table, which shows us the development of trade and of commission business (wholesale and retail) since the beginning of the Nep period.

(*In Millions of Chervonets Roubles.*)

	State Trade.	Cooperatives.	Private Trade.	Jointly.
1923/24	3025	2750	3976	9751
1924/25	5382	5231	4000	14,613
1925/26	8210	9626	5770	23,606
1926/27	9795	13,780	5200	28,775
1927/28	10,790	17,450	5200	33,440

The turnover of commodities increases year by year, but the greatest increase is in the commission business of the Soviet cooperatives.

In Chapter Five we learned that the crucial problem of the circulation of commodities in contemporary Russia was the chronic disharmony between supply and demand, which during the last few years has taken the form of an acute scarcity of goods. Let us now consider this question in fuller detail. Among Russian communists, the view generally prevails that the main cause of the scarcity of goods is the disproportion between industrial and agricultural production respectively. But this explanation is not exhaustive. As compared with pre-war conditions, industrial production and agricultural production have regained approximately the same level, so that if the cause of the scarcity of goods were a disproportion in this respect, it ought to have existed before the war. It did not so exist, and we therefore have to ask ourselves why before the war there was a certain balance between urban and rural production, a certain stability; whereas under the Soviet government this equilibrium has not been maintained. Why does the disproportion continue year after year? Why is Russian economic life subject to a condition of grave and persistent crisis, such as was unknown before the war?

It is, of course, a familiar fact that in pre-war days there was no proper balance of values as between industrial and agricultural products respectively. How could there be such a balance, seeing that the harvests are so variable? If a balance was secured in the market, this was thanks to the fact that Russia, economically considered, was not an isolated nation. Large quantities of agricultural produce were promptly exported, and the deficiency in industrial commodities was made good by imports. In every country, foreign trade is an automatic regulator, which compensates for the disharmonies that arise as between one department of economic life and another. To-day, however, when Russia has to exist apart from the economic circulation of the world at large, and is compelled to keep herself going as an almost entirely detached economic unit, the persistent disproportion between the development of industry and agriculture in the country necessarily makes itself acutely perceptible.

The "commodity famine" of Russia is a complex phenomenon, in which a number of the organic errors of Soviet political economy secure expression. That is why the causes of the commodity famine are multiple, and the intensity of this famine can only be understood when due allowance is made for the cooperation of various factors. Above all, we must never forget that between 1913 and the present day the population of the area comprised in the Soviet Union has increased by 7 per cent. Furthermore, as official data show, in many branches of production the pre-war condition has not been fully regained. Averages showing the development of production for industry as a whole can only give a hazy conception of the scope and character of contemporary production. If, for instance, a comparatively high level has been attained for the production of petroleum and coal, but only a much lower level for the production of metals, machinery, and building materials, it is obvious that percentage statements of the average development of production will give but an inadequate notion of the need for metals, machinery, and building materials. One who wants boots or sheet iron, will hardly be consoled by being informed that there are plentiful supplies of salt and matches!

In the disturbance of the pre-war balance between industrial and agricultural production, a considerable part has been played by the severance of Poland and the Baltic provinces from Russia. The industry of these regions did not supply local markets alone. In comparisons between the quantity of commodities now circulating in the U.S.S.R. and the turnover of goods in pre-war days, it is not enough to calculate the quantities that were then produced in the area which now comprises the Soviet Union, and to compare the amounts with those now produced in the same area. Finland, Poland, and the Baltic provinces were exporting regions, sending industrial products to other parts of Russia, and therefore having (as one might say), in trading relations with the rest of Russia, a favourable balance of trade. According to the reports of Professor V. Grinevetsky,[1] Russian Poland, the Baltic provinces, and Finland, produced 70 per cent of all the paper produced in the Russian empire; 74 per cent of all the jewelry, trinkets, etc.; 71 per cent of knitted goods; 33 per cent of the woollens; 53 per cent of the readymade clothing; from 60 to 68 per cent of the crude textiles; 38 per cent of the sacking; 28 per cent of the hardware; 45 per cent of the iron plates needed for building purposes and for the use of the peasants. No doubt some of these products were used where they were manufactured, in the regions which now comprise Finland, Poland, Latvia, Esthonia,

[1] [The Post-war Perspectives of Russian Industry], pp. 95–96.

and Lithuania; but most of them found their way into the general home market of Russia.

Of great moment, too, is the circumstance that many of the old factories which were taken over by the State from private owners have been kept at work without any change in their technical equipment, so that they are continuing to produce goods which are still adapted only to pre-war needs. But during the period of the revolution the entire social structure of the country has undergone radical changes, with the result that the demand for luxuries and for costly articles has been reduced to a minimum, while the demand for the articles of mass consumption has greatly increased. In addition, the disappearance of the old-time patriarchal conditions in the Russian villages has greatly modified the demands made from this quarter. That is why certain kinds of goods are so scarce, whilst of others there is a glut.

Another reason why there has been a considerable decline in the aggregate value of the products of contemporary Russian industry is that their quality is much inferior to that of pre-war days. Clothing, and boots and shoes, wear out sooner; more of the hardware is flawed; the crockery is exceptionally fragile; and so on, and so on.

Defects of organisation in the apparatus of Russian trade, account also for the increasing scarcity of commodities. A considerable part of the goods in circulation is continually being shifted from pillar to post, transferred from one owner to another, or hoarded for a long time before it reaches the consumer.

But the main cause of the scarcity of goods is that the reestablishment of foreign trade lags so much behind the advances that have been made towards the reestablishment of other branches of economic life. Whereas in industry, agriculture, and internal trade, pre-war standards have been regained or nearly so, foreign trade seems to be arrested at a figure about 40 per cent of the trade of pre-war days, or to have relapsed, as one of the Soviet newspapers wrote, into the condition of the eighteen-eighties. Owing to the decline in imports to the extent of two-thirds, the amount of goods circulating within the country has been notably reduced. Calculated in present prices, we may say that the value of the goods which ought to have been imported and have not been imported must be round about one milliard. But a mere statement of this figure does not give any clear idea of the significance of the decline in imports to Russian economic life, and of the effects of this decline upon mass consumption. In the year 1912, imports were sufficient to satisfy 40 per cent of the general demand for chemical products; 26 per cent of the demand for foodstuffs; 35 per cent of the demand for hardware; 47 per cent of the demand for raw materials needed by the textile industry; and so on. As regards machine tools, delicate mechanical apparatus, motors, small-arms, and scientific instruments, the imports exceeded Russian production by 215 per cent.

Although during the years of the Nep, the effective demand of the population (and especially of the peasants) has almost entirely revived, so that various researches show the pre-war level to have been regained, there has been a considerable decline in the amount of industrial products finding their way into circulation.[1] In Russian economic literature we find numerous attempts to estimate the extent of the deficiency of goods, but the results of such calculations differ so much one from another, and practice so persistently gives the lie to numerical forecasts, that we should do little service by reproducing the figures here.[2] I may be content to remark that since

[1] The scarcity of goods assumes especially acute forms whenever the Soviet government has recourse to the policy of inflating money or credit, whereby an artificially intensified demand from speculators or genuine consumers is stimulated. Cf. also the chapter on "Currency".

[2] At the Fifteenth Congress of the Communist Party of the U.S.S.R., Rykoff said: "I have tried to draw up a more or less accurate numerical statement of the extent of the difference between supply and demand. I must frankly admit that I cannot make up my mind to lay these figures before you, for the following reasons. First of all, there is such a multiplicity of data. Secondly, owing to inconsistencies between the various methods of calculation, they contradict one another. In the third place, they have only an extremely conditional validity, and can therefore give no more than a

1924 the Soviet economists have been unanimous in declaring that there is a shortage of industrial products.

But whereas the Soviet economists look upon this scarcity of goods as the outcome of an evil fate, as something which must be regarded as a necessary result of the objective conditions on which Russian economic structure depends, our own investigation shows that a great diminution of the scarcity might be expected to follow upon a change in the economic policy of the State. The tension arising from the persistent scarcity of industrial products makes the State regulation of the circulation of commodities at one and the same time extremely desirable and extraordinarily difficult.

As regards the regulation of the market, the most important step must be to distribute commodities to the various parts of the country in accordance with a general economic plan, and to make satisfactory arrangements for the promotion of agricultural production and for the supply of industrial commodities in the various districts. In neither one respect nor the other have the far-reaching schemes of the authorities produced satisfactory results. The requisitions of the various State organisations, competing one with another, are persistently ignored. The supplies of goods prescribed by the central authorities, and calculated in accordance with a general economic plan, fail to reach the appropriate localities; and, indeed, lack of proper knowledge of the markets and of information as to the demands of the consumers, make it impossible for the authorities to decide with any certainty what kinds and what amounts of goods are needed in particular regions. The fluctuations in the purchasing power of the agricultural producers (which vary, not only in accordance with variations in the harvests, but also as the expression of the effects of changes in the governmental policy towards the peasants) make the

distorted picture of actual market conditions. For instance, in such statements, the value of petroleum, of which we have a sufficiency, is lumped with that of cotton, of which there is a scarcity."—"Pravda", December 17, 1927.

organisation of supply to the different districts utterly impracticable. The State trading apparatus, cumbrous and bureaucratic, is incompetent to discharge its duties punctually and
intelligently. In one district there will be an excess of goods,
while in another there will be a complete lack of the same
commodities. Articles intended for the town are sent to the
countryside, while those needed by the village find their way
to an urban district. The general upshot is an overburdening
of the transport system, which must so often provide for the
needless carrying of goods to and fro, and an increase in the
activity of speculators who try to supply the articles in demand.
Since 1926 and 1927, there have been introduced two supplementary systems to regulate the circulation of goods: the entering into long-term contracts for the disposal of industrial
products as between the trusts and syndicates on the one hand
and the cooperatives on the other; and a system of contracts
entered into between the State manufacturing institutions and
the peasants for the supply of agricultural products (grain,
sugar-beets, flax, oil-containing seeds, cotton, wool, etc.). The
development of these methods is greatly hampered by the
bureaucratic procedure of the State trading apparatus, and by
the fact that the fluctuations of prices that result from market
conditions and the instability of the currency are such as cannot
be foreseen for any long time in advance.

One of the most difficult and complicated of problems is
that of fixing prices. As regards the circulation of commodities,
the State has fixed the prices of factory products,[1] and has
established a maximum cost of production in every branch.
But the attempts to carry out these regulations have been to a
large extent unsuccessful, owing to the resistance of the market
and to the inertia of the cumbrous and complicated trading
apparatus. The retail prices of industrial products are extraordinarily high. The attempts of the State to regulate such

[1] Strictly speaking, there are fixed prices for only a small number of commodities, for in the case of other commodities the State speaks only of
"directive" prices.—But in practice there is no great difference here.

matters take practical effect very slowly and to a very limited degree, partly because of the resistance of the bureaucratic apparatus, but mainly because they run counter to the laws of the market. The demand is great and the supply is small. Circumstances work in the opposite direction as regards the prices of grain and other agricultural produce.[1] Under the pressure of the monopolist consumer, the State, the prices of agricultural produce remain at a much lower level than the prices of industrial products. By taxation, by scarcity of industrial products, and by enforcing subscriptions to loans, the State compels the peasants to hand over grain, meat, flax, butter, eggs, wool, etc., to the governmental purchasing department at the prices fixed by the State. An exchange of agricultural products for industrial on unfair terms has become a daily occurrence, and is the reflection of the definite policy of the Soviet authorities, which aims at an accelerated industrialisation at the expense of the peasants' possibilities of accumulating capital. It is owing to the compulsion exercised upon the peasants in this matter of the delivery of their products to the State at fixed prices, that there are such wide fluctuations in the prices of these products from place to place and from time to time. As long as the peasants are paying their taxes and are at the same time buying the industrial products they need, and are therefore compelled to sell their own products, the prices of these latter remain low. But in the winter and the spring, when the taxes have been paid, the prices of agricultural products rise rapidly. In areas that produce a deficiency of grain, the prices are always considerably higher than in the areas that produce a surplus of grain. The prices at which the peasants sell in the open market directly to consumers are higher than the prices at which they

[1] One of the directors of the Russian State Bank, Professor S. Katsenelenbaum, writes in his book [The Industrialisation of Agriculture and the Functions of Credit in the U.S.S.R.]: "The budget policy and the industrial policy of the U.S.S.R. (involving as they do extreme economy in the domain of domestic industrial production) inevitably lead to an increase in the price of commodities. In these circumstances there can be practically no question of reducing prices."

sell to the State purchasing departments. Over and above this, it is very difficult to determine the proper ratio of prices as regards particular agricultural products. The lowering of the prices of the products which serve as the raw material of industry (flax, tobacco, cotton) as compared with the prices of grain, led, in 1926–1927, to a restriction of the area under flax, tobacco, and cotton, whereas in the year 1927–1928 an error in the opposite direction led to a restriction of the area under wheat and barley. Like phenomena are seen as regards the prices of butter, eggs, and leather.

N. Vinogradsky, one of the most noted collaborators of the People's Commissariat for Trade, admits that these fluctuations in the areas under cultivation of one kind and another and in the quantity of various products marketed, are caused "either by a radical lowering of prices, or else by glaring mistakes in regulation". He points out that such fluctuations are especially conspicuous in the case of commodities whose purchase is monopolised by the State.[1]

Down to 1928, the State has been unsuccessful in its attempts to overcome the disharmonies of prices as between industrial and agricultural products, for these attempts, in so far as they aim at reducing the prices of industrial products, can have very little effect in view of the general method of organisation of production and trade, whilst the State is prevented by its economic policy from raising the prices of agricultural products. In the middle of the year 1928, after the failure of the "swing to the left", the State was compelled to announce that its policy of keeping down agricultural prices had been erroneous; and by a decree issued on July 19, 1928, it declared that these prices were to be raised by an amount ranging from 10 to 15 per cent, according to the quality of the product and to the district concerned. There can be no doubt that this was a great concession to the peasants, but it was one whose value was to a large extent discounted, because at the same time the government declared its intention "to continue the

[1] [Theory and Practice of the Regulation of Trade], p. 41.

M

offensive against the capitalist elements in the countryside"—a phrase which in practice has been shown on previous occasions to be tantamount to a declaration of war against the peasantry aa a whole.

In the year 1928, owing to the "swing to the left", an illegal free market came into existence side by side with the legal grain market, and in the free market the peasants received much higher prices for grain. In this way, the disproportion between the prices of agricultural and industrial products respectively was diminished. The result, however, was disastrous both to the governmental schemes for a "purposive economy" and to the stability of the chervonets, since it was the outcome, not of a lowering of the prices of industrial products, but of a rise in the prices of agricultural products, above all in the free market.

Various indexes are used by Soviet statisticians to calculate the curve of prices. The commonest are: (1) the index of the Supreme Economic Council, which shows the prices at which State industry supplies its products to the State and cooperative trading organisations; (2) the wholesale index of the Central Statistical Bureau; and (3) the index of retail prices prepared by the Conjuncture Institute. Besides these, there is a standard-of-life index for the calculation of real wages, this being based upon a study of the prices of various products essential to the working-class household. The following table gives a general view of the movement of the monthly indexes[1] in October and April during recent years.

In the year 1929, the rise in prices continued. The general standard-of-life index of the Labour Statistical Department reached, on June 1st, the figure 230, and for agricultural

[1] The prices and the value of the composite commodities in the standard-of-life index of the Labour Statistical Department for 1913 are taken as 100. (The Central Statistical Bureau and the Conjuncture Institute take the figures for 1913 as 1000, but for convenience of comparison I have throughout used the customary German standard of 100 as the basis of the calculations.) —The valuation of the commodities used in the standard-of-life index and the commodities selected have been changed since October 1, 1926.

	Wholesale Index of the Central Statistical Bureau.	Retail Index of the Conjuncture Institute.	Standard-of-Life Index of the Labour Statistical Department.[1]
General—			
1923/24 October	148·8	161·0	167·0
April ..	178·0	212·0	210·9
1924/25 October	164·2	205·0	192·6
April ..	196·0	220·0	217·5
1925/26 October	175·3	216·0	196·2
April ..	197·1	246·0	232·4
1926/27 October	178·4	233·0	202·9
April ..	176·0	227·0	201·9
1927/28 October	170·4	198·0	199·2
April ..	170·8	203·0	203·3
1928/29 October	176·0	199·0	201·0
April ..	179·0	210·0	218·0
Agricultural—			
1923/24 October	87·7	92·0	104·1
April ..	153·9	181·0	190·2
1924/25 October	135·9	170·0	161·0
April ..	201·2	214·0	214·0
1925/26 October	156·6	192·0	178·2
April ..	191·3	224·0	225·8
1926/27 October	156·1	203·0	204·6
April ..	158·9	208·0	216·0
1927/28 October	154·3	189·0	206·6
April ..	155·5	199·0	212·6
1928/29 October	166·0	201·0	208·0
April ..	170·0	223·0	234·0
Industrial—			
1923/24 October	252·5	258·0	279·4
April ..	205·8	241·0	247·6
1924/25 October	198·4	245·0	248·8
April ..	190·8	226·0	223·2
1925/26 October	196·1	243·0	288·8
April ..	203·0	269·0	244·1
1926/27 October	203·8	265·0	237·8
April ..	195·0	241·0	225·0
1927/28 October	188·1	203·0	215·4
April ..	187·6	205·0	217·6
1928/29 October	187·0	198·0	210·0
April ..	188·0	203·0	214·0
Opening of the scissors[2]—			
1923/24 October[1]	288·0	280·0	—
April ..	134·0	133·0	—
1924/25 October	146·0	144·0	—
April ..	95·0	106·0	—
1925/26 October	125·0	127·0	—
April ..	106·0	120·0	—
1926/27 October	131·0	131·0	—
April ..	123·0	116·0	—
1927/28 October	122·0	107·0	—
April ..	121·0	103·0	—
1928/29 October	112·7	0·985	—
April ..	111·1	0·910	—

[1] For 40 commodities, rent, and communal services.
[2] The industrial index in percentages of the agricultural index.

products actually 258.[1] The rise in prices has been especially
great in the free market. According to the reports of the Conjuncture Institute, the market prices for flour and grain were
from 2 to 2½ times greater than the prices of last year; the
industrial index and the standard-of-life index began to rise
swiftly; there were marked divergences of prices as between
various districts and various agricultural products (as between
grain and flour, as between grain and the products destined to
form the raw material of industry, as between grain and fodder).
There was also an especially great rise in retail prices.

The rise in the retail trading index of the Conjuncture
Institute during the year 1928–1929 was as follows (reckoned
in percentages as compared with the same indexes for corresponding dates in the year 1927–1928[2]:

General Index—
General Trading Index	..	6·5	7·2	7·4
State Trading Index	..	1·3	2·1	2·6
Private Trading Index	..	16·2	16·6	16·4

Industrial Index—
General Trading Index	..	1·5	1·9	2·5
State Trading Index	..	0·0	0·4	1·0
Private Trading Index	..	4·8	4·9	5·4

Agricultural Index—
General Trading Index	..	15·2	16·6	16·1
State Trading Index	..	3·9	5·5	5·6
Private Trading Index	..	32·9	34·0	32·5

The main cause of the rise in prices is to be found in the
general disturbance of Russian economic life which occurred
towards the end of the year 1928, and above all in the obvious
inflation.

One of the causes of the failure of the attempts of the People's
Commissariat for Home and Foreign Trade to regulate prices
is that the Commissariat has been attempting, either by means
of regulations or by the supply of its own goods, to deal simultaneously with all branches of the circulation of commodities.
At a conference summoned by the Central Council of the

[1] "Vestnik Finansoff", 1929, No. 6.
[2] "Ekonomicheskaya Zhizn", December 30, 1928.

Trade Unions of the U.S.S.R. in the middle of July 1928, to consider the difficulties of food supply in the towns, the delegates were unanimous in the stress they laid upon these circumstances. There had, they said, been too much regulation. There must be no further attempts to regulate the sale of vegetables by small-scale gardeners, or the sale of milk by dairywomen. The People's Commissariat for Trade had attempted the impossible when it had tried to supervise everything. Officials with a mania for universal administration could achieve nothing. Such were the opinions expressed at this conference.

In the endeavour to effect the impossible, the People's Commissariat for Home and Foreign Trade, instead of contenting itself with the State regulation of trade (a necessary and important task under the conditions that prevail in the Soviet Union) has overreached itself in a hopeless attempt to establish a State monopoly in trade.

2. The Campaign against Private Traders

Although one of the most important elements of the New Economic Policy was a retreat in the domain of trade, was the permitting of freedom of private trade, throughout the period of the Nep the Soviet government has been vacillating in its attitude towards private traders, so that over and again there have been relapses into the methods of war communism.

During the first years of the Nep, large quantities of private capital were invested in trading concerns, and, by the end of the year 1923, according to the reports of the People's Commissariat for Finance, 84 per cent of all petty trading business was in private hands, 50·4 per cent of all retail and wholesale businesses, and more than 20 per cent of all large-scale trading enterprises. Although the turnover of each new undertaking was very small, the total turnover of private trading reached 64·8 per cent of the aggregate turnover of all trade.[1] In addi-

[1] Vorobyoff [The State of Trade in the U.S.S.R.], "Vestnik Promyshlennosti i Torgovli", 1924, No. 4.

tion, the private traders controlled almost all the trade of the rural districts, State enterprise being here forced into the background by the persistency and skill of private speculators. The Soviet economists declared that the foundations of the Soviet system were being sapped by the waters of the petty-bourgeois ocean. At the Twelfth Congress of the Communist Party of the U.S.S.R., held in the year 1924, it was decided that "the most important task of the coming year will be to regain a dominant position on the trading front. Private capital must be replaced by the cooperatives".

During the very first months of the operation of the Nep, Lenin urged the communists to learn lessons from the private traders, that they might themselves become "good traders", might get a good grip of these links of the commercial chain, so that ere long the whole chain should pass into their hands. This recommendation implied that the victory over private capital was not to be obtained by official pressure, but in the open market and in competition with private trade; yet in actual practice, immediately after the Twelfth Congress, the principle of competition on equal terms was abandoned in favour of the first phase of the persecution of private traders. Everywhere such traders were arrested, deported, deprived of their property. Economic methods of repression were also used. Some of the trusts were instructed to refuse to supply private traders with goods; others received orders to sell only to retailers; others, again, were told to sell to private dealers only the less saleable commodities, or those of which there existed a marked superfluity. The banks were to refuse credit to private traders; the railways were to give them transport facilities only in the last resort. Various special taxes were imposed upon private trade. Although the resolution passed at the Twelfth Congress had spoken of "free competition", repression and official persecution became the order of the day.

To begin with, this policy was successful in restricting the activity of the private traders. But soon there was a rally. Private enterprise accommodated itself to the new atmosphere, wormed its way into the nooks and crannies of an apparently solid wall, adopted all the devices of protective coloration. Stubbornly it fought on behalf of the "right to profit". The new generation of private traders had gathered experience when winning their spurs and accumulating their capital in the period of war communism and of civil war. The wholesale dealers disintegrated their apparatus. To outward seeming they became retailers, but in actual practice, under the masks of dozens of retailers, they sold goods just as extensively as when they had called themselves wholesalers. Armies of agents were organised to buy in the retail stores of the State trusts such goods as the private wholesaler wanted. When to some extent prevented from doing business in the towns, the private traders devoted part of their capital to the purchase of grain, meat, butter, flax, hides, wool, and other products of the countryside. They entered into close relationships with the "kulaks". It was found possible to evade the official supervision, registration, and taxation to some extent in the towns, and still more in the countryside. By degrees, the private traders were again able to play an important part in the circulation of commodities.

Towards the close of the year 1925, there was a second fierce campaign on the part of the authorities against the private traders; there was a third in the end of 1926; and there was a fourth in the beginning of 1928, as a part of the general "swing to the left". To begin with, of course, in each case, the authorities triumphed. Time after time, they were able to minimise the share of private traders, both in wholesale and in retail trade. Time after time, however, although the official organs were able to plume themselves on the fact that the State policy of repression had made the activities of the private traders impossible, they were unable to declare that either the cooperatives or the retail trading apparatus of the State had been successful in taking over the economically useful functions of the private traders as intermediaries in promoting the circulation of commodities.

According to official figures, the share of private trade in the whole internal trade of the country is as follows:

SHARE OF PRIVATE TRADE IN PERCENTAGES

1922/23	..	..	..	..	.. 64·8
1923/24	..	..	..	..	.. 40·0
1924/25	..	..	..	..	.. 26·3
1925/26	..	..	..	..	.. 23·7
1926/27	..	..	..	..	.. 18·1

During the year 1927–1928, when the "swing to the left" was in progress, the share of private trade was yet further reduced. In wholesale trade, it fell to 4 per cent; in retail trade, to 30 per cent. The number of private enterprises was reduced by 42·2 per cent between 1926–1927 and 1927–1928, the decline taking place chiefly at the expense of the large-scale trading enterprises and the mixed retail and wholesale businesses. According to the reports of Tomsky, the chairman of the Central Council of the Trade Unions of the U.S.S.R., under the pressure of the authorities and owing to the burden of taxation, during the eight months of the "swing to the left" 103,000 private enterprises were closed down, and only 4,000 new cooperative stores were opened to take their places. "It seems doubtful", remarks Tomsky, "whether one new cooperative store can effectively replace from twenty to twenty-five private shops." This, he continues, is one of those victories "in which the enemy evacuates a position when the opposing army has made no advance".[1]

In the U.S.S.R., the network of trade is poorly developed, and such retail business as there is is carried on mainly by little shops with a very small turnover. In the year 1926–1927, in the area of the Soviet Union, there were in all 648,000 shops and stores as compared with 1,011,000 in the year 1912, so that only 65 per cent of the pre-war position has been regained. One such trading enterprise has to-day to serve on the average an area of 32 square kilometres with a population of 225 persons. Especially inadequate is the supply of shops in the rural

[1] "Pravda", July 14, 1928.

districts, where one shop has on the average to serve 511 inhabitants; and there are areas of the countryside which deserve the name of "deserts" as far as the possibility of shopping is concerned, seeing that in these the only possibility of buying goods is that supplied by the weekly market and by hawkers.

These conditions are very unfortunate for the population, and greatly restrict the capacity of the home market. "The inadequacy of the commercial network of the U.S.S.R. is unanimously regarded as one of the most disastrous defects of the present organisation of Soviet trade", writes V. Kantorovich, the Soviet economist from whom I have borrowed the above figures concerning Soviet trade.[1] In such circumstances, the repressive measures that are taken against private traders, have a very unfavourable repercussion upon the economy of the Soviet Union as a whole. No doubt the effective abolition of private trade would be an excellent thing from the economic standpoint, if the functions of the private traders were to be properly discharged by a well-organised cooperative system. But in the actual condition of contemporary Soviet life, we see a very different and much less agreeable picture.

When, as we have learned, the extant trading apparatus of all kinds (State, private, and cooperative) is incompetent to supply the needs of the population satisfactorily, and when the State and the cooperatives are unable to expand their trading activities to the requisite degree, there can be no justification for the attempts of the Soviet government to restrict private trade by all possible means—including the use of force. The upshot of such attempts has been that the supply of commodities to the rural districts has become more inadequate than ever. In the towns, too, where 60 per cent of the trade in meat was in the hands of private traders, 75 per cent of the trade in vegetables, 83 per cent of the trade in eggs, and 95 per cent of the trade in milk, the destruction of private trade has caused

[Some of the Problems of the Trading Apparatus of the U.S.S.R.] Sotsialisticheskoe Hozyaistvo", 1928, No. 3.

grave inconvenience to the population. Whenever one of the periodical attempts to repress private trade has been made, there has ensued a great decline in the extent of trade in general, with a resulting reduction in the receipts of the treasury—a falling-off in that part of the State income which is derived from the taxation of economic life. The worst feature of the whole matter is that, on such occasions, private capital flows into hidden and illegal channels, especially those provided by secret speculation.[1] Of course the State is unable to control or register or regulate these underground activities of economic life.

3. SOVIET COOPERATIVES

The Russian cooperative system, as it exists to-day, has a character all its own. Outside Soviet Russia, everywhere and invariably, cooperatives have tried to promote the spontaneous organisation of the masses of consumers, to further their education and their voluntary activity. The spirit of the international cooperative movement is not purely economic, for first and foremost it is social. The movement is one for the fulfilment of social and cultural functions, as well as commercial ones. But in the U.S.S.R. there no longer exists a free and voluntary cooperative movement. Down to the end of the year 1923, the very existence of voluntary consumers' cooperatives was illegal in the Soviet State. All the workers in a particular enterprise, or all those inhabiting a particular district, were compelled by law to join the local consumers' cooperative society. Their subscriptions to this body were in most cases automatically deducted from their wages, were collected at the source. Subsequently, in order to reinvigorate the cooperative movement, on two occasions (December 18, 1923, and May 20, 1924), the Soviet government issued decrees formally

[1] "Private trade has now been completely cut off from almost all the legitimate sources of supply with the products of State industry," writes Kantorovich (op. cit.).

recognising the principle of the voluntary membership of cooperative organisations. In practice, however, a perfectly free membership of the cooperatives cannot as yet be said to exist. The question of joining a workers' and urban consumers' cooperative is decided by the votes of a small group of communists at a meeting of the workers engaged in any enterprise, the non-communists remaining passive. As soon as the resolution has been passed, all the workers in the enterprise must join the cooperative. In the countryside, it is not so easy to force people into the cooperatives; but even there official pressure plays a great part. As late as the year 1926, Smirnoff, the People's Commissary for Agriculture, had to admit that when on an official journey in south-eastern Russia, he had everywhere made adhesion to the consumers' cooperatives on the part of the peasants a precondition to the granting of State credits and other advantages.

The extant Soviet cooperatives are not the outcome of the independent activities of the masses of consumers. They have originated in accordance with the instructions of the State authorities out of the compulsory consumers' communes which were established by the card system in the first years of Soviet rule for the general distribution of the means of subsistence and other necessaries. Consequently, the membership of the cooperatives is, on paper, very large. During the years of war communism, it reached nearly 12 millions, but declined in the following years, when the system of compulsory membership was abandoned, to increase once more from 1925 onwards. According to the reports of the Centrosoyus, the membership during the last ten years has been as shown in the table on page 188.

Besides the system of consumers' cooperatives, there is in the U.S.S.R. a widely extended system of agricultural cooperatives (for credit, machinery, sowing, cattle breeding, beet cultivation, tobacco cultivation, etc.). In these, at the outset of the year 1928, 7.5 millions of peasants were enrolled. There are also cooperative organisations for the carrying-on

of small-scale industry and domestic industry—11,862 in all,
with a membership of 1,150,000.

Year.	Cooperatives.	Number of Stores.	Membership.
1918	47,000	63,200	11,500,000
1923	19,085	25,490	7,600,000
1924	22,621	37,129	7,133,000
1925	25,625	51,458	9,436,000
1926	28,658	62,736	12,462,000
1927	28,614	71,143	15,073,000
1928[1]	28,620	85,000	22,581,000

Thus the cooperative system in all its forms consisted in the
year 1927–1928 of a mighty apparatus, in which more than
60 per cent of all the organised workers and 40 per cent of the
peasant farms were enrolled. This sort of "participation" in
the cooperatives is nowise distinguishable from the ordinary
operations of the purchase and sale of goods carried on by the
governmental or private instruments of trade. The number of
active members, of those who play an effective part in the work
of their cooperatives, is, as the Soviet cooperators themselves
admit, very small. Nor are there any close ties between the
cooperatives and the consumers they supply. This is the
weakest point of the Russian cooperative system. In practice,
too, the governing bodies of the cooperatives are only to a
nominal extent elective. The lists of candidates for these
bodies, whether local or central, are drawn up by the communist
fractions, and are adopted in block by open vote. Under such
conditions, it is obviously out of the question for any group
of oppositional cooperators to put forward a list; and even
such non-party candidates as are regarded as "trustworthy" by
the communists, can only be nominated and elected with the
approval of these latter. Furthermore, the efficiency of the
communists is found to be greatest as we proceed upwards in
the hierarchal scale. According to the reports for the year 1927,
in the primary committees of the cooperatives, there were 15

[1] Provisional figures.

per cent of communists; in the district committees, 40 per cent; in the county committees, 65 per cent; and in the Centrosoyus, 90 per cent.

All independent cooperators are expelled from the cooperative organisations. After the collapse of war communism, Lenin, who based great hopes on the cooperatives, wrote: "The cooperative system throws up to the surface, with a working as accurate as that of chemical laws, menshevists and socialist revolutionaries, and for this reason, when we are making use of the cooperatives, we must drive all 'socialists' out of them, and put such persons under lock and key." By arrests and deportations, the communists have effectively "purged" the cooperatives of all the independent and active officials, and they have even got rid of the really practical workers, those who had acquired extensive experience, and who regadred their service in the cooperatives as a service to the community. In place of these, there have now found their way into the cooperatives persons who, as the communists themselves declare, know nothing about the cooperative movement, including a good many sometime private traders, tsarist officials, and illicit traders of civil war days.[1]

The Soviet cooperatives are directly dependent upon the State, alike administratively and officially. The State, which has retained a decisive influence in the cooperative organisations, makes them carry out its decisions, many of which, as we shall presently learn, conflict with the whole nature of cooperative activity. The cooperatives no longer have any collective will, are no longer able to express the will of an organised membership; all their activities are dictated and regulated by the Commissariat for Trade, by the State Planning Commission, and by other State instruments.

Even the communists had to admit this in 1926. "Pravda", the central organ of the Communist Party, pointed out that "a number of errors have been disclosed in the ways by which the State instruments regulate the work of the cooperative

[1] "Pravda", September 27, 1924.

movement". The writer went on to say: "The cooperative movement was placed on exactly the same terms as the State organisations; there were imposed upon it, under conditions prescribed by the State, a number of duties in the way of the purchase and the delivery of goods. In this way the freedom of the cooperative movement has been destroyed, for in carrying out the orders of the State, the cooperatives have often been compelled to deal with their property in a way which was injurious to the members of the organisation."[1]

Nevertheless, even after this admission, matters did not improve, as Rykoff acknowledged in July 1928, in the plenum of the Central Committee of the Communist Party of the U.S.S.R. In discharging the tasks laid upon it by the State, as main instrument in conveying goods to the countryside, and as chief purchaser of agricultural produce to supply the needs of the urban population, industry, and export, the cooperative movement has, of course, an extensive turnover of goods.

TURNOVER OF ALL BRANCHES OF COOPERATIVE MOVEMENT

				Millions of Chervonets Roubles.
1924/25	..	..	..	.. 5231
1925/26	..	..	..	.. 9626
1926/27	..	..	..	.. 13,780

In the year 1927–1928, the expected turnover of the cooperatives was 14·5 milliards of roubles, of which 12 milliards of roubles was to be the turnover of the consumers' cooperatives. Thus the cooperative turnover for that year was to be 50·5 per cent of the total wholesale turnover of goods, and 54·3 per cent of the total retail turnover. Such extensive trading is only possible because the cooperatives work with State funds and under the guidance of the State.

One of the weakest points of the Soviet cooperatives is the lack of funds of their own. In the balance sheet of the Centrosoyus for the year 1926–1927, its own funds amounted to only 6·3 per cent of the whole. In the balance sheet for 1927–1928, the proportion of its own funds has increased a little, being

[1] "Pravda", December 13, 1926.

now 9·8 per cent. In the retail activities of the cooperatives, an even smaller proportion of the working funds belongs to these bodies, being on the average only 5·2 per cent. Thus the cooperatives remain dependent upon State subventions and credits.

Nevertheless, not even the continuous financial aid of the State has put the cooperatives upon a sound footing. Again and again, the government has had to save them from bankruptcy. Often enough, cooperative bills of exchange are not punctually met. The supreme governmental authorities are continually being besieged by the cooperatives with applications for subventions. The consumers' cooperatives supply their members very badly, for neither is the supply of the working masses of the town and countryside with food-stuffs adequate, nor is the supply of the peasant producers with credit and with means of production satisfactory. The work of the urban cooperatives is carried on in a formal and bureaucratic way. There is a great scarcity of cooperative stores in the countryside, for in some regions a single store has to supply as many as ten villages within a radius of ten kilometres.

As a rule, the prices charged for goods by the cooperatives are from 5 to 10 per cent lower than the prices charged by private traders, but the cooperatives are often short of the most ordinary articles and those most in demand. A commodity taken over by the Centrosoyus from the State trusts and syndicates has to pass through four or five hands in the cooperative organisation on its way to the retail stores, and at each stage a supplement is put upon the price. The Centrosoyus adds on the average from 6 to 10 per cent, the provincial society from 5 to 7 per cent more, the district society claps on another 8 to 10 per cent, and the retail store in the town or the village adds from 15 to 20 per cent more. In some cases, therefore, the cooperatives have asked even higher prices than the private retailers.[1]

The goods handled by the cooperatives are chosen with an

[1] "Torgovo-Promyshlennaya Gazeta", June 17, 1928.

eye, not to the needs of the mass of consumers, but to those of "profitable buyers".[1] Again: "The cooperative movement aims at the accumulation of capital and at taking advantage of favourable turns in the market,"[2] that is to say it devotes itself to the speculative purchase and sale of commodities for which it has no real use. Once more: "The activities of the cooperatives are dictated by a commercial spirit; . . . in the activities of the Centrosoyus we find very little evidence of a social spirit."[3]

The agricultural cooperative system is just as little concerned to attend to the interests of its members. It participates actively in the organised pressure of the State whereby the purchase price of grain is reduced—in order to favour the export of grain. During the last months of the year 1924, though there was a famine in certain districts of Russia, a number of cooperative organisations were engaged in buying cattle, wool, and flax, when these articles were being sold at knock-down prices by the famine-stricken peasants. If, owing to scarcity, the price of grain rises in the countryside, the cooperatives make common cause with the other State instruments to force the peasants to hand over grain and agricultural raw materials at low prices, below the cost of production. Hence it comes to pass that the peasant seeks to protect himself against the cooperatives as buyers by selling to private traders, who are willing to pay higher prices.[4]

The Soviet cooperatives have departed so far from the cooperative spirit that when, in the beginning of the year 1924, there was one of the periodical movements against private trading, and the monopolistic wholesale instruments of the State were forbidden to supply goods to private traders, the cooperatives rallied to the side of the private traders, and organised the purchase of goods from the State on behalf of these, but in the name of the cooperatives. This was not done

[1] "Ekonomicheskaya Zhizn", February 26, 1927.
[2] "Soyus Potrebitelei", Nos. 13 and 14.
[3] "Ekonomicheskaya Zhizn", July 18, 1928.
[4] "Ekonomicheskaya Zhizn, October 8, 1927.

only here and there, but was so general a phenomenon that "Ekonomicheskaya Zhizn", the economic organ of the government, published an alarmist article concerning the danger that the retail cooperative stores would become salaried buyers in the service of private traders. In the summer of 1928, when there was a manifest scarcity of grain and flour in the market, a number of urban cooperatives (for instance, in Maltsev, Bezhetsk, and Zlatoust) sold their stores of grain, to the amount of several hundreds of thousands of poods, to private dealers![1]

In the phase of primary accumulation through which the U.S.S.R. is now passing, the cooperatives could perform important economic and social duties. But in this omain, likewise, as in so many others, the economic possibilities created by the Nep encounter the restrictions imposed by the dominant political regime. A genuine cooperative movement cannot be conjured into existence by a "friendly" dictator; it can only arise as a product of communal activities, and must be based upon the spontaneity of the masses. In a land where social and political rights are denied to the generality, the conditions for the upbuilding of such organisations are not forthcoming. Even in tsarist Russia, the cooperative movement could not flourish until the arbitrariness of the old regime had been somewhat mitigated, and the authorities had ceased to interfere in the internal life of the cooperatives.

There exists to-day in the U.S.S.R. a widely ramified trading apparatus with a gigantic turnover of goods. It works under the cooperative label, but neither in respect of its essence, its structure, or its principles, has it anything in common with the true nature of cooperation. It is nothing more than an organisation which runs parallel to that of State trading, and it is liable to all the errors and tainted with all the vices of State bureaucracy.

[1] "Ekonomicheskaya Zhizn", July 15, 1928.

N

CHAPTER TWELVE

FOREIGN COMMERCE, COMMERCIAL TREATIES, CONCESSIONS

1. CONDITION OF FOREIGN COMMERCE.

DURING the last years before the war, Russian foreign commerce expanded rather rapidly, although in respect alike of scope and of structure, it reflected the backwardness of Russian economic life. In the year 1913, the total turnover of Russia's foreign commerce amounted to 3·8 per cent of the aggregate commerce of the world, and was valued at 2894 millions of roubles. If we calculate the extent of exports and imports in percentages of the total production, in the area which now comprises the U.S.S.R., we find that Russia's imports in the year 1913 were equivalent in value to 7 per cent, and the exports to about 6 per cent, of the value of the total home production.

TURNOVER OF FOREIGN TRADE IN MILLIONS OF ROUBLES[1]

Yearly Average.	Exports.	Imports.	Balance.
1901/05	941·1	637·2	+ 303·9
1906/10	1204·6	910·3	+ 294·3
1911/13	1543·8	1235·8	+ 308·0

The turnover of foreign commerce is shown to have increased rapidly, the balance of trade remaining favourable to Russia, and the excess of exports over imports during the last 10–15 years before the war amounting to round about 300 millions of roubles. The backwardness of the industrial development of the country, and the predominance of agrarian production, had a decisive influence upon the characteristics of the foreign commerce. Russian exports consisted mainly of grain, timber, hides, flax, and other rural produce in the crude state. During

[1] The figures relate to the Russian empire of pre-war days.

the period 1908–1912, approximately 35 per cent of the whole export of the most important grains throughout the world were Russian. The imports into the Russian empire consisted mainly of the raw materials for industry, machinery, and manufactured goods. As regards the production of machinery, tools, motors, and apparatus of all kinds, Russia was wholly dependent upon the world market. A considerable proportion of the raw materials exported by Russia (hides, timber, iron ores, furs, gut, and even grain) subsequently found their way back into the country in the form of manufactured goods. The backwardness of industrialisation in Russia accounted for the peculiar characteristics of the imports and exports, but these characteristics, in their turn, reacted unfavourably upon the speed of the process of industrialisation.

The Great War, and subsequently the intervention of the foreign powers and the civil war, reduced Russian foreign commerce to a minimum. In the year 1919–1920, the value of foreign trade was only 1/77 of what it had been before the war. In 1922, a slow reestablishment of Russian foreign commerce began. According to data published by the Central Statistical Bureau, the imports and exports have been as follows:

(*In Millions of Pre-War Roubles.*)

Year.	Imports.	Exports.	Total.
1913[1]	1350·0	970·0	2320·0
1920/21	20·0	208·0	228·0
1921/22	64·5	270·0	334·5
1922/23	133·2	147·8	281·0
1923/24	369·1	233·5	602·6
1924/25	370·8	411·5	782·3
1925/26	470·6	464·5	935·1
1926/27	558·0	497·4	1055·4
1927/28	480·3	640·5	1120·8

The foreign trade of the U.S.S.R. in the year 1927–1928 amounted to only 45 per cent of that in the year 1913, so that

[1] In the area now comprising the U.S.S.R.

the share of Russia in the aggregate trade of the world had fallen to 1·5 per cent. It is interesting to note that the present foreign commerce of the Soviet Union is smaller than that of Denmark, Sweden, or Switzerland, and that the aggregate exports and imports are equal to the value of those of the sometime constituents of the tsarist realm, Poland, Lithuania, Latvia, and Esthonia, taken together, whose area is only 12 per cent of that of the U.S.S.R. and whose population is 22 per cent.[1]

There has been some change in the nature of the exports since pre-war days. This is shown by the following table:[2]

(In Percentages of the Total Exports.)

	1913	1926/27.	1927/28.
Grain and Fodder	45·0	30·2	5·4
Butter	4·7	5·1	6·2
Eggs	5·9	4·3	6·4
Poultry	0·4	1·0	1·7
Flax and Hemp	7·7	2·8	3·3
Bristles	0·6	1·0	1·0
Gut	0·7	1·4	1·7
Furs	1·1	11·8	17·9
Other rural products	8·6	10·0	14·0
Total rural products ..	— 74·7	— 67·6	— 57·6
Timber goods	11·4	10·4	12·6
Petroleum products	3·4	12·2	15·4
Manganese ores	1·3	3·6	2·2
Other industrial products ..	9·2	6·2	12·2
Total industrial products	— 25·3	— 32·4	— 42·4
Grand Totals	100·0	100·0	100·0

Now, as before the war, rural products take the premier place, but their share in the totals is smaller than it used to be. In 1913, it was 74·7 per cent; in 1924–1925, it was 53·2 per cent; in 1925–1926, 62 per cent; in 1926–1927, 67·6 per cent;

[1] Data published by the People's Commissariat for Home and Foreign Trade in "Ekonomicheskoye Obozreniye", 1928, No. 1.
[2] [Encyclopaedia of Soviet Exports] and [Survey of Foreign Commerce], in "Ekonomicheskaya Zhizn", October 30, 1928.

in 1927–1928, 57·6 per cent. The percentage amount of the export of grain, and especially of wheat and barley, has been greatly reduced. There are various causes of these changes, the most important being: the comparative detachment of contemporary Russian agriculture from the market; the increased home consumption of agricultural produce, and especially of those articles which used to be exported; the falling-off in the area under cultivation and in the yield of wheat and barley, which were two of the chief exports.

Tabulating the exports of the various kinds of grain, in thousands of tons, we get the following table:

Year.	Total Grain.	Wheat.	Rye.	Barley.	Oats.
1913	9583·4	3329·0	646·5	3926·0	599·5
1924/25	598·7	167·4	72·1	199·1	3·3
1925/26	2068·6	737·1	158·3	836·0	22·8
1926/27	2177·6	1198·5	417·4	262·2	66·0

The export of the agricultural products that form the raw material of industry has varied greatly in amount. In 1925–1926, the export of flax was 23 per cent of the pre-war amount, and in the year 1927–1928 it had fallen to 14 per cent; the export of oil-containing seeds was in the year 1924–1925, 60 per cent of the pre-war amount, and in the year 1925–1926, it was 44 per cent, while in the year 1926–1927, it had fallen to 10 per cent. In 1925–1926, the export of vegetable oil was 400 per cent of the export of pre-war days; in 1926–1927, it was only 50 per cent. The pre-war standard of export has not as yet been regained for butter (40 per cent); eggs (26 per cent); meat, poultry, and game (49 per cent).

The export of industrial products has exceeded the pre-war level in the case of some groups of commodities, but in the case of others it remains far below the level of pre-war days. The total exports of industrial products in the year 1926–1927 were valued at 298·8 millions of roubles. Here are the exports of certain important commodities:

(*In Millions of Roubles.*)

	1913.	1923/24.	1924/25.	1925/26.	1926/27.
Timber goods	165·0	70·5	72·5	58·2	79·7
Petroleum products ..	50·0	37·3	66·6	76·0	89·2
Manganese ores	14·5	14·3	17·8	21·2	24·0
Sugar	27·0	6·5	13·9	18·9	31·1

In the years 1926–1927 and 1927–1928, owing to the decline in the export of grain, the Soviet government began to do its utmost to promote the export of certain products of minor importance, such as caviare, poultry, down, feathers, horn, horse-shoes, bones, fruit, mushrooms, berries, etc.

In the imports to the U.S.S.R. during the first years of the Nep, articles needed for mass consumption played a considerable part. Since 1925-1926, however, the import of raw materials and means of production has come to the front:

(*In Percentages of the Total Imports.*)

	1913.	1924/25.	1925/26.	1926/27.
Machinery and means of production	14·0	7·4	12·0	21·0
Raw materials, half-manufactured goods, and accessories	40·8	50·9	56·5	62·3
Machines and manufactured articles for agricultural production ..	5·1	6·2	8·5	5·9
Materials for the transport system	2·1	3·3	3·4	2·4
Fuel	7·4	0·1	0·6	0·9
Articles for mass consumption ..	23·3	28·5	13·5	4·9
Hygienic, medical, and sanitary requisites and appliances ..	1·2	1·8	1·9	0·8
Articles of luxury	5·4	0·1	0·1	0·0
Other commodities	0·7	1·7	3·5	1·8
Totals	100·0	100·0	100·0	100·0

The preliminary data relating to imports for the year 1927–1928, show that the proportion of machinery, raw materials, and half-manufactured goods has continued to grow, now reaching 81·6 per cent of the total imports; but that at the same time there has been an increase in the proportion of articles of mass consumption (at the cost of other imports) to the extent of 11·7 per cent of the total imports.

Turning to consider to what countries Russian exports go, and from what countries Russian imports come, we get the two following tables:

(In Percentages of the Total Exports or Imports.)

Exports to	1913.	1924/25.	1925/26.	1926/27.	1927/28.
Great Britain	17·5	33·2	28·7	29·1	23·2
Germany	29·9	15·2	16·5	24·7	29·2
Holland ..	11·7	3·6	3·1	3·4	2·6
U.S.A. ..	0·9	4·9	4·5	2·5	3·5
France ..	6·7	3·8	5·9	8·0	6·4
Italy ..	4·9	2·7	4·9	5·6	4·1
Latvia ..	—	10·9	9·4	8·5	12·6
Persia ..	3·8	5·0	5·2	5·4	5·7
Turkey ..	2·4	1·7	2·6	1·9	2·2
Esthonia ..	—	2·4	2·5	1·0	0·8
Finland ..	3·7	0·4	0·7	1·5	1·2
China ..	1·9	1·6	2·5	2·7	2·6
Japan ..	0·1	2·2	1·9	2·0	2·3
Other countries ..	16·5	12·4	11·6	3·7	3·6
Totals ..	100·0	100·0	100·0	100·0	100·0

Imports from	1913.	1924/25.	1925/26.	1926/27.	1927/28.
Great Britain	12·6	15·3	18·6	15·6	5·5
Germany	47·5	14·2	25·6	25·6	29·2
Holland ..	1·6	4·8	1·0	0·8	0·5
U.S.A. ..	5·8	27·9	16·1	23·0	22·1
France ..	4·1	1·3	2·6	3·5	4·3
Italy ..	1·2	6·7	3·1	0·5	1·4
Latvia ..	—	1·3	0·6	0·3	0·7
Persia ..	3·2	7·2	5·8	5·4	5·3
Turkey ..	1·3	0·4	1·3	1·5	1·6
Esthonia ..	—	1·1	1·0	0·6	0·3
Finland ..	3·7	2·6	2·0	2·8	2·0
China ..	5·5	2·3	4·1	4·2	3·8
Japan ..	0·4	0·4	0·3	0·4	0·5
Other countries ..	13·1	14·5	17·9	15·8	22·5
Totals ..	100·0	100·0	100·0	100·0	100·0

The data relating to the turnover of the foreign trade of the
U.S.S.R. for the year 1927–1928, present, as the table shows,
a somewhat new picture. Germany has come to the front,
whereas trade with England is on the down grade, owing to the
rupture of Anglo-Russian relations. Despite the best endeavours
of the Soviet government to promote the export of industrial
products and of agricultural by-products, while restricting
imports, the notable decline in the export of grain, on the
one hand, and the urgent need of Russian industry for raw
materials and machinery of foreign origin, on the other,
combine to make the balance of trade unfavourable. If we
calculate exports and imports in chervonets roubles, that is
to say in the currency in which they are actually paid, we get
the following trade balances for the various years:

(*In Millions of Roubles.*)

	1913.[1]	1923/24.	1924/25.	1925/26.	1926/27.	1927/28.
Imports	1350·0	523·4	575·2	676·6	770·5	783·7
Exports	970·0	430·2	723·5	756·3	712·7	944·7
Balance	+ 380·0	+ 93·2	− 148·3	− 79·7	+ 57·8	− 161·0

In the five-year period which has elapsed since foreign
commercial relations were resumed, there have been only two
years in which the balance of trade has been favourable to
Russia.

The first of the Soviet government's decrees relating to the
regulation of foreign trade was the decree of October 28 (old
style), 1917, prohibiting the import of articles of luxury, and
prescribing measures to prevent smuggling. But during the first
months of the Soviet regime, when the only outlet from the
country was towards Finland, the amount of export trade was
so small that not until well on into the year 1918 was a radical
reorganisation of foreign commerce begun. On April 22, 1918,
the Council of People's Commissaries issued a decree national-

[1] Within the area now comprising the U.S.S.R.

ising foreign trade in its entirety. Down to the beginning of
the year 1920, however, this decree remained nothing more
than a declaration regarding the State monopoly of foreign
commerce. Not until the first of the peace treaties had been
signed, that with Esthonia on February 2, 1920, did the foreign
trade relations of the U.S.S.R. begin to expand a little.

In the year 1920, trade relations were opened up chiefly with
Esthonia, Turkey, and Persia. Since 1921, Soviet Russia has
been endeavouring to promote commercial relations with other
countries, and from time to time was able to enter into trade
conventions and commercial treaties with these. The first trade
convention was that made between the U.S.S.R. and Great
Britain on March 16, 1921. In the same year, commercial
treaties with Turkey and Persia were signed. On April 16, 1922,
a general agreement was entered into with Germany at Rapallo,
and this included a number of economic stipulations. In the
same year, commercial relations were resumed with Holland,
Sweden, France, and Italy. By the year 1927, the U.S.S.R.
had signed commercial treaties with Germany,[1] Turkey,
Persia, Sweden, Italy, Norway, Latvia, Greece, Finland,
Esthonia, Poland, Lithuania, Czecho-Slovakia, Austria, Denmark, China, and Japan.

In the year 1924, proposals for the replacement of the trade
convention with England by a detailed commercial treaty were
being discussed, but the fall of the MacDonald government
prevented the ratification of this treaty. In 1927, diplomatic
relations between Britain and Russia were broken off, and this
has had a very unfavourable effect upon the trade relations
between the two countries. In 1928, the trade convention with
Greece expired, and Greece has not renewed it.

Among European countries, the following have no trade
conventions or commercial treaties with the U.S.S.R.: France,
Belgium, Holland, Jugo-Slavia, Spain, Portugal, Bulgaria,
Rumania, Switzerland, Hungary. The exception of France is

[1] The commercial treaty with Germany was signed in the year 1925. In
the year 1928, negotiations were in progress for the revision of this treaty.

remarkable, seeing that this country formally recognised the Soviet Union as long ago as 1924. Although the United States has never conceded diplomatic recognition to the U.S.S.R., and although there is no commercial treaty between the two countries, the U.S.A., as the table shows, occupies a high place among the countries trading with Soviet Russia, coming second only to Germany, as far as Russian imports are concerned.

The Soviet government has done all it could to promote trade relations with eastern countries, such as Persia, Turkey, China, and Afghanistan. Political considerations have played their part here; but the ease with which Russian industrial products can be sent to these countries has likewise something to do with the matter. Although the total trade of Russia with eastern countries is not very large, the balance is one favourable to Russssia.

The foreign trade of the U.S.S.R. is carried on upon principles which differ from those customary in capitalist countries. The foreign trade is nationalised. Trading operations in foreign markets, whether purchases or sales, can be carried on only by the instruments of the People's Commissariat for Home and Foreign Trade. The sale of exports and the purchase of imports is effected by this Commissariat, either directly, through its trading apparatus (the Gostorg administrations in Russia and the commercial delegations abroad), or else by special societies organised for State import and export (Hleboexport for grain; Lesoexport for timber; the Naphtha Syndicate for petroleum products; the Tea Administration; the Textile Syndicate, etc.). The leading cooperative organisations, such as Centrosoyus, Selskosoyus, etc., are likewise impowered to carry on foreign trade within certain specified limits.

All the other State organisations must do whatever foreign trade they want to do through the instruments of the People's Commissariat for Home and Foreign Trade, after procuring a special licence for the export or import of particular goods. Not even the smallest quantity of goods can be imported and exported without a licence. In the case of every commodity, the Commissariat for Trade lays down the maximum quantity to be imported or exported, as the case may be.

Customs tariffs do not, in the U.S.S.R., play the part they play in other countries, although in certain respects they have the usual effects here. In the first place, prices are raised by high import duties, and thus particular branches of home industry are protected against foreign competition; and, in the second place, the customs dues are a considerable source of revenue to the State. But under the Soviet system of foreign commerce, these aims of protection and of levying of revenue are also fulfilled in other ways.

Goods imported by the State are handed over for sale to the State syndicates or trusts (textiles, to the Textile Syndicate; agricultural machinery, to the Selmash Trust; electro-technical articles to the Elektro-Trust, etc.). These organisations fix the sale prices of the imported articles in a way which is designed to bring the greatest possible revenue to the State, and at the same time to prevent any interference with the market for home products.

The question of the desirability of continuing the present system of foreign trade has been repeatedly discussed by Soviet economists during recent years, and hitherto these authorities have remained in favour of it.

2. The Soviet Governmental Monopoly of Foreign Commerce

Russian communists maintain that the governmental monopoly of foreign commerce is one of the most important and valuable achievements of the Russian revolution; and that its maintenance preserves the national economy of Russia from disintegration and from exploitation by foreign countries. Now that the Soviet control of foreign trade has been in force for more than a decade, we are in a position to draw up a sort of balance sheet, and to study the results of this monopoly. We are not here concerned with examining the monopoly of foreign trade as a matter of principle or of program. In the chapter on the Nationalisation of Industry I pointed out that the most perfect of systems would have been rendered nugatory by the backward condition of Russian economic life and by the methods of the communists. But our present purpose is to examine in the light of actual facts the concrete system of foreign trade now on its trial in Russia—a system which differs in many respects from that proposed for the monopolisation of foreign trade as part of the programs of many of the socialist parties in other European countries.

The reason why the foreign commerce of the U.S.S.R., imports and exports together, amounts to only about 40 per cent of the total foreign trade of pre-war days, is to be found, not so much in the general political hostility between Soviet Russia and capitalist countries, as in the foreign commercial policy of the Soviet government, in the peculiar system of self-imposed blockade to which the Russian communists gave the name of a monopoly of foreign commerce.

Though the renunciation of the utopian idea of the immediate realisation of communism has opened possibilities for the economic reconstruction of the country, the utopian insistence upon maintaining the present system of foreign commerce imposes artificial difficulties in the way of this commencing process of reconstruction. Alone among the departments of Russian economic life, that of foreign commerce still retains the basic form imposed by the decrees of the year 1918. Industry, agriculture, internal trade, and finance, have all been radically transformed by the Nep, but there has been no corresponding change in the matter of foreign commerce.

Yet practical experience has shown that the Russian State is incompetent, with the apparatus at its disposal and with no aid but its own resources, to perform the complicated functions involved in the conduct of the exports and imports of this gigantic country. Above all, there is a shortage of the means required for this purpose. The State has not enough money to finance the nationalised industry or to provide for the needs of home and foreign trade. Owing to its lack of funds, the State cannot pay a proper price for the surpluses of grain produced by the peasants or for the agricultural raw materials required by industry. It forces down prices, thus causing widespread discontent among the peasantry, and hindering the reestablishment of peasant agriculture. Consequently it is compelled, year after year, to restrict imports. Furthermore, the defects of the foreign commercial policy of the country are intensified by the characteristics of the monopolist apparatus of foreign trade, which is bureaucratic, over-centralised, cumbrous and immobile owing to its immense size, unduly speculative, and worm-eaten with official corruption.[1]

The root cause of all these troubles is that the State apparatus is unable to cope with the complicated task of providing raw materials in the huge territories of Soviet Russia, and with the task of buying foreign goods to supply the manifold needs of the country. Let me give two examples to substantiate this assertion. First of all, private traders, operating in the home market, disposing of amounts of capital which are trifling in comparison with those available to the State, and paying much better prices to the peasants, were able (thanks to a rapid turn-over) to purchase 25 per cent of all the grain and 30 per cent of the agricultural raw materials available throughout the country. Again, the State imports of tractors, ploughs, scythes, and manures, are far from sufficient to satisfy the demands of the peasant population. Since 1925, there have been repeated complaints in the Russian economic press that the peasants' demand for agricultural machinery was being satisfied only to the extent of 40, 50, or 60 per cent. The imports, said the

[1] In proof of these statements it will suffice to refer to certain great trials which have taken place during the last two years: the proceedings against the commercial administration of the north-west in Leningrad, and the Arcos in London, etc.; and also to the reports of revisionary committees (drafted by Avanezoff and Roisman) concerning the results of changes of the personnel in the commercial delegations in Berlin, Paris, Riga, Constantinople, etc.

Soviet papers, were being restricted because the country had not enough equivalents to offer in exchange. Surely this carries with it a direct admission that the present system of foreign commerce is bankrupt. Neither the Gostorg, nor the State Bank, nor the Centrosoyus, has equivalents to offer, and the State has none. But the main consumers, the peasants, have equivalents to offer! The peasants of Northern Caucasia, who have ordered cord for their binders; the Ukrainian farmers, who were supplied with tractors without spare parts; the Siberian peasants, who were unable to get the separators they wanted; the Astrakhan fishers, who could not get any nets; the northern hunters, who could not procure the necessary equipment; the peasants in general who, in the year 1927–1928 were able to obtain only from 50 to 60 per cent of the agricultural machinery and the textiles they wanted, and only 32 per cent of the metal goods—one and all these represent, not merely a demand, but an effective demand, the demand of those who are willing and able to pay. They can supply ample equivalents in the form of grain, furs, dairy produce, fish, and so on.

That which, before the war, numerous private exporters and importers and branches of foreign firms were able to do well enough, while earning considerable profits, is beyond the power of the Soviet State, with its monopoly of imports and exports. The State is unable to mobilise the values in the hands of the peasants, the grain, the agricultural raw materials, etc.; and is therefore unable to provide the peasants with the requisite means of agricultural production and the other industrial goods they require. Not only does the Soviet government refrain from attracting the capital and the energy of private traders and from guiding these, in the interests of the Russian national economy, into the channels of foreign commerce, but it centralises the whole of Russian foreign commerce in the hands of a State department equipped with monopolist powers, while the State trading and industrial instruments which are directly interested in the foreign commerce of the country are not allowed to say a word in the matter. The State trusts, the

State trading organisation, the State sanitary authorities, the municipal enterprises—each and every one of them can only place orders abroad through the instrumentality of the Commissariat for Home and Foreign Trade. The essential feature of this Russian monopoly of foreign trade is a narrow-minded and obviously absurd determination that the whole stream of exports and imports shall flow through the one door known as the "operative section" of the department for foreign trade.

All these restrictions are maintained in the interest of a fixed plan of imports and exports. But, in existing circumstances, the program of foreign trade drafted by the People's Commissariat for Home and Foreign Trade necessarily remains fictitious. The Russian market was little studied even before the war; and indeed, after the convulsions of recent years, there is no practical possibility of drafting a detailed program for imports and exports. Thus, in the years 1924–1925 and 1927–1928, grain was still being exported at a time when it was already plain that there was going to be a failure of the crops in Russia; and indeed shortly afterwards it became necessary to import grain from Britain, Germany, and America. At the very time when flax, sugar, and butter are urgently needed at home, these commodities are busily sent across the frontier. Machinery for industry and agriculture, and half-manufactured goods for further elaboration, are not imported to the necessary amount. High-powered locomotives are imported at a cost of many millions of roubles, and only when it is too late do the authorities discover that they are far too heavy for the tracks and the bridges of the Russian railway system. Machinery needed for new or reconstructed enterprises is ordered in accordance with specifications that are out of date, and make no allowance for the acquirements of modern technique.

It would hardly be possible to conceive anything more hopelessly bureaucratic than a system in which for the import of every machine, and even for that of every spare part, a special licence must be obtained from the supreme department for foreign trade. The apparatus controlling foreign commerce is burdened with responsibilities for studying the minutest details of the demand for imports, with the result that in the Russian homeland the wheels of enterprises cease to turn because the necessary licences for the import of spare parts have not been obtainable.

No less unhappy in actual working is the communist idea of industrial protection. Unquestionably, for some time to come protection will be needed by Russian industry, which is economically and technically enfeebled; and this need is reinforced by the scope and nature of unemployment. Above all, protection is indispensable in days when even the most highly developed industrial countries of the world erect tariff barriers along their frontiers, and at the same time compete furiously one with another for foreign markets. But the communists, with their usual tendency to exaggeration, have carried to an absurd pitch their endeavours to perform a necessary task. No doubt for the consolidation and rationalisation of home production, there was temporarily forced upon them a policy aiming at the protection of key industries against dangerous foreign competition, and at assisting these industries to supply a sufficiency of the commodities in general demand, at prices which should be within the purchasing power of the population, even if rather high. But that is not how things have worked out in practice! In practice, the import of foreign machinery, tools, etc., indispensable to Russian enterprises, is often prohibited simply for the reason that some commission or other has decided that a Russian enterprise shall devote itself to that particular branch of production.

When such a decision is come to, it will be without any regard to the question how long must elapse before the necessary machinery or tools can actually be produced in Russia, or how the price of the home-made articles will be affected by the fact that the production of a small quantity of a particular product will necessitate the reequipment of a number of factories, and very likely their rebuilding as well.

Thus the inauguration of textile factories will be delayed because, as a preliminary, machine-construction works for the making of textile machinery must be reorganised, rebuilt, and technically transformed. In order to make twelve grain elevators needed in the Black Sea harbours of the U.S.S.R., an enterprise quite unsuited for making these machines had to be radically transformed. Certain works where machinery made by particular German and English firms was used, applied for a permit to telegraph for some spare parts that were needed. Permission was refused on the ground that the orders ought to be placed in Russia. Machinery which is always on sale in Germany will be made in Russia, and, after months have elapsed in the making, will be found to be useless.

In its practical working, industrial protection of this kind becomes a system of self-imposed isolation.

Economic science has long since made it perfectly clear that a protectionist system can only exert a favourable influence on a national industry when the tariff or other protectionist measures afford no more than a moderate degree of protection against foreign competition, so that it is still incumbent upon the industry to cheapen and improve its products. A very high tariff, which amounts to an embargo upon imports, can only serve to encourage a weakly, infirm, and hopelessly uneconomic system of industry. In tsarist days, the truth of this contention was made manifest by the condition of a great many of the branches of industry. Nevertheless, the Soviet government has followed in these misdirected footsteps. Soviet industry, protected by high tariffs, and above all by a licensing system which is often equivalent to the total prohibition of imports, produces goods which are not only too costly, but also of very poor quality.

The State, possessing a monopoly of foreign commerce, fixes the prices of imported goods at from 10 to 30 per cent higher than the average prices of home products, although the prices of Russian textiles (for instance) are 238 per cent higher, and the prices of Russian metal goods 250 per cent higher,

o

than the prices in the world market. An enquiry made by the Commissariat for Trade has shown that the Russian buyer of foreign textiles and boots and shoes is charged 345 per cent above cost.[1]

Agreed that this monopoly system in Russia does not serve, as it would serve in a capitalist country, for the enrichment of the bourgeoisie or of great landed proprietors. Still, neither this fact nor the fact that the monopoly of foreign trade is unprofitable to the Soviet government which holds it, can be regarded as proofs that the monopoly, as exercised, is a good thing for the country.

In the year 1927, the Workers' and Peasants' Inspection published a fulminating criticism of the activities of the department of foreign commerce. The management of foreign commerce was said to be "unsatisfactory", "purposeless", "inadequately controlled". There was "unwholesome competition"; "the goods imported were sold under unsatisfactory conditions"; "obviously unprofitable contracts were entered into"; "the costs of management amounted to 140 per cent of the total cost of providing the articles"; "foreign credits and advances were made under extremely unfavourable conditions, interest of 40, 50, and even 100 per cent per annum being demanded"; "the exports did not pay, and in the case of some articles involved considerable losses"; and so on.[2]

Many of the Soviet economists are aware that the present organisation of the monopoly of foreign trade is quite unsuitable, and is disastrous to the general economic life of Russia. They contend, however, that the mischief lies in the bad organisation of the system, in the defects of the apparatus, and that reorganisation would put matters right. They wish to retain the present system of monopoly as a foundation, and merely desire to get rid of the bureaucracy, the bungling, the incapacity, and the extravagance that hamper the working of the extant apparatus. But the monopoly of foreign trade has continued

[1] "Pravda", August 17, 1927.
[2] "Ekonomicheskaya Zhizn", September 1, 1927.

for more than six years, under the guidance of some of the most
efficient and energetic communists (such as Krassin, Frumkin,
Stomonyakoff, etc.), the Commissariat for Trade and the
commercial delegations have during this period been several
times reorganised, changes have been made from a centralised
to a decentralised system and back again. There have been
thoroughgoing overhauls and legal proceedings, attempts have
been made to manage the affair with the aid of tried and
trusted communists exclusively, and at other times commercial
specialists have been called in. Nevertheless, the cumbrousness,
inertia, and incapacity of the State apparatus for foreign trade
have persisted unchanged. The reason is that what is wrong
with the Russian monopoly of foreign trade is not the existence
of casual defects in the mechanism, not the flaws of the present
system of organisation, but the very nature and scope of the
monopoly istelf.

The drawing up of programs of export and import without
a knowledge of the market and its needs, the paralysis of the
commercial relations between the U.S.S.R. and the outer world
by excessive nationalisation and monopolisation, together with
the centralised and bureaucratic construction of the whole
apparatus—these are links in a single chain. Each feature helps
to determine the others. Just as in the domain of the nationalisation of industry, so also in the domain of foreign commerce,
for the sake of the preservation of those elements in the
nationalisation of foreign trade which are economically
beneficial, it is essential to liquidate a condition of affairs which
with its utopian methods and results is hampering the development of Russian economic life as a whole. Rebuilding and
patching, "petty reorganisations", will no longer suffice.
The whole system of foreign commerce in Soviet Russia must
be radically reconstructed.

The social democrats agree with the communists that in
contemporary Russia the State must be able to regulate foreign
commercial policy in a way that will minister to the economic
interests of a country that is economically weak, and that the

hands of the government must not be tied in this respect. The question at issue is, what forms State regulation is to take, and to what extent the State should participate in foreign commerce.

In the programs of many of the socialist parties of Europe, a State monopoly of foreign commerce is one of the most urgent demands. See, for instance, the socialist programs of Sweden and of Switzerland, the Austrian agrarian program, and the Kiel agrarian program of the German social democracy. But what all these programs demand is, not the complete nationalisation of foreign commerce once and for all, but the progressive nationalisation of certain departments of foreign commerce. Thus the Austrian and German agrarian programs and the Swiss program demand a State monopoly in the export of grain. The general view of socialists is, not that the State apparatus should monopolise the conduct of foreign commerce as a whole, but that particular branches of foreign commerce should be guided and regulated by a special State authority. Within limits imposed by the State, and within the range of prices fixed by the State, the actual trade operations should be conducted by private persons as well as by the State and by cooperative organisations. Nay more, the authority to which the control of foreign trade is entrusted, should contain representatives of private traders and of the consumers as well as representatives of the State.

There are two important distinctions between the system thus proposed and that now practised in the U.S.S.R.: for, first of all, it aims only at the nationalisation of particular branches of foreign commerce, and, in the second place, within the nationalised branches, there is not to be a State monopoly of trade, but only a State monopoly of the economic direction of trade. Thus the State would guide and regulate foreign trade without creating a great bureaucratic machine, unfitted by its very nature, by its inelasticity, for the conduct of commercial undertakings.

It would unquestionably be to the interest of Russia as a

whole, if in the U.S.S.R., there were to be a State monopoly of foreign trade in certain commodities, such as the export of grain and of petroleum products, and for the import of materials for railway construction, cotton, tea, coffee, etc. If such a system were instituted, the State would need to have a definite economic plan for foreign trade, to follow a definite commercial policy, and would require in addition to regulate the foreign trade in all other commodities than those just specified. But this is far from implying that there should be a system of licences for every sending of hides abroad and for every consignment of machinery imported. During the centuries of commodity production, very effective measures for enforcing a clearly conceived and differentiated commercial policy have been elaborated, such as: the prohibition of the export and import of certain goods; the fixing of definite proportions in which certain other goods shall be imported or exported; the imposing of high, medium, and low tariffs for various goods; the abolition of duties in some cases, and the payment of premiums upon the import and export of other goods; granting permission that certain goods shall be imported only on condition of their reexport; and so on. In addition to adopting such measures, the State, controlling as it does the transport system, exchange business, the banks, and the machinery of credit, is able to enter into separate economic agreements with other countries, and has the choice of various expedients for the promotion of any commercial policy it may prefer.

Under such a system, the State would, in the first place, be immediately freed from its present concern about the financing of exports and imports in their entirety. The capital at its disposal would thus be liberated for immediate use in those branches of industry which would remain nationalised. For the fostering of exports, which offer great possibilities in the U.S.S.R. if a rational economic policy be adopted, recourse could be had to the initiative, the activity, and the capital of private individuals, as well as to those of the State. The Russian and foreign private firms allowed to undertake import business, entering into direct contact with the consumers, could import all goods for which there is a demand, and their mutual competition would keep the prices of imported goods down to a reasonable figure.

The endeavours of the foreign firms to increase the market for their wares would entitle them to credit on a larger scale and under more favourable conditions than is possible to-day under the monopoly system. Unquestionably, the country would no longer be compelled to pay from 16 to 20 per cent interest, as it must to-day. The system of licences would be maintained only for the commodities whose import or export remained conditional. Other commodities than these would merely be subject to the tariffs and to the general customs control.

Those who to-day guide the policy of the Soviet government declare, appealing to the authority of Lenin, that the formulas which apply to the protectionist policy of other countries have no bearing upon the problems which face the U.S.S.R. The Soviet Union, they say, is encircled by capitalist powers, which would, if they could, reduce Russia to the status of a colonial country. Nothing but the monopolisation of foreign commerce can protect Soviet Russia from its enemies. Thanks to this monopoly, say the Russian communists, Russia is able to resist all the unjust claims of capitalist firms. By taking advantage of the competition between the foreign capitalists, she can secure the best possible conditions for herself, and is able to place her orders abroad wherever prices are most advantageous.

The events of the last seven years have shown clearly that Lenin was wrong both in his estimate of the economic aggressiveness of the capitalist world as against Soviet Russia,[1] and in his view that the monopoly of foreign commerce was a

---

[1] Enough to remind the reader of Lloyd George's cynical remark that Britain was ready to do business with Russia without concerning herself as to the nature of that country's constitution, just as she was willing to trade with cannibals. The danger of an armed conflict between capitalist countries and the U.S.S.R. remains very great, but the root causes of this danger are political, and have nothing to do with the question of the efficiency of this or that system of foreign commerce.

system which would prevent foreign capitalists from making undue profits at the cost of the Soviet State. Since 1921, since the collapse of the policy of foreign intervention, no capitalist country (whether Britain, Italy, Germany, France, or the United States) has attacked the sovereign rights of the Soviet Union, or endeavoured to reduce Russia to a "colonial status". Far from it, these countries, wishing to expand their foreign markets, and competing one with another, have tried to extend to the utmost their commercial relations with the Soviet Union. On the other hand, experience has shown that the monopoly of foreign trade has not prevented the foreign firms doing business in Russia from making fabulous profits. Indeed, the system has promoted the gaining of profits of the kind known as premiums for risk. We shall return to this matter when we come to consider concessions.

Let us, however, suppose for the sake of argument that capitalist countries would really like to impose economic slavery upon contemporary Russia. Beyond question, a complete closing of the frontiers of the Soviet Union would be the most certain way of preventing the growth of economic relations with the outer world. But in so far as Russia wants to trade with the capitalist world—whether by selling grain, raw materials, and petroleum products, or by importing machinery, cotton, medicaments, etc.—the system of monopoly is a system of self-blockade which conflicts with the interests of the Russian national economy and of the population at large.

The hope that the monopoly of foreign commerce would enable Russia to derive an advantage from the mutual rivalries of the capitalist firms, has likewise proved illusory. Apart from the fact that the commercial treaties between the Soviet Union and foreign countries have not been so designed as to allow Russia to turn to the best advantage her favourable situation as State monopolist, and putting aside for the moment the consideration that the huge expenditure upon credit, transport, and administration, more than counterbalances any advantages secured in the way of rebates and the like, we find that the main trouble of Soviet Russia is that the capitalist world speedily discovered a means of paralysing the monopoly powers of the Soviet State. Three years' experience of commercial relations with the Soviet Union have taught foreign traders and manufacturers how to contrapose a monopolist organisation of their own to the monopoly of the Soviet government. In the negotiations for the revision of the Russo-German commercial treaty, one of the main demands was for the formation of a German industrial and commercial committee, entrusted with the task of giving advice and information, which in practice would mean that it would keep itself well-informed regarding the interests of the German firms as against the Russian commercial delegation, and would regulate the prices, conditions, and scope of all transactions.

In a number of the press organs of the French bourgeoisie it was openly declared that France was following with keen interest the commercial negotiations between the Germans and the Russians, and would pursue the same course when negotiations were entered into between Russia and France. We do not know whether the Soviet government will succeed in inducing the foreign capitalists to withdraw their demands, and what price will have to be paid to secure the withdrawal. It is, however, of the first importance that in the future the Soviet government will not have to negotiate with fiercely competing foreign firms, but with foreign capital which has closed its ranks firmly and is working as an integrated force. The existing system of the monopoly of foreign commerce has served only to increase the pressure exercised by the capitalist organisations, for it has made an end of the competition of the capitalists among themselves, and has induced them to form a united front in this matter of business with Russia.

However, a rational policy of regulation and a wisely directed tariff system would promote the real interests of the Soviet Union quite satisfactorily under present conditions.

In the years 1922 and 1923, when the value of the Russian currency was rapidly declining, and when the difference between prices in Russia and in foreign countries had become enormous, it was, of course, impossible that any tariff could safeguard the country against being plundered by its neighbours, and the necessary protection could only be secured by a system of licences and prohibitions.[1] This was Lenin's chief argument in those days on behalf of the governmental monopoly of foreign commerce. But where is the need for maintaining this monopoly to-day, when the difference in the levels of prices in Russia and in foreign countries respectively, though still considerable, has now become one which can be equalised by protective tariffs? Besides, the Soviet State would still have the power, should there be any reason to suppose that one country or another was making aggressive onslaughts on the Russian market, of breaking off economic relations with the offender. Imperialist excesses, which are always possible, may for the time being necessitate the adoption of extraordinary precautions, but they do not make it necessary to hamper foreign trade in perpetuity by the establishment of what is tantamount to a state of siege.

No doubt a system of protective tariffs does not provide any guarantee that the quantity of imports and exports of a particular commodity (apart, of course, from those for which a definite quantity is prescribed) will correspond with mathematical accuracy to the amount required by a State economic plan. But the present system does not provide any such guarantee! Do we not find that the defects of the existing apparatus, under the system of the monopoly of foreign trade and the licencing of imports, have reduced the most detailed and precise of plans to a mere semblance? Moreover, has not smuggling attained unprecedented dimensions in the Soviet Union?

Doubtless a tariff system and State regulation can do no more than prescribe the nature and extent of the market for particular

---

[1] It was no chance matter that Germany, likewise, at the time of the greatest depreciation of her currency, had to have recourse to a system in which imports were only allowed on special licence.

groups of commodities, but they can do that much without paralysing the whole economic life of the country.

The communists have another reason for maintaining the monopoly of foreign trade, and a reason which in practice is one of the most cogent, although it is seldom pushed into the foreground. The State is in perpetual need of an influx of foreign bills of exchange, and has to keep a careful watch on the outflow of currency. It is easiest under the monopoly of foreign trade to ensure that exporting organisations shall deliver over currency to the State, and that importing organisations shall get the bills of exchange they need from the State. But, first of all, the problem of regulating currency has no direct relationship with the system on which foreign trade is organised. In all countries, this problem comes within the domain of banking and financial policy. But when the State tries to regulate the currency, not by financial and political measures, but by police and administrative measures—as happens to-day in the U.S.S.R. —this has a disorganising effect upon foreign trade and upon the national economic life in general. Besides, is the desired end attained by the present currency policy under the monopoly of foreign trade? How many foreign bills of exchange can be kept in the U.S.S.R., thanks to the working of the monopoly system, when the balance of trade, year after year, is an unfavourable one to the extent of many millions of roubles? Can we say that the nationalisation of foreign trade has had beneficial results, when the recent budget estimates that the entire business of foreign commerce will produce no more than a revenue (in round figures) of 4 millions of roubles?

The experience of the New Economic Policy has shown that in all departments of economic life the abandonment of the utopian system of war communism has led to a great development of the productive forces of the country. But the Soviet monopoly of foreign commerce is a vestige of war communism! With a turnover of foreign trade which is arrested at 40 per cent of the pre-war level, it is impossible that the monopoly can produce a favourable balance of trade. Only a reorganisation of the whole system of foreign commerce on the lines above suggested, abolishing as it would the obstacles now interposed between peasant agriculture and the world market, can lead to an increase in exports, and thus ensure for the State a steady inflow of currency.

What is wrong with the capitalist system of foreign commerce is not that there is any inadequacy in its organisational structure, its methods, or its technique. What is wrong is that the policy on which capitalist foreign commerce is based is itself wrong. What we have to fight against is the social (or, rather, anti-social) trend of the commercial policy of capitalist countries. Through the conquest of political power by the working class, we must bring about a change in the class significance of the policy of foreign commerce. But this does not mean that we must all in a moment destroy an instrument which it has taken centuries to perfect, one which has with all its faults done good work under extremely complicated economic conditions. The Russian communists have found it necessary to reestablish the banking and credit system, after scrapping them. The interests of the national economy will compel them, in like manner, to resuscitate many of the methods and forms of capitalist regulation of foreign commerce which they have too hastily rejected.

In present-day Russia, any attempt to discuss the desirability of the existing system of a monopoly of foreign commerce is regarded as an attack upon one of the main buttresses of the Soviet State. When Sokolnikoff, in the year 1927, being at that time people's commissary for finance, ventured to criticise the State monopoly, he had to pay for his frankness by the loss of his position and by becoming the object of general odium. It will be interesting, therefore, in this connexion, and as my closing contribution to the topic, to recall a fact which has been generally forgotten. Towards the close of the year 1922, a resolution, proposed by Kameneff and seconded by Zinovieff, was adopted by the Political Bureau of the Central Committee of the Communist Party of the U.S.S.R., to the

effect that the gradual liquidation of the State monopoly of
foreign commerce was to be undertaken. The only reason why
this resolution was never acted on was that Lenin considered
the time was not yet ripe.[1]

The sooner the whole system of the State monopoly of
foreign commerce has been radically reorganised, the better
will be the effects of such a reorganisation, both for the Russian
currency and for the industry and agriculture of the U.S.S.R.

By the end of the year 1928, the need for a radical change in
the existing system of foreign commerce had become so plain,
that the "right opposition" (consisting of Rykoff, Kalinin,
Tomsky, and others) made a demand for "the mitigation of the
monopoly of foreign commerce" one of the planks in its
platform.

3. CONCESSIONS

Although the policy of the Soviet government in the matter
of concessions does not fall entirely within the domain of
foreign commerce, seeing that some of the concessions are for
industrial production, still, in so far as this policy determines
the economic relationships of the U.S.S.R. with foreign
industry and commerce, it is closely connected with the Russian
system of the monopoly of foreign commerce.

Even before the introduction of the Nep, the Soviet government had made various attempts to encourage the inflow of
foreign capital "upon a basis which would not be incompatible
with the foundations of the Soviet economic system". When it
had become plain that there was no possibility of floating loans
abroad, because the political and economic obstacles were
insuperable, and when it was obvious that the Soviet State
would only be granted credits for the purchase of imports for
small amounts and on very short terms, the Soviet government
resolved to grant concessions to various capitalists, and by a
decree dated November 23, 1920, it decided to lease industrial

[1] See the memoirs of Frumkin, one of the notables in the Commissariat
for Trade, published in "Ekonomicheskaya Zhizn", February 20, 1927.

and commercial enterprises to foreign capitalists, on a concessionary basis. In the year 1923, a decree was issued concerning the organisation of mixed commercial and industrial societies in which foreign capital was to participate with capital provided by the Russian State, the preponderance of Soviet influence in the management being secured by the proviso that the government was to hold at least 51 per cent of the share capital.

The positive results of this policy of concessions have been small. According to official data, by January 1, 1928, a total of 2200 demands for concessions had been considered. In the course of seven years, however, only 163 contracts for concessions had actually been entered into. Information regarding the assignment of concessions to various branches of economic life are as yet only available down to January 1, 1927.[1] Down to that date, the concessions granted were distributed as follows:

	Number of Concessions.	Percentages.
Trade	36	25·0
Forestry	6	4·2
Agriculture	0	6·8
Fishing, hunting, etc.	6	4·2
Mining	24	16·6
Elaborative industry	41	28·5
Transport, Posts, and Telegraphs	12	8·4
Building	3	2·1
Other enterprises	6	4·2
Totals	144	100·0

Of the 144 contracts, 27·8 per cent had been signed by Germans; 15·3 per cent, by Englishmen; 10·4 per cent, by United States citizens; 3·5 per cent, by Frenchmen; and the remaining 43 per cent, by the nationals of other European,

[1] A. Yoffe [The Concession Policy of the U.S.S.R.], "Planovoye Hozyaistvo" 1927, No. 1.

Asiatic, and American countries. During the same period, 31 mixed joint-stock companies for export and import had come into existence.

The hopes of the Soviet government that the policy of concessions would ensure a steady and considerable flow of foreign capital into the country have proved fallacious. Notwithstanding the very large profits that some of the concessionaries derived from business done in Russia,[1] the amount of capital introduced into Russia by the concessionaries has been trifling. Taken all in all, 58 millions of roubles of new capital has been invested in Russian economic life, and 32 millions of roubles have been made available in the form of credits for commodities. Three-quarters of this amount are assignable to trading enterprises, and only 13 millions to industrial enterprises. The State revenue from the concessionary enterprises has also been small, the yearly average being about 5 millions of roubles in the way of direct payments, and about 7 millions of roubles in the way of taxes and excise.

The main causes of this slow progress in the development of concessions are identical with those which have been responsible for the persistent crises in industry and for the stagnation of foreign commerce.

Let me enumerate them once more: the lack of a proper legal system, and especially of definite legal provisions for the regulation of economic life; bureaucracy, venality, and peculation on the part of the State authorities of all grades; enormous difficulties in the way of the provision of raw materials, in the freighting of products, in the carrying-on of business relations with private customers, and in the appointment of the personnel of the concessionary enterprises. If a concessionary enterprise requires new machinery of a kind obviously unobtainable in Russia, it may have to wait months

[1] The Central Concessions Committee has published data to the effect that the average interest paid on invested capital in the year 1926–1927, as shown by the balance sheets of 17 concessionary undertakings, was 35·2 per cent on the total capital, and 76·5 per cent on the fixed capital. "Ekonomicheskaya Zhizn", April 1, 1928.

before getting an import licence, and may never succeed in getting one at all. Similar difficulties have to be overcome when experts or skilled workers who are not to be found in Russia have to be recruited from abroad. Further and very serious complications arise from the circumstance that, according to the terms of most of the concessions, the concessionary has no right to engage in the direct disposal of his products in Russia or elsewhere. The aggregate product must be handed over at specified prices to the State or cooperative instruments. However precise the stipulations in the agreement, in actual practice the concessionary, after investing his capital, finds himself impotent as against the monopolist State if there are any difficulties in the marketing of his products. When disputes arise, he can get no remedy in the Soviet courts, which are under the thumb of the government, and have to carry out the governmental policy. Should a concessionary propose arbitration for the settlement of a dispute, the Central Concessions Committee of the Soviet government almost always rejects the application. Of late, however, in some of the contracts relating to concessions made to French and American firms, a clause providing for arbitration has been introduced.

But the main cause of the slow development of the concessions is to be found in the currency policy of the Soviet government, in the general prohibition of the free export of foreign bills of exchange, and in the fixed rate of the chervonets. Foreign bills of exchange must be discounted at the State Bank and at the official rate. In most cases, moreover, the profits made in a concessionary undertaking may not be sent abroad until the contract expires. Only in some of the most recent agreements has the right to do this been granted to a limited extent. In any case, a concessionary finds it very difficult to secure an official permit for the export of his profits or for the use of them in the purchase of foreign bills of exchange. The result is a considerable reduction in the high profits for whose sake a concessionary is willing to accept all the risks and complications involved by undertaking to produce or to trade in Soviet Russia.

These various circumstances account for the fact that fewer and fewer concessions are being asked for, and that some of the existing concessionary enterprises are being wound up. Of the 163 concessions granted prior to January 1, 1928, only 92 were actually functioning at that date.[1] It is significant that during the last three years 32 concessions have been annulled, and among them the most important, those of Krupp, Wolff, Wirth, and Harriman. In like manner, the foreign concessionaries have withdrawn from a number of the mixed societies for export and import, so that of the 31 that had been inaugurated, only 8 remain in existence.

In support of the first decree relating to concessions, Lenin declared, in a report under date November 27, 1920: "Concessions—these do not mean peace with capitalism, but war upon a new plane." Down to the present day, the whole concessionary policy and concessionary practice of the Soviet government have been guided by this spirit. That accounts for the failure of the policy of concessions. In the year 1927–1928, it is plain that concessions have been a failure. The stubborn refusal of foreign capitalists to make long-term investments of capital in Russia under existing conditions is no secret for the leaders of Soviet policy. The doubts concerning the possibility of collaboration with the Soviet Union which have been voiced by prominent members of German industrial and commercial circles in connexion with the negotiations for the revision of the Russo-German commercial treaty, and the lessons of the last five years, have led the Soviet government to make a change in its concessionary policy. On July 24, 1928, the Council of People's Commissaries came to a new decision concerning concessionary policy.[2] On the basis of this decision,

[1] V. Butkoffsky [Foreign Concessions in the U.S.S.R.], Moscow, 1928.
[2] The decision of the Council of People's Commissaries was published in the "Torgovo-Promyshlennaya Gazeta", on September 15, 1928, and was sent to all the commercial delegations.

a decree is to be elaborated and submitted for approval to the presidium of the Central Executive Committee. The decision involves important changes in the extant concessionary system. By the terms of the first decree concerning concessions, in the year 1920, they were to be granted only in the frontier areas of the U.S.S.R., and never in the key industries. The first departures from this principle were made in respect of the concession to Harriman (manganese ores) and in the Lena Goldfields Concession. By the new decision, all restrictions as to the nature of a concessionary enterprise are to be abolished. The Central Concession Committee is to be empowered to take the necessary steps for attracting capital into all branches of the transport system, of elaborative industry (including the metal industries), mining, the provision of fuel, electrification, forestry and agriculture, the making of synthetic textiles, and even municipal enterprise. The new decision gives concessionaries the right of selling their products freely. The taxation of concessionary enterprises is to be unified, the various national and municipal taxes being replaced by a single tax which is to be levied by an ad hoc authority in a specified manner. Tariff privileges are to be granted to concessionaries in respect of the import of machinery, tools, building materials, etc. There is to be a speeding-up of the process of granting licences for the import of machinery, spare parts, raw materials, etc., so that a licence is to be delivered within a month of the application. Privileges are also to be given to the concessionaries in respect of the recruiting of experts and skilled workers from abroad and in respect of the engaging of Russian workers. Finally, the Commissariat for Finance is to see to it that concessionaries shall be able to do exchange business promptly.

Owing to the economic conditions that prevail in Soviet Russia at the time when these new decisions have been arrived at (failure of the crops, a further fall in the purchasing power of the chervonets, difficulties in industry), and owing to the state of the relations between the Soviet government and the capitalist great powers, we cannot but doubt whether a radical

P

change in the concessionary policy will be followed by a speedy influx of foreign capital. Foreign firms already working in Russia know that in that country, where industry and commerce are under the monopolist control of the State, and where security before the law is lacking, the verbal tenor of concessions has much less effect than have political considerations upon the practical conditions of daily work.

The new law relating to concessions is not yet drafted, and the published decision upon which it is to be based is couched in such general terms that no precise and concrete deductions can readily be made from it. Every section contains a rider, or a proviso, which, as experience shows, can nullify the proposed privileges and alleviations. Agreed that the concessionary is to have the right of selling his products; but this right is granted only "as a rule", which means that there are to be exceptions, and these will be subject to special stipulations. Again, the concessionary is to be allowed to export his profits in the form of foreign bills of exchange, but here also there is a proviso, "in accordance with the concessionary agreement". We naturally have to ask ourselves whether the concessionary agreements of the future are likely to contain more favourable conditions as regards the date, the amount, the rate of discount, etc., of foreign bills of exchange, now that the financial position of the U.S.S.R. has changed for the worse, now that the value of the chervonets has undergone a further decline, and now that the monetary reserves are lower than they were in the years 1925 to 1927. The new privileges are only to be valid "in accordance with the agreement". Obviously the real effect of the new decision, as determined by the wording of the legislation, will depend upon the general course of Soviet policy in the near future. There will be no likelihood of any considerable activity on the part of foreign capitalists in Soviet Russia unless the Soviet government abandons its present utopian policy. These considerations should prevent our basing larger expectations as to the practical possibilities of the latest change in concessionary policy.

As far as principle is concerned, however, the significance of the change is considerable. The new decision implies that the Soviet government finds itself compelled to permit the establishment of large-scale private industrial enterprises in the U.S.S.R. (though for the time being they are to be owned by foreigners exclusively)—to tolerate them in the widest possible measure, and even in the key industries. Should the decision take practical effect, this would involve the abandonment of the State monopoly even in large-scale industry, and would therefore signify the modification of nationalised industry in a way that would enable it to enter into competition with foreigners engaged in private industrial enterprise in Russia.

The new program for the "activation" of the concessionary policy signifies, not only the abandonment of the economic monopoly of the State and the handing-over of the most important departments of industry to private capitalism, but also the recognition that a partial denationalisation of industry is indispensable. Concessionaries will be allowed, not merely to establish new enterprises, but to invest money in already existing factories, mines, and electrical power stations.[1] The abandonment of State monopoly even in the key industries, the practical recognition of the need for a partial denationalisation, and the demand for an increase of the share of private capitalistic production in Russian economic life—these signify the relinquishment of three of the basic principles of the communist program. "The extent of denationalisation will be directly dependent upon the policy of the Soviet government"; denationalisation will be more extensive "in proportion to the degree to which the national economy is disturbed, and in proportion to the time for which a comprehensive system of nationalised industry unsuitable to the present economic

[1] Under date September 15, 1928, the "Torgovo-Promyshlennaya Gazeta" writes unambiguously regarding the new decision in this matter of concessionary policy: "This will make it possible [for the State] to withdraw large amounts of capital from the branches of economic life into which the concessionaries are to be attracted."

conditions of the country is maintained"—such were the prophecies made a good many years ago by Russian social democrats. In the year 1922, L. Martoff wrote: "A time may come in which no help from outside will any longer suffice to make it possible to maintain that social control of the productive forces which is desirable in the interest of the workers."[1]

In the year 1928, the Soviet government already finds it necessary to evacuate its positions on the most important sectors of the economic front. The government, which has prided itself so greatly upon its policy of socialisation, is now ready to auction to private capitalists even that minimum of publicly-conducted enterprises which in tsarist Russia were conducted by the urban and rural self-governing authorities— the enterprises which all the democratic elements in the country were struggling to extend. Instead of undertaking an organised denationalisation, beginning with the less important enterprises and passing only so far as is necessary to the more important ones, the Soviet government has to make a disorderly retreat, leaving to private capital the choice of investment in petroleum, coal, metal ores, municipal enterprise, and railways.

Nothing but bitter need can have induced the Soviet government to sacrifice its economic monopoly and partially to denationalise industry for the sake of "accelerating the development of the country and of satisfying the needs of the population". These things being so, it is hard to understand why the right to establish new industrial enterprises is to be granted exclusively to foreign capital. When the first decree relating to concessions was promulgated in the year 1920, the Communist Party's organ for agitation and propaganda explained in the following terms the reasons for issuing the decree: "The fundamental significance of the concessions is political. They will be made to foreigners in order to increase hostile opposition within the capitalist world. By bringing our bourgeois opponents into enmity one with another, by arousing in them envy, rivalry, and alarm, we shall weaken the

[1] [Our Platform], "Sotsialisticheskyi Vestnik", October 4, 1922.

bourgeois alliance." How childishly naive does this argument sound in the year 1928! Even the most credulous of the communists no longer believe that the attraction of foreign capital into the Soviet Union can be regarded as one of the revolutionary fighting methods of the Comintern, and that the capitalists of the whole world are jostling one another in their eagerness to secure concessions from the U.S.S.R.

Eight years ago, however, there was a second argument used, a politico-economic one. "The Soviet government is attracting foreign capital upon a concessionary basis for the sole reason that this capital is not at the disposal of the Soviet government, whereas Russian private capital belongs to us in any case." I have already shown that, after seven years' experience of the Nep, it cannot be said for a moment that the Soviet government has learned to make an effective use even of the small amount of capital in the hands of Russian private entrepreneurs, or of the savings of the Russian population. It is true that the Soviet State is able to reduce the "private economic sector" in the general national economy by the persecution of private entrepreneurs and by closing down private enterprises; but it is not able to mobilise private funds for the productive purposes of the State economy in the form of loans, savings, or bank deposits.

Certainly the attraction of Russian private capital to an extent worth considering will only be possible if the dominant political and economic conditions undergo a change and if the productive accumuation of capital in the homeland increases. But even the attraction of foreign concessionaries will only be possible, as the experience of recent years indubitably shows, if certain legal guarantees are provided, and if a normal course for the economic activities of these concessionaries can be ensured. The latest decisions of the Soviet government show that it is prepared (in defiance of its own principles) to allow foreign capitalists "the necessary freedom of economic activity". But this will involve for the Russian national economy the creation of abnormal conditions, analogous to those which obtain under the capitulations in force in colonial and semi-colonial countries. The struggles in China have given a vivid demonstration of the fierce conflicts to which foreign concessions can and must lead; and the concessionary practice of the Soviet Union up to the present time has also shown all too plainly how inevitable is the interweaving of considerations of "high policy" with economic interests in almost every important concessionary undertaking. In a concessionary system, every difference of opinion, every dispute, becomes magnified into a conflict of worldwide significance. There can be no doubt that the Soviet Union's need for capital is so acute that it will be necessary for those who now direct its policy to accommodate themselves to the promotion of an influx of foreign capital under the most diversified auspices, including that of granting concessions. But what grounds are there to justify the rejection of all possibilities of accumulating private capital within the country, for refusing on principle to promote private initiative within the Russian frontiers, and for exclusively reserving for foreign capital those opportunities for that profit-making which is repugnant to socialists in any and every form?

In the reorganisation of the concessionary policy of the U.S.S.R., special anxiety is felt concerning the problem of the relations between foreign concessionary capital and the Russian workers. How can the communists justify the fact that the Russian workers in the enterprises of the private concessionaries are deprived of the possibility of carrying on the class struggle in the customary way and of combining to form independent trade-union organisations? The ordinary contention that the Soviet State as employer has no interest hostile to the working class (a contention whose validity has never been admitted by the social democrats) cannot be regarded even by the communists as having any bearing upon the concessionary enterprises of foreign capitalists. The fact that the nationalised Soviet trade unions, when a conflict arises between Russian workers and foreign concessionaries, are not guided by the interests of the working class, but by a medley of political considerations, has been made plain more than once by the practice of recent years. There can be no doubt that concessionaries whom the State regarded with disfavour have sometimes been subjected to "pressure on the part of the trade unions". That was what happened when the authorities wanted to squeeze Harriman out of the manganese-ore concession, and when a struggle was going on to secure a revision of the contract with the Indo-European Telegraph Company. In most cases, however, the trade unions have been instructed by the government to see to it that the foreign concessionaries are not "annoyed". This will be plain to any one who takes the trouble to read the interviews with concessionaries that are published from time to time in the Soviet press. These concessionaries, wishing to make themselves agreeable to the Soviet government, declare with much satisfaction that "with the support of the trade unions" they have been able "to introduce a piecework system into their enterprises"; that "the trade unions have not put any obstacle in the way of securing a higher output"; and one of them even admits with enviable frankness that "in no other country does the employer find such peaceful labour conditions, for it is enough that he should be on good terms with the trade union, and then any possibility of a strike will be out of the question".[1]

The foregoing is in full accord with the remarks made by S. Araloff, a member of the presidium of the Supreme Economic Council of the Soviet Union: "It is especially noteworthy that we do not regard the concessionary as a private employer whose work and success are no concern of ours. We regard work with the concessionaries as a reasonable and harmonious cooperation." When Lenin first made up his mind that concessions were to be granted, he had in view a "competition between a socialist economy and a private capitalist economy". By the year 1928, his disciples have retrogressed so far as to approve of a harmonious cooperation!

[1] "Izvestia", October 7, 1928.

Should the foreign concessions attain considerable proportions, the suppression of the right of combination by the Soviet government cannot fail to create a situation that will be menacing and even disastrous to the Russian workers.

The present economic position of the Soviet Union makes it indispensable to attract an inflow of foreign capital, and this need would be just the same whatever the nature of the government. But owing to the lack of the most elementary legal securities, and owing to the determination of the Soviet government to persist in a disastrous policy at home (one which nips in the bud any attempt to accumulate capital in town or countryside), the State finds it necessary to allure the foreign capitalists by granting them all kinds of special privileges, such as are unfavourable to the prospects of industrialising the Soviet Union, and are unlikely to provide a satisfactory foundation for the development of economic relations between Russia and the world market.

CHAPTER THIRTEEN

CURRENCY AND STATE FINANCE

1. CURRENCY

DURING the period of war communism, the Russian currency underwent a complete collapse. The depreciation of the currency was so extreme that the cost of printing paper money exceeded the value of the notes. Inflation reached its logical doom by devouring itself.

No doubt, the disorganisation of the Russian currency had begun already during the opening weeks of the Great War. On August 9, 1914, the supply of gold in exchange for notes was suspended, and at the same time increased power of emission was granted to the State Bank. The printing of notes became one of the main expedients for the financing of the war. The following table shows the amount of money in circulation during the war period:

					Millions of Roubles,
July 16/29, 1914	..	..	..	..	1633
Jan. 1/14, 1915	..	..	..	..	2945
Jan. 1/14, 1916	..	..	..	..	5617
Jan. 1/14, 1917	..	..	..	..	9103
Oct. 23/Nov. 5, 1917	..	..	..	..	18,917

At the time of the communist revolution, the purchasing power of the paper rouble was from 0·10 to 0·12 of that of the pre-war rouble. Owing to State action, the value of the rouble in the foreign exchanges was somewhat higher, ranging to from 0·25 to 0·30 of a gold rouble.

After the establishment of the Soviet State, notwithstanding that the expenditure of milliards for war purposes had now come to an end, the increase in the amount of money in circulation and the depreciation of the currency proceeded even more rapidly. This was due to the arrest of normal production, to the dependence of the whole financial system of the government upon the income from the note issues, and to the deliberate (though utterly utopian) attempt of the Soviet government "to liquidate money as the foundation of the capitalist economy by making it entirely valueless". The amount of money in circulation at various subsequent dates was as follows:

Jan. 1, 1918	..	..	27·3 milliards of roubles
Jan. 1, 1919	..	..	63·8 milliards of roubles
Jan. 1, 1920	..	..	225·0 milliards of roubles
Jan. 1, 1921	..	..	1·1 trillions of roubles
Jan. 1, 1922	..	..	17·5 trillions of roubles[1]
Jan. 1, 1923	..	..	2·6 quadrillions of roubles
Jan. 1, 1924	..	..	178·5 quadrillions of roubles
Mar. 1, 1924	..	..	865·5 quadrillions of roubles

At the time of the reform of the currency, in 1924, the value of all the paper money in circulation amounted to 25 millions of gold roubles.

The reform of the currency in the U.S.S.R. was effected by two stages. On July 27, 1922, the new monetary unit, the chervonets, was introduced into circulation, while the old monetary unit, the "Soviet token", still remained current. This new currency was guaranteed by a 25 per cent reserve of the precious metals and of foreign bills of exchange, and was kept stable in its relation to gold (one chervonets representing 174·24 dolyas[2] of pure gold), although the right of exchanging the chervonets notes for gold was "postponed for an indefinite period". The stability of the chervonets was evidenced by the fact that the State Bank was prepared to exchange Soviet tokens for chervontsy at the current rate. The coexistence of the two currency systems soon eventuated in the complete depreciation of the Soviet token. The chervonets became the principal medium of exchange, being used almost exclusively in the towns, whereas the Soviet token continued to circulate in the countryside. The chervonets was used especially to

[1] To facilitate a comparison between the state of affairs at the various dates, the cancelling of the noughts in some of the note issues during the years 1922 and 1923 has been ignored.
[2] 1 dolya = 0·044 of a gramme.

finance State industry, while the Soviet token was used to pay private traders and in the peasant economy.

By degrees the Soviet token was entirely replaced by the chervonets. In January 1923, 91·4 per cent of the currency was in Soviet tokens; in January 1924, the percentage had fallen to 15·7; and in February 1924, to 11.

At length, on February 5, 1924, after the budget, the credit system, and the national economy had been reduced more or less to order, the definitive reform of the currency was effected. The issue of Soviet tokens was discontinued. A stable currency, on a gold basis and reckoned in gold roubles, issued by the Treasury, was introduced by a decree, the amount of the issue being fixed. The chervonets was retained as the currency of the State Bank, to be covered by a gold reserve. One rouble of the Treasury currency was to be worth one-tenth of a chervonets. Chervontsy and Treasury roubles were to be legal tender everywhere, and must be accepted and exchanged one for another at all the paying departments of the State and the State Bank. In the year 1927, the emission of the Treasury currency was likewise put in the hands of the State Bank, and the distinction between the chervonets and the Treasury rouble has, for the most part, gradually disappeared.

Thus in the year 1924, after the depreciation of the currency had been going on for six or seven years, a stable currency was established. The establishment of a stable currency was not possible until after the adoption of certain elementary principles of a sound economy (the transition to the Nep); but as soon as this had been effected, the stabilisation of the currency became itself one of the factors promoting the reestablishment of the national economy. Industry, agriculture, and commerce, were now able to be carried on with the aid of notes which did not lose some of their value from day to day, and they thus acquired trustworthy foundations. In like manner, when a worker was paid his wages, it was henceforward in a currency which did not lose part of its real value from day to day.

The financial authorities have since then been doing their

utmost to maintain the stability of the new currency. During the five years which have elapsed since the currency reform was effected, the People's Commissariat for Finance has displayed the greatest possible caution. Proposals made by the authorities and by the managers of the State industrial undertakings have been ruthlessly curtailed whenever they involved considerable expenditure. At all economic congresses and similar gatherings there have been incessant complaints of the dictatorship of the Commissariat for Finance. But it is only thanks to the policy pursued by this Commissariat that so far, down to the end of the year 1928, despite fluctuations in the value of the chervonets, the Soviet currency has been saved from a further disastrous collapse.

The amount of currency in circulation since the introduction of the chervonets is shown in the following table[1]:

(In Millions of Roubles.)

	Chervonets Notes.	Treasury Currency.	Totals.
1922/23	—	156·9	156·9
1923/24	207·4	74·5	281·9
1924/25	346·5	280·7	627·2
1925/26	652·0	490·9	1142·9
1926/27	780·6	562·6	1343·2
1927/28	989·8	638·5	1628·3
1928/29	1063·7	907·7	1971·4
1929 (July)	1192·4	1020·5	2212·9

Notwithstanding all the precautions of the Commissariat for Finance, there have nevertheless during the last five years been repeated indications of an open or concealed inflation. This is because, owing to the unfavourable balance of trade, it has been impossible to retain the reserves needed to safeguard the chervonets; because the granting of credit and funds for industrial development has gone on at an increasing pace; and because, at the same time, there has been a slackening in the growth of commodity production.

[1] "Finansy i Narodnoye Hozyaistvo", 1928, Nos. 11 and 42.

During three of the last five years the balance of trade was unfavourable, the excess of imports over exports aggregating 260 millions of roubles. In order to pay for this excess of imports it was necessary to hand over a considerable proportion of the State reserves of gold and foreign securities. Whereas during the first year of the currency reform the chervonets issue was covered by a reserve amounting to 38 per cent (289 millions of roubles), in the year 1928 the reserve amounted to only 14 per cent (290 millions of roubles). In countries with a stabler currency and a healthier economic life, the gold and other reserves covering the note issues play a less important part; but in Russia, where economic life is continually being disturbed by paroxysms of inflation fever, the psychological importance of having large reserves is enormous. Besides, the reserve which safeguards the chervonets happens to be the only gold fund to which, in case of need, the State can have recourse in order to pay for imports. Professor Katsenelenbaum, one of the directors of the State Bank and a leading figure in the financial administration of Soviet Russia, in his report on the fifth anniversary of the introduction of the chervonets, says: "Our main task in this matter of the currency, and that which must be the chief plank in our platform for the next few years, is the formation of a gold reserve, which will safeguard the chervonets more effectively than at present. In this respect, during the last two years, there has in actual fact been a certain weakening on our currency front."[1]

Increased national expenditure upon industrialisation has involved a heavy, and sometimes an almost intolerable, burden upon the currency. During the last four years, three and a half milliards of roubles, in round figures, have been invested in industry, either in the form of cash or in that of long-term credits. During the years when industrial production was being expanded by a more vigorous using-up of the old industrial capital, the direct or indirect financing of industry by note

[1] [Five Years of Stable Currency in the U.S.S.R.], "Ekonomicheskaya Zhizn", November 27, 1927.

issues was less dangerous than it has become of late. In that earlier period, the State investments served to strengthen the capital of enterprise, and thus very soon after the issue of new paper money, new commodities could be placed on the market. It is different to-day, when the money supplied by the State is needed for the starting of entirely new enterprises, and when, according to the Soviet program of industrialisation, it is needed mainly to provide new means of production. Speedily, and in large quantities, the money gets into circulation (being used to pay the workers their wages, to pay for raw materials supplied by the peasants, and so on), whereas the new commodities will not find their way into the market for from five to seven years at least, when the works where the new means of production are to be made will have been set a-going, and when, with the aid of the machinery made at these works, the articles of mass consumption will have been brought into being. But the putting of these excessive quantities of money into circulation burdens the market and gives rise to phenomena of inflation. The forcing-house growth of industry, brought about, not by the normal accumulation of capital but by extensive State subventions, has, in the course of the last few years, more than once given rise to phenomena of inflation, for which the only possible remedy has been a spasmodic restriction of the issue of notes. The disproportion between the growth of the currency, on the one hand, and the circulation of commodities on the other, is shown in the following table:

	Yearly Increase in Currency.	Yearly Increase in Circulation of Commodities.	Purchasing Power of the Chervonets.[1]
	Percentage.	Percentage.	Roubles.
Oct. 1, 1923	—	—	5·99
Oct. 1, 1924	+ 124·0	+ 40·0	4·85
Oct. 1, 1925	+ 100·0	+ 64·0	4·65
Oct. 1, 1926	+ 18·5	+ 22·0	4·35
Oct. 1, 1927	+ 22·8	+ 18·0	4·42
Oct. 1, 1928	+ 21·1	+ 16·0	3·82

[1] According to the retail trade index of the Conjuncture Institute.

Owing to the peculiarities of the Soviet economy, the phenomena of inflation do not manifest themselves as an obvious depreciation of the currency taking the form of a general rise in prices, as usually happens in such cases in capitalist countries. The State, which controls the exchanges and the banks, fixes the value of money. In the U.S.S.R., as in no other country, the value of money, as prescribed by the State, persists without fluctuation. Business done in the so-called black exchanges is illegal. Alike for State trade and for private trading, prices are fixed by the State; and often enough during periods when the value of the currency is really fluctuating, prices are compulsorily kept down. Furthermore, the monopoly of foreign commerce makes it possible for the State to regulate all foreign import and export business with an eye to currency considerations. No price for the chervonets is quoted on the foreign exchanges, so that its fluctuations are not officially recorded in the international money market. Yet when in one way or another the customary outward symptoms of a disease are repressed, this by no means signifies that the disease no longer exists, but only that it has been driven inwards.

In order to stabilise the chervonets at home and abroad, it is necessary to prohibit its exchange for foreign currency, to give it an arbitrary value, to forbid the export of foreign bills of exchange, and, finally (when the foreign banks which carry on business with the Soviet Union notify a fall in the value of the chervonets) to forbid the import of chervontsy into Russia.[1] Assuredly this is an entirely new phenomenon in the history of currency.

The fall in the value of the chervonets manifests itself in Soviet Russia as an incerase in the scarcity of commodities. Those who are paid in chervontsy for their labour or for the products they sell, hasten to rid themselves of the depreciating

[1] In November 1928, some of the German banks valued the chervonets at 9 marks, when the Soviet government was declaring its value to be 21 marks; and already in the beginning of 1928, the Garantie und Kreditbank für den Osten, the Berlin agents of the Russian State Bank, had discontinued the acceptance of chervonets notes.

currency units by buying new goods. On the other hand, the peasants prefer to keep their products, which are real and stable values, in their own hands, and to restrict to the utmost the sale of agricultural produce.

The difference between the nominal value of the chervonets at home and abroad is also a heavy burden on foreign trade, which now to a great extent ceases to pay. In the organ of the People's Commissariat for Finance we read: "The profits made by the State as importer in the present condition of our currency (which now has a different value at home and abroad respectively), can by no means make good the losses incurred by the State as exporter."[1] The State Planning Commission likewise admits the difficulties that arise from this abnormal situation: "The problem of equating the home and the foreign value of our currency must be solved in one way or another."[2] But the writer does not tell us how this problem is to be solved.

In the middle of the year 1928, when the unfavourable balance of trade, the failure of the harvest, and the impracticability of getting further credit abroad, were all working together, the value of the chervonets was fluctuating more ominously than ever.[3]

2. BANKING AND CREDIT

One of the first steps taken after the establishment of the Soviet government was the nationalisation of all the banks and credit institutions. On December 27, 1917, the banks were

[1] "Vestnik Finansoff", 1927, No. 5.
[2] [Perspectives of the Development of the Economy of the U.S.S.R.], Gosplan Publishing House.
[3] L. Yuroffsky, one of the most noted of the Soviet financiers, writes in "Finansy i Narodnoye Hozyaistvo", September 16, 1928: "Such manoeuvres as the provision of the necessary monetary resources by means of pressure on the monetary system can only be successful at the cost of injury to the national economy as a whole, and in the course of the year 1927–1928 (just as once before in the year 1925–1926) the results of inflation have shown how inconvenient it is to try and bring about economic development in such a way. The situation resulting from inflation has become very grave."

nationalised and were amalgamated with the State Bank, which was then given the name of People's Bank. But during the period of war communism, when Russian economic life was completely nationalised and centralised, and when a monetary economy had been abolished, the People's Bank was a functionless organisation, and by degrees all its branches were closed.

At length, however, the reestablishment of a commodity economy, the putting of the State enterprises upon a basis of commercial calculation, and the development of private industry and private trade after the inauguration of the Nep, compelled the Soviet State to create the banking and credit system anew. On November 16, 1921, the first Soviet bank, the State Bank, was called into existence. When it was founded, the assumption was that it was to be the only banking institution in the U.S.S.R. But the development of Russian economic life has made the functions of the credit system extremely complicated, and has compelled a further differentiation of the banking system. By degrees special banks have come into existence to finance the cooperative system, municipal enterprise, industry, agriculture, foreign commerce, and private trade as well. All the banks, with the exception of the private credit institutions which finance private industry and private trade, receive their monetary resources from the State, are subject to State control, and are of the nature of State banks. The right of issuing notes is the prerogative of the State Bank.

On October 1, 1927, there were more than 400 banks in Russia, their capital and the business done by them being shown in the table on the next page.

During the short period for which the Soviet banks have existed, there have already become manifest a number of defects in their organisation. For instance, branches have been founded where there was no urgent need for them, and there has been a good deal of competition between the branches of the respective State credit institutions. It therefore became necessary to consider the question of restricting the number of

branches, and of closing some of them. By the end of the year
1928, the number of branches, which had been 1435 in the
year 1926, was reduced to 985. For the granting of long-term
credits, it was decided to establish a special bank, called into
being by the reorganisation of the Industrial Bank. When
economic life is financed with means voted in the budget, the
State Bank and the appropriate special banks undertake this
operation. The importance of the banks in the financing of the
national economy increases from year to year.

	Banks.	Branches	In Millions of Roubles.		
			Total Balance.	Credits and Loans.	Deposits.
State Bank	1	418	4844·7	2135·2	926·2
Cooperative banks	2	81	277·5	159·6	101·0
Municipal banks	51	127	932·8	732·0	223·0
Agricultural banks and Agri-cultural Credit Societies..	76	195	1468·7	1128·7	84·8
Commercial and Industrial bank	1	34	681·7	312·2	130·1
Bank for Foreign Commerce	1	5	171·7	107·7	16·8
Bank for Electrification ..	1	1	191·2	—	—
Credit Societies	289	289	60·3	33·8	22·7

Although there are so many branch banks, and although the
banking turnover is now very large, the credit system of
Russian banking is still in its initial stages of development.
There is a comparatively small aggregate sum on deposit and
current account. The deposits made by private individuals are
insignificant, partly because the accumulation of money goes
on so slowly in Russia, and partly because those who have put
any money by are afraid of drawing attention to the fact by
depositing their savings in the State institutions. Nor have the
State authorities, departments, etc., any considerable sums at
current account in the banks, for these various organisations
are continually short of funds, and the amount of the deposits
undergoes marked seasonal variations. As far as concerns the
State as a customer, credit and loan business has not yet

acquired a stable foundation. The factors of a "purposive economy" are perpetually in conflict with the commercial principles of banking business. Often enough, the granting of credit does not depend upon the solvency of the borrower, but upon political considerations. For this reason, short-term credits become long-term credits. Bills of exchange are renewed upon instructions from the State authorities. Long-term credits granted to the State instruments sometimes bear interest and at other times not. Special difficulties are imposed upon the granting of credit to private individuals. There is but a small amount of capital in the State credit institutions, and these institutions grant credits to private borrowers only in exceptional instances. For this reason there is a marked tendency to the development of an underground speculative credit business.

Since the reform of the currency, there has been a revival of the State savings banks, which did an extensive business before the war. The capital in the hands of the savings banks was more than 1·5 milliards of roubles at the outset of the war. During the war, the real value represented by this sum had greatly declined; and after the revolution of 1917 a decree was issued repudiating State responsibility for the deposits in the savings banks. When savings-bank business was resumed, the growth of the deposits was at first very slow, but as confidence in the financial stability of the State has increased and the accumulation of capital has made progress, there has been a considerable growth in savings-bank deposits.

	Number of Savings Banks.	Number of Depositors.	Aggregate Deposits (Roubles).
On October 1, 1924	7482	537,406	11,200,000
On October 1, 1925	9756	817,735	33,493,000
On October 1, 1926	11,360	1,315,053	90,468,000
On October 1, 1927	14,589	2,211,730	186,969,000
On October 1, 1928[1]	16,170	3,826,800	314,800,000

[1] Provisional figures.

It is interesting to note the sources of the deposits in the savings banks. According to a report of October 1, 1927, 32·5 per cent of all the deposits belonged to governmental authorities and organisations; 33·8 per cent to employees; 10·6 per cent to workers; 2 per cent to home workers and handicraftsmen; 2·8 per cent to members of the liberal professions; 2·2 per cent to non-workers; 4 per cent to peasants; 12·1 per cent to unclassified persons. One of the greatest hindrances to the growth of deposits made by private persons, among whom come the peasants who form the preponderant mass of the Russian population, is the lack of any guarantee that the savings banks will keep their business private as regards the tax authorities and the political police (G.P.U.).

3. State Finances, Taxation, Loans

Only after the currency had been stabilised, could the Soviet government make detailed proposals for the conduct of the nationalised economy as a whole; only then, that is to say, could it draft a State budget. Until then, all that had been possible had been to draw up vague schemes of income and expenditure for the next few months; but in view of the progressive depreciation of the currency, these schemes were hardly worth the paper they were written on. The first stable budget, the first well-balanced plan for the next year's financial and economic activities of the State, was drafted in the year 1924–1925, the items being given in the new monetary unit, the chervonets.

The structure of the Russian budget has altered considerably during the ten years of Soviet rule. The period 1918–1921 was that in which the former monetary economy was dying out; the State revenue during these years consisted to the extent of from 67 to 87 per cent of note issues, and only to the extent of from 13 to 33 per cent of genuine sources of national income. Of this real income, 75 per cent was in kind, consisting of the products of State enterprises and of agricultural produce which the People's Commissariat for Food Supply levied by force upon the "grain surplus" of the peasants. Since the introduction of the Nep, revenue has no longer been collected in kind, and from 1922 to 1924 there was an increase in the revenue from taxation, although during this period revenue from note issues still played a considerable part. At length, after the currency reform in the year 1924–1925, note issues ceased to constitute an official item of revenue in the budget, and since then the State revenue has been of three main kinds: revenue from taxes; revenue derived from State property and State enterprises, from the transport system, and from the post office; and revenue from loans.

Since the year 1924–1925, the budget of the U.S.S.R. has assumed a definite form. By degrees there has been an improvement in budgetary technique, and the budgets of the central authorities of the U.S.S.R. are now kept distinct from those of the various republics of the Union and those of the local soviets. To-day, the revenue and expenditure of the State is estimated in two main budgets: the united budget of the U.S.S.R.; and the local budget of the urban and village soviets. The State budget and the local budget combine to form the general budget of the U.S.S.R. A proper assignment of budgetary responsibility to the U.S.S.R. and to the isolated republics respectively is at present impossible, for the budgets of four out of the six separate republics of the Union show a deficit, and moreover the burden of taxation varies greatly in different parts of the Union.

During the five years that have elapsed since the reform of the currency, the budget has grown considerably. A comparative survey of the unified budget at various dates is given in the table on page 246.

By 1927–1928, as we see from the table, the budget of the U.S.S.R. exceeded the budget for the same area in pre-war days. Nevertheless, the factors of the budget of the U.S.S.R. are of a very different kind from those of the Russian budget of pre-war days. The Soviet State, whose economy is in the main nationalised, has to finance at the cost of the State almost the whole of industry, home and foreign trade, and banking. There is hardly any private capital in the country, and no influx from abroad worth considering, so that the State treasury has to provide for everything.

UNIFIED BUDGET

	In Millions of Pre-war Roubles.		In Millions of Roubles at the Rate of the Day.	
	Absolute.	Percentages of 1913.	Absolute.	Year's Increase in Percentages.
1913[1]	3140	100·0	3140·0	—
1924/25	1453	46·3	2929·0	—
1925/26	1867	59·4	3948·0	34·7
1926/27	2387	76·0	5125·0	29·8
1927/28	3764	119·1	6350·0	23·2

The size and character of the budget for 1928–1929 is shown by the estimates approved by the Central Executive Committee on December 15, 1928 (see pages 248–249).

There has been a further marked increase in the estimates for 1928–1929, an increase of about 15 per cent.[2] The budget is increasing to keep pace with the general expansion of the national economy, and outstrips this. Thus the expansion of the budget is largely explicable, as we shall see, by phenomena of the nature of inflation. The growth of the aggregate national income, and the growth of the total production of the country (including both agriculture and industry), lags, in fact, far behind the growth of the budget. Of course, calculations of the income of the State and of the aggregate production of the country are open to many sources of inaccuracy, but still, since the methods of calculation are identical for successive years, the figures given above, inaccuracies notwithstanding, enable us to ascertain the general developmental trends.

[1] The figures under this year are given for the area now comprised in the U.S.S.R.
[2] The local budget for 1928–1929 amounts to 1370 millions of roubles.

The following table shows the growth of the national income,[1] the gross production, and the combined (local and central) budget of the Union in millions of chervonets roubles:

	National Income.		Gross Production.		Combined Budget.	
	Absolute.	Annual Increase in Percentages.	Absolute.	Annual Increase in Percentages.	Absolute.	Annual Increase in Percentages.
1924/25	14,376	—	24,088	—	3706	—
1925/26	18,475	28·5	30,990	28·7	5022	35·5
1926/27	20,389	10·3	31,741	2·4	6593	31·3
1927/28	21,709	6·5	32,528	2·5	7724	17·1

The proportion of the national income redistributed by the State budget increases year by year. In the year 1924–1925, the unified State budget represented 20·3 per cent, and the combined State budget 25·8 per cent of the national income; in the year 1927–1928, the corresponding figures were 30·5 per cent and 35·5 per cent.

So comprehensive an absorption of the national income by the State budget need not interfere with the growth of the national income if the State, by its guidance of capital into new channels, were opening new sources of income (from the State enterprises, the increase of exports, etc.). But the budget of the U.S.S.R., as far as revenue is concerned, is mainly composed of taxes. The percentage parts played by the various sources of revenue in the total revenue (calculated in the currency of the year to which the figures relate), are seen in the table on page 250.

These figures show very clearly how large a proportion of the revenue is derived from taxation, and they throw a very strong light upon the unfortunate outcome of the State control

[1] The Soviet statisticians have not given us a trustworthy and unified estimate of the national income. For the year 1927–1928 alone, there are seven different estimates, and even the members of the State Planning Commission produce different series of figures. The ones printed in the text are derived from [Control Figures of the National Economy for 1927–1928], which is certainly the most trustworthy of the official sources.

UNIFIED BUDGET FOR 1928–1929

(In Millions of Roubles.)

REVENUE

1. DIRECT TAXES:

Agricultural tax	400·0
Business tax	1005·0
Income tax	272·0
Other direct taxes	23·3
	1700·3

2. INDIRECT TAXES:

Tax on consumption	1735·5
Customs dues	255·0
	1990·5

3. STAMP DUTIES OF VARIOUS KINDS .. .. .. 138·0

Total Taxes .. .. 3828·8

4. REVENUE DERIVED FROM OTHER SOURCES THAN TAXES:

Revenue from Natural Resources	65·0
Revenue from Banks	103·0
Revenue from Forests	272·4
Revenue from State Industry	275·0
Revenue from Home trade	28·0
Revenue from Foreign commerce	4·0
Revenue from Concessions	4·0
Other State property (including realisation of State property)	33·3
Other sources	66·9
Repayment of loans	41·5
	893·1

5. REVENUE FROM STATE LOANS .. .. 800·0

Total Revenue, apart from Transport, Posts, and Telegraphs .. .. 5521·9

6. TRANSPORT .. .. 1904·5

7. POSTS AND TELEGRAPHS .. .. 190·0

Grand Total .. .. 7616·4

8. REVENUE CARRIED OVER FROM LAST YEAR .. .. 115·1

Revised Total .. .. 7731·5

UNIFIED BUDGET FOR 1928-1929—*continued*

(*In Millions of Roubles.*)

EXPENDITURE

1. FINANCING THE NATIONALISED ECONOMY:

Industry	942·4	
Electrification	184·0	
Agriculture (including 107·0 for the organisation of Soviet and Collective Farms)	334·0	
Internal Trade and Cooperatives	200·0	
Municipal enterprise and Housing Schemes ..	70·0	
Railway construction	225·0	
Other economic purposes	102·1	
		2057·5

2. STATE DEPARTMENTS AND INSTITUTIONS:

Commissariat for Transport	2133·4	
Commissariat for Posts and Telegraphs	190·0	
Commissariat for War	855·7	
Other Departments and Institutions of the U.S.S.R. (Central Executive Committee, Council of People's Commissaries, Commissariats for Foreign Affairs, Finance, Trade, Labour, Workers' and Peasants' Inspection, Supreme Economic Council, Central Statistical Bureau, State Planning Commission, State Political Administration[1]) ..	283·1	
Departments and Institutions of the federated republics (Executive Committees of the republics, People's Commissariats for Home Affairs, Justice, Public Health, Agriculture, Education, Social Insurance, etc.)	566·8	
		4029·0

3. SPECIAL FUNDS	206·8
4. EXPENDITURE FOR STATE LOANS	293·0
5. SUMS TRANSFERRED TO THE LOCAL BUDGET	999·8
6. EXPENDITURE OF THE AUTONOMOUS REPUBLICS ..	95·4
7. STATE RESERVE FUND	50·0
Total Expenditure	7731·5

[1] Formerly the Cheka.

of economic life. In this country where industry and trade are nationalised, the revenue from State property and State enterprises forms only a small proportion of the general revenue!

(In Percentages of the Total Revenue shown in the Budget.)

	1925/26.	1926/27.	1927/28.	1928/29.
1. Taxes	73·8	73·2	67·2	67·8
2. Sources of revenue other than taxes (Transport and Posts and Telegraphs not included)	19·9	18·2	16·9	15·9
3. State loans	5·3	8·2	14·8	14·3
4. Carried over from the previous year	1·0	0·4	1·1	2·0
Net totals	100·0	100·0	100·0	100·0

The revenue from the State property and the State enterprises (transport not included), that is to say the revenue derived from the whole of the nationalised industries, the banks, commerce, and the exploitation of natural resources, was for the year 1924–1925, 347 millions of roubles; for the year 1925–1926, 532 millions of roubles; for the year 1926–1927, 670 millions of roubles; for the year 1927–1928, 806·8 millions of roubles; and for the year 1928–1929, it is estimated at 893·1 millions of roubles—about 16 per cent of all the revenue. We have to note that the revenue from these sources remains very low, notwithstanding the fact that the high prices charged for industrial products extract very large sums from the population. Year after year, the balance sheet of the transport system shows a deficit, the amount having to be made good from the State resources being 63 millions of roubles in the year 1927–1928; and according to the estimates for 1928–1929, the deficit on transport will be 89·9 millions of roubles. All these figures combine to show that the methods by which the Soviet State is managing the economic life of the country are extremely unsatisfactory. But even these figures give an illusory impression, unless we also take into account the expenditure column, and note that year after year huge sums are paid for the requirements of industry, trade, and electrification. The State enterprises are not paying concerns; their conduct represents a loss for the Soviet economy as a whole; the deficits upon them having to be made up chiefly out of the funds obtained by taxation.

It is usual, of course, in capitalist countries, to find that the receipts from taxation constitute the main sources of revenue; but as far as Soviet Russia is concerned, this circumstance has a peculiar meaning, in view of the radical transformation which has been effected in the social structure of the country. In the capitalist lands of the west, the working class is always fighting to transfer the main burden of taxation to the shoulders of the bourgeoisie, which has enormous amounts of capital and income at its disposal. In Russia, since the expropriations of the period 1917 to 1920, the great capitalists and the middle class, those who comprise the bourgeoisie in other lands, have practically disappeared. The State has taken their place. But if the State enterprises do not pay, if they have to be financed by continually renewed investments, the shifting of the burden of taxation from the shoulders of the mass of the population is impossible.

The table on page 252 shows the direct taxes of the U.S.S.R., and what proportion each tax contributes to the whole:

Indirect taxation, that levied upon articles of consumption and that levied by means of customs dues, has increased even more rapidly. The revenue derived from this source was 308·1 millions of roubles in 1923–1924; 609·7, in 1924–1925; 992·1, in 1925–1926; 1365·07, in 1926–1927; 1632, in 1927–1928; and according to the estimates it will be 1890 millions of roubles in 1928–1929.

Most of the indirect taxes (70–80 per cent) fall upon articles of consumption. In the year 1927–1928, the taxation of articles of mass consumption (tea, sugar, coffee, salt, matches, and textiles) brought in 610 millions of roubles, and according to the estimates for 1928–1929, the revenue from this source during the current year is to be 650 millions of roubles. The revenue from the vodka monopoly was 705 millions of roubles in 1927–1928, and is expected in the year 1928–1929 to reach the amount of 795 millions of roubles, a sum almost equal to the total revenue from the other State enterprises and State property. Vodka is becoming a more and more important source of national revenue—while, as before the war, it wreaks devastation in the economic, social, and cultural life of the country. According to the calculations of the State Planning Commission, the consumption of vodka per head of population increased from 0·6 of a bottle[1] in the year 1924–1925, to 6·5 bottles in the year 1927–1928; and the Five Year Plan looks for an increase in the consumption to 9·5 bottles per head of population by the year 1930–1931.

DIRECT TAXES
(*In Millions of Roubles.*)

	1923/24.	1924/25.	1925/26.	1926/27.	1927/28.[4]	1928/29.[5]
Unified agricultural tax	231·0	326·2	251·8	300·6	350·0	400·0
Business tax	113·1	157·3	229·2	290·5	745·0[6]	1005·0[6]
Income tax	64·1	94·3	151·4	168·1	232·0	272·0
Special tax	—	14·5	1·1	—	—	—
Super tax on profits[2] ..	—	—	1·5	7·5	—	—
Land tax[3]	0·8	2·7	5·9	6·0	23·0	23·3
Other direct taxes ..	1·1	0·4	0·3	0·6	—	—
Totals	410·1	595·4	641·2	773·3	1350·0	1700·3

[1] One bottle is a little more than an English pint of 20 fluid ounces.
[2] This super tax is levied on the profits made by private employers.
[3] By a decree under date September 12, 1923, town land and the strips of land lying along the railways are subjected to a land tax. The State enterprises, too, have to pay the land tax, although at a very moderate rate. Peasant farms are not subject to the land tax.
[4] Provisional figures.
[5] Estimates.
[6] In the year 1927–1928, the business tax was levied jointly for the State budget and the local budget, and the whole sum was assigned to the revenues of the U.S.S.R. That explains the sudden increase in the revenue from the business tax for this year. From 1928–1929 onwards, the business tax has been reorganised. Absorbing various other taxes previously levied, it has now become a unified tax upon the turnover of a business.

Very little can be gleaned from Russian economic literature concerning the problem of the way in which the burden of taxation is borne by various strata of society. The data published by the People's Commissariat for Finance are contradictory; the State Planning Commission pays no heed to the problem in its "Control Figures"; and the information given in the works of individual authors is of a casual and often of a tendentious nature. The most trustworthy enquiries into the distribution of the burden of taxation which have been made are by two members of the People's Commissariat for Finance, P. Mikeladze[1] and V. Strogy,[2] who have been engaged in an enquiry into this topic for several years.

The following table, showing the distribution of the burden of taxation (both direct and indirect, and municipal as well as national) has been compiled from the data of the Department for Taxation,[3] and from the articles mentioned in the last footnotes.

	1925/26.		1926/27.	
	In Roubles per Head of Population.	In Percentages of the Income.	In Roubles per Head of Population.	In Percentages of the Income.
Rural working population ..	8·43	9·96	13·20	10·81
Non-rural working population	41·89	14·24	50·87	13·84

In the U.S.S.R., no precise data have been published to show the amount of the aggregate national income, or the distribution of the population in various social strata, or the income of various social strata and of the groups of persons engaged in different kinds of occupation, or the differences between the ways in which the burden of taxation imposed by

[1] [How Taxation bears on the Non-Rural Working Population], "Vestnik Finansoff", 1927, No. 2.
[2] [How Taxation bears upon the Rural Working Population], "Vestnik Finansoff", 1925, No. 10, and 1927, No. 2.
[3] [Report of the Taxation Department of the People's Commissariat for Finance], in "Finansy i Narodnoye Hozyaistvo", 1927, No. 18.

indirect taxes falls upon various social strata in town and countryside, or upon the extent to which the burden of direct taxation can be evaded, or upon the amount of "self-taxation", etc., etc. In these circumstances, it will be obvious at the first glance that the figures in the foregoing table can only be approximate, and can only to a very restricted degree disclose the actual burden of taxation. Indeed, the above-quoted authors, Mikeladze and Strogy, admit this frankly. Still, the general trend of the tax policy of the Soviet government as regards the non-rural working population is disclosed plainly enough by the figures.

Much more complicated is the problem of the burden of taxation as regards the rural population. In the first place, the rural population of the U.S.S.R. has to pay what is equivalent to a supplementary tax owing to the high price of industrial products and the low price of agricultural products (the "scissors"). Furthermore, it is extremely difficult to make a valid comparison between the burden of taxation upon the rural working population and the non-rural working population respectively. A mere juxtaposition of the figures showing the average height of taxation and its relation to the incomes of the respective strata does not give us the information we want, for the reason that Russian agrarian production is carried on under conditions approximating to those of a natural economy.

For instance, according to the calculations of Mikeladze, in the year 1925–1926, an urban worker was taxed to the amount of 12 per cent of his net income, and a peasant to the amount of 10 per cent. We must remember, however, that the gross taxation of the workers during this year was very much higher, seeing that the average annual income of a worker was 284 roubles, and that of a peasant 85 roubles. This problem of the burden of taxation in the U.S.S.R. needs for its elucidation far more concrete and far more precise methods of comparison.

Notwithstanding the lack of detailed information, it is obvious that the burden of taxation is now very high. According to data published by Professor P. Genzel,[1] in the year 1913 the burden of taxation per head of population was 11·18 roubles, this being 11·17 per cent of the income per head of population. By the year 1926–1927, the burden of taxation had already exceeded that of pre-war days, and it increased yet further in 1927–1928.

In fact, the burden of taxation in the U.S.S.R. has nearly reached the limit. In the [Control Figures for 1927–1928], we find the following remarks, based upon a study of the budget of 1926–1927: "When we consider the revenue for the year 1926–1927, we come to the conclusion that in the immediate future there can be no reason for introducing new taxes, or for increasing the amount of extant taxes or tariffs. The lessons of the recent increases, made in the interests of the budget of 1926–1927, convince us that the financial system is strained very nearly to the uttermost, if not quite." Nevertheless, in the year 1927–1928, as we have already learned, additional taxation was imposed upon private traders in the towns, and upon the rich peasants and upon the middle peasants in the countryside, by the introduction of "self-taxation" and "individual taxation". (See above, in Chapter Ten and Chapter Eleven.)

The drying-up of the sources of taxation has compelled the Soviet government to consider the possibility of increasing the borrowing operations of the State. Until a few years ago, the Soviet loans were not loans in the ordinary sense of the term. First of all, the main contributions to the loans took the form of forced subscriptions by the State and cooperative industrial and trading enterprises, this signifying that the loans did not mean any influx of fresh funds into the channels of the State finances, but only a redistribution of funds as between the various organs of the State. Down to the year 1927–1928, most of the Russian State loans were of this character.

But in the beginning of the year 1925, the method of compulsory subscription to State loans was extended by demanding

---

[1] [Taxation in the U.S.S.R.], published by the People's Commissariat for Finance, Moscow, 1926, p. 21.

such subscriptions, not only from the State cooperative organisations, but also from the workers and employees. Various methods of securing the desired subscriptions were used, ranging from the payment of a part of wages and salaries in loan scrip, to the levying of collective subscriptions from the working staffs of enterprises by "resolutions" passed by the workers' committees.

Of course, this compulsory method of raising loans had a very bad effect upon their financial yield. People wished to rid themselves as speedily as possible of loan scrip which they had taken against their will, and the effective value of the State loans soon fell to 40 per cent of the nominal value. Each new loan was encountered by a more vigorous resistance, and the population gradually learned how to avoid subscribing.

These unfortunate experiences convinced the People's Commissariat for Finance that the system of compulsory loans must be abandoned; and it tried to regain the confidence of the general population, which had been shattered by the expropriations, inflations, and compulsory loans. In the organ of the Commissariat for Finance we read: "There can be no doubt that the maintenance of State credit will depend upon the renunciation of any methods of pressure (even indirect), and of measures which might be interpreted in this sense."[1]

For "educative" purposes in the years 1926 and 1927, small voluntary loans were issued, the unit of subscription being a very low one, and numerous though small lottery prizes being obtainable by lucky subscribers. Thanks to the high interest (ranging up to 30 per cent per annum) and to the prizes, it was possible, though with difficulty, to float these loans, the chief subscribers being town dwellers. Encouraged by this experience, in the same year larger loans were issued, so that the total income from loans that year amounted to 300 millions of roubles; and in the year 1927–1928, it reached 689 millions of roubles. According to the estimates for 1928–1929, the State revenue from loans is to be 740 millions of roubles.

[1] "Finansy i Narodnoye Hozyaistvo", 1927, No. 21.

The total national debt amounted to 1019 millions of roubles[1] on March 1, 1928. Out of this sum only 500 millions of roubles was due to private persons, including the subscritions of the savings banks. The amount of loan stock directly held by private persons amounted to 350 millions of roubles. But even these subscriptions to loans are not wholly voluntary. Although from 1925 onwards the use of compulsion has formally been renounced, in actual fact a certain measure of compulsion has been retained. The raising of the loan of 200 millions for industrialisation in the year 1927 was to some extent effected by the use of compulsion (applied also to private individuals). "Under moral pressure, many workers and employees have subscribed sums out of proportion to their financial capacity", wrote Vulf, the director of the State Credit Department of the Commissariat for Finance.[2] Coercion was more openly practised in raising the loans of the year 1928. The "swing to the left" was making itself felt in the financial domain as well as elsewhere. When the village authorities were being ordered to supply certain quantities of grain, they were also told to subscribe certain sums to the peasants' loan. In actual practice, contributions to the loan were secured by way of assessment. The upshot was that the loans to a considerable extent represented new taxes, which differed only in externals from ordinary taxes. In a word, the levying of compulsory loans had been resumed, and in this way the laborious efforts on the part of the Commissariat for Finance during previous years to restore the confidence of the population were to a great extent rendered nugatory.

Since the first loan of 1922, the Soviet government has, down to the year 1928, raised nineteen loans, totalling a sum of 2220 millions of roubles. The cost of raising this money has been enormous. Down to the year 1924, it amounted to from

---

On January 1, 1914, the national debt, as far as home loans were concerned, was 4735 millions of roubles. After the communist revolution, the old national debts were annulled.
[2] "Finansy i Narodnoye Hozyaistvo", 1928, No. 4.

40 to 50 per cent of the loan, and only of late has it sunk to from 13 to 15 per cent.

The amount of the national debt on October 1st, in various years, is shown in the following table:

Year.				Millions of Roubles.
1922	..	..	..	..	2·5
1923	..	..	..	..	118·2
1924	..	..	..	..	244·8
1925	..	..	..	..	367·3
1926	..	..	..	..	417·3
1927	..	..	..	..	741·1
1928	..	..	..	..	1210·7

We see that the increase in the debt has been rapid. In September 1928, the government issued a new loan, amounting to 500 millions of roubles, the proceeds being intended mainly for industrialisation. When the first loan was issued, the government promised that it should not be made compulsory. Most of the loans, including the last, have been lottery loans.

The floating of loans in the U.S.S.R. is a very difficult and complicated task. The trouble does not arise only because the confidence of the population has been shaken by compulsory loans. The main reason for the difficulty is that the accumulation of capital in town and countryside goes on very slowly, and that the process of accumulation is hindered by the policy of the Soviet government towards the comparatively well-to-do members of the population.

Turning to consider the expenditure side of the budget, we are at once struck by the large amounts disbursed in order to finance economic life. In the year 1925–1926, the State spent 782·6 millions of roubles on this account; in the year 1926–1927, 1207·5 millions of roubles; in the year 1927–1928, 1316·4 millions of roubles; and according to the estimates for the year 1928–1929, the sum will be 2055·8 millions of roubles. The items under other heads in the estimates for 1928–1929 really belong to this section, so that the financing of the national economy this year will demand, in round figures, two and a half milliards of roubles, this being one-third of the total expenditure. It was inevitable that the industrialisation of Russia should impose a considerable burden upon the State finances. But in Soviet Russia, owing to the inadequate accumulation of capital, the small influx of foreign credit, poor harvests, and the sluggish payment of taxes, the government has often been compelled to finance economic life with the aid of note issues, and this practice, as we have learned, has frequently led to inflation of the currency.

The item of national defence plays a considerable part in the budget expenditure. In the year 1924–1925, the amount under this head was 435 millions of roubles; in 1926–1927, it had risen to 692 millions of roubles; and in the estimates for 1927–1928, the sum assigned to military purposes was 813 millions of roubles, being 13·5 per cent of the aggregate expenditure. If we exclude the expenditure upon the transport system from the budget, the share of expenditure upon purposes of national defence rises to 21·5 per cent. This, being a fifth of the available resources, is a very heavy burden on economic life.

Down to the year 1924–1925, the expenditure upon the political police (G.P.U.) and the troops under their command ("troops with a special function") was not disclosed in the budget. We must assume that this item was financed by deductions from other departments, or out of a special fund not included in the estimates. From 1925–1926 onwards, the expenditure on the political police has been included in the budget, amounting for that year and for 1926–1927, to 38 millions of roubles each year, and for the year 1927–1928, to 47 millions of roubles, an additional sum of 57 millions being required for the "troops with a special function".

The campaign for the reduction of administrative expenses has had an effect in moderating the increase in this item of the budget. The State budget and the local budget taken together, in the year 1926–1927 had amounted to 832 millions of roubles; but in the year 1927–1928, to only 780 millions of roubles. Nevertheless, owing to the bureaucratic nature of the Soviet apparatus, the item remains a very large one.

A positive acquirement in the budget is the growth of the expenditure upon social and cultural purposes (schools, popular education, hygiene, social insurance). The expenditure for these purposes (including the local budgets, in which it is mainly comprised) amounted in the year 1924–1925, to 521·3 millions of roubles; in 1925–1926, to 738·4 millions of roubles; in 1926–1927, to 940 millions of roubles; and in the year 1927–1928 (according to the estimates), to 1071·6 millions of roubles. The sum allotted to elementary education was 635·1 millions of roubles in 1926–1927, and 833·5 millions of roubles in 1927–1928. Per head of population this amounts to 5·55 roubles; or calculated in commodity roubles to 3·15 roubles, whereas the budgetary expenditure for educational purposes in the year 1913 was, in the combined budget, only 2·13 roubles per head of population. No doubt in pre-war days, both in the domain of education and in that of public health, the State expenditure was supplemented by considerable expenditure on the part of various organisations and individuals. Still, the taxpayer has to-day more attention paid to his social and cultural needs by the State than was paid to them in pre-war days. But the funds are insufficient to satisfy the popular needs. The introduction of universal compulsory schooling, the establishment of a comprehensive public-health service, and the enlargement of the scope of social insurance, are hindered by the scarcity of means in the local budget and the State budget.

The budget of the U.S.S.R. is unfavourably affected by the lack of an influx of foreign capital. All the funds to meet the diversified State expenditure, and to finance the performance of the complicated tasks undertaken by the Soviet government, have to be provided from home sources.

During recent years, the estimates have been published by the People's Commissariat for Finance, and are submitted for approval to the Budget Committee and to the plenum of the Central Executive Committee; but there is no detailed public discussion of the estimates, such as takes place in the parliaments of most modern countries. Nor is there any proper auditing of

State expenditure. The lack of public control makes it very difficult to ascertain what is really done with public funds. We do not know, for instance, what use is made of the reserve fund of the Council of People's Commissaries (125 millions of roubles in the year 1927–1928), and of the special reserve of the Union (50 millions of roubles). When we consider the budget of the U.S.S.R., we are faced with many unsolved problems. Whence come the millions expended by the Comintern and the Communist Party of the U.S.S.R.? Why have there never been any accounts published concerning the expenditure of the sums obtained by the confiscation of ecclesiastical property?

Even under the tsars, there was in latter days, after the establishment of the Duma, more public control of the use of State funds than there is to-day, and more trustworthy accounts were issued.

Russia has relapsed into the conditions of long ago, into the conditions of the eighteenth century, when one of the financial advisers of the Russian government, Lyuberas, made the following characteristic declaration regarding the publication of accounts: "In order that the secrets of State finance may be kept, only privy councillors in the strict sense of the term must be allowed access to financial information."[1] Just as in eighteenth-century imperial Russia, so in the U.S.S.R. to-day, the masses of the people are not "allowed access to financial information".

[1] [Memorial concerning the Formation of a Finance Committee.]

CHAPTER FOURTEEN

THE HOUSING PROBLEM

ONE of the most important obstacles to the effective industrialisation of the Soviet Union and to the general cultural
and social advance of the country, is the housing shortage.
The lack of housing accommodation, high rents, and
overcrowding of the unhealthy working-class habitations,
were already in tsarist days characteristic of the proletarian
quarters of the towns. During the war, owing to the cessation
of building, the situation in this respect changed for the worse.
After the communist revolution, in almost all the large centres
of population, there was in practice a communalisation of
private houses effected in accordance with resolutions of the
local Soviet authorities. Members of the bourgeoisie were
compulsorily expelled from their quarters, and the evacuated
premises were handed over to workers and Soviet employees.
The abuses which followed upon this disorderly reassignment
of housing accommodation, and the absence of any authority
to deal with housing problems, induced the Soviet government
to extend its formal sanction to the communalisation of houses,
and on August 20, 1918, there was issued a decree "for the
abolition of private property in urban dwellings". By the terms
of this decree, only very small houses were left in the hands
of the sometime owners. The soviets were to appoint housing
and land departments whose business it would be to control
the whole matter, and to allot free housing accommodation.
The State prescribed the amount of floor space to be allowed
per person. Vacant rooms, and even the spare parts of already
inhabited houses, were assigned to new tenants, the working
elements of the population being given a preference. Rents
were likewise specified, but owing to the extreme depreciation
of the currency, and in accordance with the general spirit of
the period of war communism, on January 27, 1921, the
payment of houserent was abolished.

The housing policy of the period of war communism was certainly one calculated to fulfil the natural desire of the working masses for the abolition of the previously existing gross inequality in the distribution of housing accommodation, but its result was only to accentuate the intensity of the housing crisis, and to lead to a rapid diminution of the available accommodation. Amid the general decay of economic life, no attempt was made to build new houses, or to keep existing ones in proper repair, while the practice of continually shifting the tenants from house to house deprived them of all interest in taking care of their rooms. Houses that happened to be empty were torn down, and the wood in them was used as fuel, while others fell to pieces.

According to the housing census of 1923, of the 2·6 millions of inhabited houses which had existed in the year 1913 within the area now comprising the U.S.S.R., 316,000 had by the date of the census fallen down or become uninhabitable, this amounting to about 12 per cent of the whole.

The end of the policy of war communism was attended by a radical change in the housing policy of the State. Small houses [1] were decommunalised, and a number of decrees were issued restricting the right of expulsion. Rents were reintroduced. From 1923 onwards, the State began to undertake the repair of old houses and the building of new ones. Decrees were issued allowing private persons to build small houses, but making it incumbent upon the house-owners to leave part of the floor space of the new houses available to the State, and to follow the State prescriptions as regards inhabited area and rents. These measures did not suffice to relieve the housing shortage, which became more acute year by year.

The intensity of the trouble is above all dependent upon the increase in population. Whereas in the year 1913, the population of Russia was 139·7 millions, by 1927–1928 it had increased

[1] In the provinces, a small house is one with a floor space of not more than 25 square sazhenes (a sazhene being approximately 7 feet); in Moscow and Leningrad it is a house containing not more than five tenants.

to 149·6 millions. The urban population, which in the year 1913 had been 25·7 millions, had in the year 1927–1928 grown to 26·9 millions. During the last three years, the average increase in the entire population of the U.S.S.R., has been 2·3 per cent per annum, and that of the urban population 5·6 per cent per annum. The rural areas, whose economic advance is hindered by the policy of the Soviet government, flood the towns with the surplus population for which there is no occupation in the countryside.

An additional and hardly less important factor of the trouble is that during the period of war communism there was a decrease in the area of habitable floor space amounting to about 20 per cent, and a yet further decline during the first four years of the Nep.

(In Millions of Pre-war Roubles.)

Year.					Aggregate Value of Dwelling-houses.
1913	..	..	..	..	10,008
1922/23 ..	..	..	..	..	7960
1923/24 ..	..	..	..	..	7728
1924/25 ..	..	..	..	..	7631
1925/26 ..	..	..	..	..	7593
1926/27 ..	..	..	..	..	7643

During the first years of the Nep, very few new houses were built, and it was not always possible to repair the old houses soon enough to save them from destruction.

The present condition of the available housing accommodation in the U.S.S.R. is shown clearly enough by the results of the census of 1926, the last housing census. The total number of inhabited houses in the towns of the Soviet Union at that time was 2,882,000, with a floor space of 154 millions of square metres. In these houses, there were 4,526,000 tenements, and 27,000 communal homes (including hospitals, prisons, and boarding schools). There were in all 9,012,000 living rooms, and 3,133,000 kitchens.

The census showed that there was very great overcrowding. Owing to the shortage of housing accommodation, the governmental allowance of floor space per head of population has been fixed at 8 square metres, which is far less than the amount regarded as hygienically essential. But in actual practice, the average allowance of floor space is less even than this, and declines year by year. In the year 1924-1925, the average floor space per head of population in the towns of the U.S.S.R. was 6·1 square metres; in the year 1926-1927, it was only 5·6 square metres; and in the year 1927-1928, it had fallen to 5·5 square metres. According to the building schemes of the State Planning Commission, and taking into account the prospects of private building as well as public, the inhabited floor space per head of population will attain 5·7 square metres in the year 1931-1932.[1] In the industrial centres, according to the census of 1926, the floor space per head is even smaller. For instance, in Ivanovo-Voznesensk, one of the main centres of the textile industry, it is only 4·3 square metres per head; and in Sormovo and Izhevsk, centres of the metal industry, it is only from 4·6 and to 4 square metres respectively.

The scarcity of housing accommodation in the U.S.S.R. becomes even more obvious when, instead of talking about the floor space per head of population, we use the system of calculation common in other European countries, that is to say when we consider the ratio between the number of families and the number of tenements, and between the number of persons to be housed and the number of rooms. On the average, in the towns of the U.S.S.R., there are 168·7 families per 100 tenements. The density of urban population implied by these figures is indicated by the fact that in Germany there are 108·2 families to every 100 tenements [2]—although, as every one knows, there is a great scarcity of housing accommodation in modern German cities. And whereas, when we consider the average of all towns in the U.S.S.R., the ratio of families to tenements is more than 3 to 2, matters are still worse in the very large towns, for we find that in Kharkov there is only one

[1] "Planovoye Hozyaistvo", 1928, No. 1.
[2] "Wirtschaft und Statistik", 1927, No. 16.

tenement for every two families, in Leningrad only one for every two and a half families, and in Moscow only one for every three. The numbers of inhabitants per room is two on the average, including large and small dwellings; but when we consider exclusively the small one-roomed tenements inhabited by the poorest strata of the population, we find much more serious overcrowding, for in these there are often as many as four inhabitants per room.[1]

The scarcity of housing accommodation, overcrowding, and its unwholesome consequences, are especially conspicuous in the large towns and in the industrial centres. The difficulties that are thus placed in the way of the government's policy of industrialisation deserve special consideration. Industrial reconstruction, and, above all, the building of new factories, are made very much more expensive than they otherwise would be, since when a new factory is built it is likewise necessary to erect new habitations, or in some way or another to provide quarters for the workers. The adoption of a two-shift or three-shift system leads to terrible overcrowding. Nine out of ten of the decisions of the economic planning authorities relating to the construction of new factories in the regions where raw materials are elaborated and fuel is provided, are never carried out, mainly for the reason that there is not a sufficiency of vacant dwellings in the areas which are especially suited for industrial development.

All the inhabited dwellings at present (1927–1928) existing in the U.S.S.R., may be classified in accordance with the table on page 267, as regards their ownership.

These figures show that the majority of inhabited buildings in the U.S.S.R. are owned by private persons, but that the houses which are State property are much larger than the others.

During the first period of the Nep, the Soviet government tried to have its housing schemes financed locally, by the

[1] R. Sifman [Housing Conditions in the West and in the U.S.S.R.] "Statisticheskoye Obozreniye", 1927, No. 12.

municipalities. But the extensive deficits that arose, and the increasing extent to which the houses were being allowed to fall into disrepair, forced the State to abandon this idea, and at present only 14·8 per cent of all the repairing and building of houses is undertaken by the local authorities, the rest of the work being done by the State authorities (38·7 per cent), tenants' cooperatives[1] (40·2 per cent), and individual tenants (6·3 per cent). An enquiry among the municipalities has shown that the houses left in their care are those in the worst condition. "In this respect, unquestionably, there is going on an extensive wastage of our basic capital."[2]

	Inhabited Buildings.		Floor Space. Percentages.	Particulars of Inhabited Rooms per Building. Averages.
	Absolute.	Percentages.		
State	512,100	17·8	46·2	7·3
Building and other co-operative societies..	11,200	0·4	0·8	6·4
Private persons ..	2,358,700	81·8	53·0	2·2
Totals	2,882,000	100.0	100.0	—

However, even the dwellings that are managed directly by the State, and let out on lease by the central authority, are not kept in proper repair. The deficit on the State housing fund was in the year 1923–1924, 193 millions of roubles; in the year 1924–1925, 164 millions of roubles; and in the year 1925–1926, 111 millions of roubles. In the year 1926–1927, rents were raised, and the deficit was thus reduced to 49 millions of roubles.[3] Rents have twice been raised, in 1927 and 1928 respectively, owing to losses incurred by the State housing department. In Soviet Russia there is a "class system" of assessing rents,

[1] There are cooperative building societies for the building of new houses or the repairing of old ones to fit them for cooperative use. The tenants' cooperatives are societies formed among the tenants of a tenement house, which is leased to them by the municipal authorities.
[2] "Statisticheskoye Obozreniye", 1928, No. 7.
[3] V. Balaban and V. Shavran [The Problems of Financing Municipal Economy], "Vestnik Finansoff", 1927, No. 10.

in accordance with which the rent is proportional to the tenant's income. This makes things easier for the workers, but does so at the expense of the State housing enterprise in general. All over the world the houserent question is a very difficult one, for housing accommodation cannot permanently be provided at a loss, and yet rents must not be fixed at a figure beyond the financial capacity of the tenant.[1] The difficulty is especially great in the U.S.S.R., for, since the communist revolution, there has been no well-to-do class worth speaking of, and the whole burden of providing satisfactory housing accommodation has to be borne by the working masses.

On January 4, 1928, the Central Executive Committee decided that thenceforward rents were to be fixed sufficiently high to make the provision of housing accommodation a paying proposition, and that rents were to be charged even for the tenements which industrial enterprises put at the disposal of their workers. Nevertheless, the assessment of rent in proportion to a tenant's income was to be retained. No statistics are as yet available to show to what extent the new policy has been put in force. As far as information goes, it would seem that the deficit incurred by the State housing department has been somewhat reduced, but that the real wages of the workers have been proportionally depressed.

During the first years of the Nep, it was proposed to establish a State monopoly in the building of houses. The increasing scarcity of housing accommodation has made it necessary to abandon this idea. At the present time, new houses are being built, not only by the State instruments (the soviets, the industrial trusts, the transport enterprises, and various State authorities), but also by cooperatives (building societies) and by private individuals. The expenditure upon building by these

[1] The German social democracy, in its campaign against the raising of houserents, has been faced with this difficult problem of combining with the interest of the working class, due regard for the principle that housing schemes must be made to pay. Of late, the problem has likewise become very acute for the Austrian social democracy, which is doing its best to protect working-class tenants.

various sections of the community is shown in the following table:

EXPENDITURE UPON BUILDING HOUSES[1]

(In Millions of Roubles.)

	1924/25.	1925/26.	1926/27.	1927/28.
By Industrial enterprises	63·7	87·5	110·2	111·5
Transport enterprises	9·3	22·5	33·2	38·4
Soviets and other State instruments	26·6	63·2	101·0	128·9
Cooperatives..	5·9	26·5	38·6	57·0
Private persons	51·0	87·0	110·0	120·0
Totals	156·5	286·7	393·0	455·8

The soviets build houses for the urban population, and hand them over to be managed and kept in repair by the municipal authorities or by tenants' cooperatives. The industrial enterprises, transport enterprises, and State institutions, build houses for their workers and employees. The aim of allowing the formation of building societies was to mobilise the private means of workers and employees for building purposes. Such cooperative building societies had, at the beginning of the year 1928, approximately 200,000 members; but since the funds these have at their command are small, the building of houses is still mainly (about four-fifths) financed by State funds. During the last few years, the cooperative building societies have developed to become building enterprises working on commission for the State authorities.

As the foregoing table shows, private enterprise plays a considerable part in the provision of new housing accommodation. During the last four years, one quarter of all expenditure in this field was by private persons; but the importance of private enterprise in this respect is shown to be much larger when we consider, not merely the question of expenditure, but also that of the amount of habitable floor space provided. In the last four years (1924–1928) the State

[1] Control Figures for 1927–1928.

and cooperative organisations provided 6·38 millions of square metres of new habitable floor space, whereas private individuals provided 7·82 millions of square metres. While spending only one-fourth of the total capital invested in building new houses, the private builders have provided more than one-half of the new habitable floor space. The explanation of this remarkable fact is partly that State and cooperative building is far more expensive than private building, and is less thriftily conducted; but also that the housing accommodation provided by private enterprise is of an extremely primitive character, the dwellings being unsatisfactory both technically and hygienically. Furthermore, especially in small towns and in workers' settlements, private builders are saved a good deal of expense because the would-be tenants give a considerable amount of unpaid help while the building goes on.

In the U.S.S.R., the State and cooperative organisations build expensively and slowly, and, it must also be added, they build badly. The new workers' settlements, and the new workers' tenement houses in the towns, are usually in need of repair from the very first. The rooms are cold and damp, very uncomfortable, and built without any regard for the most elementary needs of the tenants. The columns of the Soviet press are full of complaints from the workers upon these matters. Such complaints are underlined by the following remarks of Shmit, the People's Commissary for Labour: "Our efforts to provide housing accommodation have not had an effect proportional to the expenditure. We have built houses without due regard to the nature of the demand. . . . We have not as yet been able to establish a normal type for the buildings, whether in respect of the way in which the work is financed, or in respect of the provision of building materials, or in respect of securing skilled workers to carry on the building operations."[1]

The experience of the provision of housing accommodation in the U.S.S.R. during recent years has shown that the State,

[1] "Vestnik Truda", 1928, No. 2.

despite its best endeavours, is not able to ensure a gradual mitigation of the housing scarcity. Nor, in existing circumstances can the building societies or the private builders cope with the difficulty. According to the calculations of the State Planning Commission, to provide the whole urban population with sufficient housing accommodation during the next five years (allowing for the growth of population and paying due heed to the minimum housing space specified as essential to health), it will be necessary to supply new floor space to the extent of 99 millions of square metres, and the cost of this will be approximately 10 milliards of roubles. When we remember that during the years 1924–1928, only 1·3 milliards of roubles were devoted to building, and that only 13·2 millions of square metres of new floor space were provided, we can readily understand that the Soviet government is eagerly trying to discover new sources from which building operations can be financed.

On August 28, 1928, a decree was issued to the effect that special privileges should be provided in this matter of house building to private capital, both Russian and foreign. Private individuals and private joint-stock companies building houses with a floor space of not less than 700 square metres in Moscow and Leningrad, and of not less than 200 square metres in other towns, are to be granted special facilities for obtaining the necessary land, and the newly-built houses are to remain under the control of the builders as private property, no matter how large the building may be. Further, the formation of private building firms to build large houses is to be allowed, without any restriction as to the number of wage workers employed on the scheme. The builders will be empowered to lease tenements or individual rooms in their houses by agreement with the tenants without any restriction as to the length of a lease or as to the amount of floor space required by an individual tenant; and in the case of such houses, the officially prescribed rent restrictions may be disregarded. The building of business premises and warehouses, and the letting of them out on lease will likewise be allowed. Moreover, in these new houses, the authorities will have no right to clear out old tenants and instal new ones. The land required for the new buildings will be leased to the builders for long terms, ranging up to 80 years. The builders will be exempt from taxation upon the income derived from the new houses, and from the obligation to pay the municipal taxes upon house property, while the land tax will in their case be reduced to 50 per cent of the usual amount. The new decree also provides that no legacy duty shall have to be paid when the new buildings and the leasehold areas on which they stand are transmitted by inheritance.

In existing circumstances, under the political conditions that now prevail in the U.S.S.R., this new decree cannot be expected to produce great results. What we have to note is, however, that it implies, not only a complete reversal of all the principles of Soviet policy, but also an unconditional abandonment of the State regulation of housing accommodation —so far as privately-owned houses are concerned.

CHAPTER FIFTEEN

LABOUR

DURING the years of the revolution, there were extensive changes in the numerical strength and in the composition of the Russian working class. Throughout the period of civil war and war communism, the proletariat was undergoing a process of rapid pulverisation, large sections of the working class being extruded from the process of production. Since most of the factories were idle, there was an exodus into the countryside on the part of all those members of the proletariat who had maintained ties with the villages, and who might hope to secure at least a subsistence in the rural districts. After the idtroduction of the Nep, and when a brief period of transition was over, a new phase in the existence of the Russian workers began. The dwindling in the number of the urban operatives soon came to an end; and, owing to the reconstruction of industry, transport, and trade, there occurred, not only a reflux into the towns of a considerable proportion of the old proletariat elements, but likewise an influx of new recruits for developing trade and industry from the proletarianised strata of town and countryside. The return of population from the open country to the town was favoured by the general backwardness of agriculture and by the over-population of the agricultural districts.

The table given on the next page shows the decline and the subsequent growth in the numbers of the wage earners and salary earners.[1]

The table shows that during the years of war communism the number of workers fell to 40 per cent of the number during 1913, but that by the year 1928, the number of workers and employees had approximately regained the pre-war level.

[1] Control Figures of the State Planning Commission for 1927–1928. A. Rabinovich [Problems of Labour in the U.S.S.R.], "Ekonomicheskoye Obozreniye", 1927, No. 10.

S

	1913.	1922/23.	1927/28.
Rural workers	3,000,000	1,000,000	2,041,000
Industrial workers ..	} 3,636,000 {	2,043,000	3,115,000
Building workers..		137,000	544,000
Trade	451,000	306,000	548,000
Transport, Posts and Telegraphs	777,000	1,185,000	1,420,000
State and Public Institutions ..	} 3,336,000[1] {	1,409,000	2,041,000
Domestic workers and workers by the day		456,000	791,000
Totals	11,200,000	6,636,000	10,500,000

As long as it was possible to continue the reconstruction of industry by using up the extant fixed capital, there was an accelerating process of enrolling labour power in industry. In the year 1925–1926, the increase in the number of wage earners was 19·8 per cent; in the year 1926–1927, the increase fell to 5·1 per cent; and in the year 1927–1928, it was only 3·8 per cent. The figures showing the increase in the number of workers engaged in large-scale State industrial enterprises tell the same story:

	Number of Workers.	Percentage Increase upon the Previous Year.
1921/22	998,600	—
1922/23	1,161,100	16·3
1923/24	1,308,700	12·8
1924/25	1,529,900	16·9
1925/26	1,919,300	25·4
1926/27	2,021,000	5·2
1927/28	2,113,000	5·2

In seven years, the number of workers employed in large-scale industry has more than doubled, so that the number of workers in large-scale industry in the year 1913 (2,518,000) has nearly been regained. But during recent years the speed

[1] Before the war, the domestic workers and the workers by the day were not separately itemised in the statistical tables.

of increase in the number of workers has fallen off greatly. Even in the year 1927–1928 there was very little increase, notwithstanding the introduction of a third shift in the textile industries, the reason being that simultaneously in these industries there was a speeding-up of the labour process.

During the years of war and revolution, there was also a notable change in the composition of the proletariat. There was a considerable increase in the proportion of workers in small-scale industries and petty enterprise, of commercial employees and of State employees. There was, on the other hand, a decline in the number of skilled workers of the old kind. The proletarianisation of urban strata consisting of persons who had until recently belonged to the possessing classes, and the new process of differentiation in the countryside, have contributed to supply to the working class a great number of recruits who were not class conscious and had had no technical education of any kind.

During the war, a great many women were enrolled in the process of production. In 1913, 33·3 per cent of industrial workers were of the female sex, and in 1916 the proportion of women had risen to 39·9. By the end of 1917, the proportion of female industrial workers had increased to a considerably greater extent. After the end of the war, although Soviet legislation aimed at favouring the retention of women in industry, there was an increase in the proportion of men engaged in the process of production. A decisive factor in this movement has been that the Soviet legislation for the protection of working women makes their labour dearer than that of men, with the result that the cost of production increases as the proportion of female workers in an enterprise grows. In practice, therefore, unless the wages of women can be forced down, female labour is replaced by male. The proportion of women among the workers in large-scale and medium-scale industry was 29·7 in the year 1923, and had fallen to 28·7 in the year 1928.[1] These figures must not be uncritically

[1] "Statisticheskoye Obozreniye", 1928, No. 7.

compared with those relating to the proportional employment of women workers in war time and before the war, for the scope of the various enterprises considered in the statistics has changed. A. Rashin, a Soviet statistician, who has made calculations relating to enterprises of like scale before, during, and after the war, comes to the conclusion that the percentage employment of working women in industry is somewhat higher to-day than it was before the war, but is considerably lower than it was during the war period.[1]

The number of workers under eighteen years of age has fallen off considerably. Whereas in the year 1913, 10·6 per cent of all industrial workers were under eighteen, and whereas the proportion had increased to 14·3 in the year 1917, it fell to 6·5 in the year 1923, to 5·7 in 1927, and to 4·7 in 1928. The reason why there was so large a percentage of child labour during the war and in pre-war days was that the employment of the cheap labour of youthful workers was extremely profitable to the employer. From this outlook the falling-off in the number of workers under eighteen is certainly a phenomenon upon which Soviet Russia can be congratulated; but it assumes a somewhat different aspect when we contemplate it from the outlook of occupational training, and from that of the reproduction of skilled labour power. The possibilities of technical training outside the actual productive process are so small in the Soviet Union that the State has found it necessary to prescribe, by legislation, that there shall be a certain minimum of workers under eighteen engaged in particular branches of industry. In practice, moreover, owing to economic pressure, and as an outcome of the desire to lower the cost of production, this minimum has often been disregarded.

The problem of the reproduction of skilled labour power has become a very serious one for Russian industry. Even before the war, there was a great scarcity of skilled workers in Russia, and very little was done in the way of technical education. Of late years, not only has there been a further decline in

[1] [Women's Labour in the U.S.S.R.], 1928, p. 11.

the number of skilled workers, but there is not taking place any reproduction of skilled labour power competent to keep pace with the natural wastage. According to the calculations of the Supreme Economic Council, the loss of skilled labour power from death is so extensive that within the next five years at least half a million new skilled workers must be provided to make good this loss and to cope with the demand that will arise from the expansion of production. But in quite a number of branches of industry (metal work, coalmining, electrical undertakings, textiles, chemical work, building, etc.) there are no reserves of skilled workers, or none to speak of. With the best will in the world, and with the utmost effort, it seems likely that only three-fourths of the requisite skilled workers will be forthcoming, even if the term "skilled" be interpreted in a very liberal sense.

Technical education and occupational training in the U.S.S.R. are most unsatisfactory, both quantitatively and qualitatively. Every one knows that there are very few technical schools, that the courses of instruction are too short, that for the most part technical training must be left to the foremen in the various enterprises, that there is a great lack of preliminary training in theory, and that a very low standard of skill has to pass current. For these reasons, as far as concerns the program of industrialisation and the need for rationalising production, the problem of the scarcity of skilled labour power is almost as serious as the problem of the exhaustion of the reserves of fixed capital.

Notwithstanding the extreme scarcity of skilled workers in certain branches of production, Russia is afflicted with an unemployment problem of increasing gravity, the out-of-works being mainly unskilled workers and employees. The characteristics of unemployment in Soviet Russia are quite different from those of the unemployment among industrial workers in other lands, for in Russia unemployment is not due to a restriction of the basis of production as the outcome of a crisis of over-production or of a depression of trade. In Russia, since the introduction of the Nep, there has been a fairly steady increase in production, with a concomitant increase in the number of workers engaged, and nevertheless unemployment has increased more and more rapidly:

(In Percentages of the Previous Year.)

	Increase in the Number at Work.	Increase in the Number of Unemployed.
1925/26	25·4	25
1926/27	5·2	33
1927/28	5·2	34

The main cause of this phenomenon is that, owing to the levelling-down of ownership in the urban population, the number of persons seeking occupation as wage workers has considerably increased. Above all, that is why there are so many out-of-works among the employees and the young workers. But there is also going on a steady influx into the towns of peasants who can no longer find work on the land, and this results in a continuous increase in the number of the unemployed. Agriculture, as we have already learned, is unable to provide nourishment for the increase in the rural population, and for that reason millions of peasants seek bread and work in the towns. According to the census of 1926, year by year about a million peasants in want of work drift into the towns, and some of the newcomers elbow the urban operatives out of the process of production. The government does what it can to prevent this influx. Sometimes persons seeking work are directly forbidden to enter the towns; sometimes the labour bureaus refuse to register peasants in search of employment. But such expedients can have no lasting effect. The number of unemployed registered at various dates at the labour bureaus is shown in the table on the next page.[1]

The actual number of unemployed is not known.[2] The trade

[1] "Pravda", September 20, 1928.
[2] In the Control Figures of the State Planning Commission for 1927–1928,

unions register only unemployed trade unionists; the insurance
bureaus register only the unemployed who are entitled to
unemployed benefit; the labour bureaus register only the
unemployed who are entitled to registration. A comparison
of the figures published by these authorities with the published
estimates made by various Soviet notables shows that the

October 1, 1925	..	..	..	920,400
April 1, 1926	..	..	..	1,056,500
October 1, 1926	..	..	..	1,070,800
April 1, 1927	..	..	..	1,477,900
October 1, 1927	..	..	..	1,041,000
April 1, 1928	..	..	..	1,596,000

actual extent of unemployment must be from 30 to 40 per
cent higher than the figures given by the labour bureaus.
According to these latter, the total number of unemployed in
the U.S.S.R. was from 1·0 to 1·3 millions in the year 1926–
1927, whereas in the same year the trade unions reported that
the unemployed among their members numbered 1·6 millions.
According to the State Planning Commission, there were
1·7 millions of unemployed in 1926–1927, and more than
2 millions in 1927–1928. But even these last figures must be
regarded as understatements.

Interesting data regarding unemployment in the years 1925
and 1926 have been published by L. Mints.[1] Among the
unemployed, 17·1 per cent were skilled and semi-skilled
industrial workers; 19·6 per cent were brain workers; and
55·1 per cent were unskilled workers and persons who had not
previously been wage earners. The proportion of women
was 48 per cent, and that of young persons under eighteen
was 13·1 per cent. Most of the unemployed were fairly young,
44 per cent being under 25, 38 per cent being at ages between

we read: "An analysis of the state of unemployment is rendered difficult
because the registration of unemployment is incomplete and untrustworthy"
(p. 212). The Supreme Economic Council, in [The Five Year Plan for the
Development of Industry], declares: "Unfortunately we have no accurate
statistics of unemployment, so that we are not in a position to say how
many unemployed there are" (p. 67).
[1] [The Present State of Unemployment], "Statisticheskoye Obozreniye",
1927, No. 3.

25 and 40, and 18 per cent being over 40. The figures for 1927 give similar results. Among the unemployed, the percentage of persons who have come to the towns from the countryside is very large, varying from month to month between 15 and 32 per cent. On the whole, however, the figures show that a very large majority of the registered unemployed belong to the urban population.

One of the greatest acquirements of the revolution was the introduction of the eight-hour day. A shorter working day had been one of the main demands of the Russian proletariat in the class struggle under tsarism, and for this reason the need for an eight-hour day was insisted on in resolutions passed by various local revolutionary bodies in the early months after the March revolution of 1917, and the eight-hour day was actually introduced in most large-scale enterprises. On November 11/24, 1917, that is to say almost immediately after the November revolution, the Soviet government made an eight-hour day legal for all wage earners, thus adopting with certain modifications a law that had already been drafted by the Provisional Government. Before the revolution, the working day in most industrial enterprises had been ten hours, as prescribed by law; but in handicraft, small-scale industry, and commerce, there was no legal limit to the working day. The Soviet government's decree, while fixing the working day for adults at eight hours, prescribed a working day of six hours for young persons from 16 to 18. For underground workers, a working day of six hours was also prescribed. In the case of children under 16, the working time was not to exceed four hours. At the All-Russian Trade Union Congress in December 1928, it was stated in one of the reports that for children the prescribed limit was often exceeded: "Of children, 35 per cent work six hours instead of four!" [1] For employees and brain workers, the working day was to be six hours. The general rule in modern Russian industry is that the working day does not exceed eight hours, but there are many exceptions.

[1] "Pravda", December 21, 1928.

Of late years, in industry, overtime has been common, so common that in many branches it has become practically normal. According to the reports of the Central Council of Trade Unions, in the year 1926 overtime represented 2·4 per cent of the whole working time. In the petroleum industry, 55 per cent of all the workers worked overtime; in the metal industry, 4·1 per cent; in the chemical industry, 37 per cent; in the coalmines, 20 per cent.[1] A number of enquiries have shown that the official statistics underestimate the extent to which overtime is worked. Besides, various decrees have been passed allowing a disregard of the eight-hour day in the building industry, in agriculture, and in other seasonal occupations.

In certain respects the Soviet State still remains revolutionary, and one indication of this is afforded by the maintenance of the eight-hour day in industry. There are, however, economic factors also at work here, and especially the need for restricting as far as possible the growth of unemployment. Inasmuch as the State is not only the monopolist of industry, but is also responsible for relieving the pressure of unemployment, it is compelled to maintain the eight-hour principle. Furthermore, the main object of the Soviet government as employer must be to make the utmost possible use of its machinery and technical equipment (of which it has an inadequate supply, and which would be extremely costly to replace), while showing moderation in the exploitation of labour power (of which there is a superfluity, and which is comparatively cheap). That is why the State, as employer, aims, not at increasing the length of the working day, but at speeding-up the labour process, and at increasing the number of shifts. Actuated by these considerations, in the beginning of the year 1928 a three-shift system was introduced for about 22 per cent of the workers in the cotton industry, and for about 7 per cent of the workers in the woollen industry. The strike movement of 1925–1926 showed that such attempts at speeding-up labour are apt to lead to acute dissatisfaction among the workers. The State, therefore,

[1] "Torgovo-Promyshlennaya Gazeta", June 8, 1927.

when the three-shift system involving night work was introduced in the year 1927, proposed to cut down the working day to seven hours for those who were working three shifts. In part, this proposal has now come into effect, but the reduction in the length of the working day has not sufficed to make the workers content with the inauguration of a night shift, for, under the housing conditions that prevail in the U.S.S.R., and in view of the fact that the transport system for the most part ceases operations during the night while the food shops and the children's homes and crêches are only open in the daytime, night work is extremely inconvenient for the workers —and all the more so, seeing that most of the textile workers are women.[1]

One very considerable advantage the workers have gained by the revolution is the introduction of a compulsory weekly holiday of 42 consecutive hours, and a fortnight's holiday each year for all workers and employees. But, owing to the abolition of a number of public holidays that existed in pre-war days, the working year has in practice been increased by 22 days, from 278 to 300. Allowing for the fortnightly annual holiday and the week-end holidays, the working year since the introduction of the Nep has on the average been 262 days, this being 5 days more than the average working year before the war.

The decline in the value of real wages, which had set in even during the war (a fall to from 85 to 88 per cent of the pre-war condition), became catastrophic after the November revolution, so that the real wage in money and in kind fell to 10 per cent of the pre-war standard.[2] After the introduction of the Nep, wages began to rise, and, according to official

---

[1] Both the male and the female workers in the textile industry live for the most part in barrack-like habitations, and the introduction of the third shift, with the changes of shift that take place at various hours of the day and night, leads to a perpetual noise and bustle in these dwellings, so that it is very difficult for the workers to get proper rest.

[2] S. Strumilin [Wages, and the Productivity of Labour in Russian Industry], Moscow, 1923.—For further information as to the movement of wages in the period of war communism and during the first years of the Nep, see S. Schwarz, Der Arbeitslohn und die Lohnpolitik in Russland, Jena, 1924.

data, taking industry as a whole, the pre-war level was slightly exceeded by the year 1926–1927. The following table shows, in chervonets roubles, the average monthly earnings of the workers in large-scale industry, as calculated by the Central Bureau for Labour Statistics: [1]

	1924/25.	1925/26.	1926/27.	1927/28.
Metal Industry	49·71	62·91	70·87	80·50
Textile Industry	37·32	45·30	51·35	54·68
Mining	38·34	51·97	58·05	61·57
Chemical Industry	44·06	54·23	60·38	67·13
Printing Industry	71·19	76·63	79·91	89·49
Leather Industry	60·61	70·18	78·22	85·69
Average for large-scale industry ..	43·48	54·04	60·38	66·52
Average for Moscow	65·15	74·90	81·90	88·67
Average for Provinces	39·24	49·66	55·97	61·74

In the year 1926–1927, the average real monthly wages of workers in industry amounted to 32·65 commodity roubles. Real wages in Russia are calculated with the aid of the standard-of-life index which is worked out every month on the basis of the varying prices for food, clothing, shelter, and municipal services. (See above, Chapter Eleven.) The movement of monthly real wages in percentages of what they were in 1913 is shown in the table prepared by the State Planning Commission and relating to the individual branches of industry and transport as given on the next page.

The pre-war standard of wages was regained most rapidly in those branches of industry in which before the war wages had been lowest. (For instance, before the war the textile workers and the workers in the chemical industry received only about half the wages paid to the metal workers.) There was also a comparatively quick recovery in the rate of wages in those branches of industry which were concerned with

[1] A. Rashin [Wages in the U.S.S.R. during the Reconstruction Period], published by the Central Committee of the Trade Unions, p. 11.— "Ekonomicheskoye Obozreniye", 1928, No. 9.—The figures for 1927–1928 in the relevant table are based on provisional calculations.

supplying the needs of the mass of consumers, for here reconstruction was rapid (food industry, leather industry). Recovery
was slowest in the heavy industries, in the industry of extracting
ores, in the elaboration of metals, in mining, and in the railway
services. In these branches of industry, the pre-war standard
of wages has not even yet been regained. But the piece-work
system has been very greatly extended, so that now more than
60 per cent of all the workers are on piece work. This has
led not only to an increase in wages, but also to a marked
speeding-up of labour.

REAL MONTHLY WAGES

(*In Percentages of Pre-war Roubles (1913 reckoned as 100).*)

	1924/25.	1925/26.	1926/27.
Metal Industry	67·5	77·4	86·9
Textile Industry	102·3	111·9	129·2
Mining	55·5	71·1	81·1
Chemical Industry	104·9	116·9	130·5
Leather Industry	116·4	122·0	136·8
Paper Industry	115·3	126·3	134·4
Food Industry	141·4	143·5	154·2
Timber Industry	97·6	102·3	108·8
Average for large-scale industry ..	82·6	93·7	105·3
Railway Services	59·2	74·9	82·5

There are still a good many departments of small-scale
industry and petty industry in which the standard of wages
is considerably lower than in pre-war days. On the whole,
however, it must be admitted that the average height of real
wages, when due allowance is made for all the social and municipal services, such as the reduction of rents, of municipal
taxation, etc., has during the last two years (1927 and 1928)
been stabilised at a level somewhat above that of pre-war days.
The communists declare that this has been a great achievement
of the Soviet system. It is hard to say what right they have
to plume themselves on the fact that after ten years of revolution
and after private capitalism has been put out of action, the

workers should at length be once more earning wages as great as those which, despite an incredible degree of exploitation, they were earning under the tsarist regime.

The pre-war level of production has been regained, and so has the pre-war level of wages. Both these things are a common-place of post-war days all over Europe, and there can therefore be no reason for regarding them as peculiar achievements of the Soviet system. There is all the more reason for this criticism seeing that the pre-war level of wages in Russia and the pre-war level of wages in other European countries meant very different things. We have to remember that the most advanced sections of the Russian proletariat before the war were fighting stubbornly to effect an advance in their wages because they regarded the Russian standard of life as a slave standard. But since the revolution of 1917, the needs of the workers have considerably enlarged, and there has been an advance in the cultural level of the worker and his family. For these reasons, he wants higher wages than before, to say nothing of the need for the replacement of the clothing, furniture, crockery, etc., which it was impossible to replace during the years of the war and revolution. Inasmuch as before the war the standard of life of the Russian workers was lower than that of the workers in any other European country, there can be no reason for boasting of the Soviet system because under it the pre-war level of wages has been regained.[1]

Living conditions in Russia are especially difficult for the salaried employees of industrial enterprises, and of municipal and State institutions, for the salaries are very low. Apart from a few exceptionally skilled experts and from certain high dignitaries, the salaries of Russian employees are on the poverty level. A university professor, for instance, receives from 85 to 90 chervonets roubles a month; a doctor, 75 roubles; a school teacher, from 40 to 50 roubles; a post-office official,

[1] During the last months of 1928, owing to the scarcity of food and the rise of prices in the towns, there was a renewed decline in the real wages of the workers.

48 roubles; a factory watchman, 41 roubles; a washerwoman in a children's home, 40 roubles. The payment of the employees in all these categories is not merely far below the pre-war standard, but is insufficient to provide the necessaries of life.

Since the introduction of the Nep, there has been in Russia a renewed and marked differentiation in the amount of wages paid to different categories of workers. There are whole groups of privileged workers who are able to earn wages from six to seven times as great as the wages earned by those who come lowest in the scale. Although nominally the labour of women is paid at the same rate as the labour of men, in practice women earn much less than men, this being brought about by enrolling the women in a lower grade. On the average, in the year 1926, a woman's wage was 63·4 per cent of a man's wage, although there were certain branches of industry in which women could earn from 80 to 90 per cent as much as a man. An unskilled female worker usually received about 30 per cent less in wages than an unskilled male worker.[1]

In the Soviet press, the question of the mutual reactions of the productivity of labour and the rate of wages are a frequent topic of discussion. The managers of industry, and the economic press, endeavour to show that the wages now paid in Soviet industry are too heavy a burden, since they increase more rapidly than the productivity of the workers. The trade unions endeavour, although tentatively, and with reserves' concerning truancy and idleness, to refute the accusation that the workers are hindering the advance of industry. It is very difficult to ascertain the actual productivity of labour, and Soviet statisticians have not yet succeeded in elaborating a trustworthy method of doing so. That makes an effective comparison between the present productivity and the pre-war productivity of labour almost impossible. This much is certain, that wages to-day represent a larger proportion of the cost of production than in pre-war Russia, and often a larger proportion

[1] A. Rashin [The Wages of Working Women in the years 1924–1926], 'Statisticheskoye Obozreniye", 1927, No. 2.

than in other European countries.[1] In conformity with this we find that during the year 1927–1928 in a number of branches of production there was a slackening in the increase of the productivity of labour, whereas the increase in wages was going on somewhat more quickly. But in spite of the contentions of the managers of Soviet industry, this does not apply to industry as a whole, for, according to the official data for 1927–1928, even nominal wages for the average of the whole of industry increased only by from 6 to 7 per cent, whilst the productivity of labour increased by 13·16 per cent. It does, however, apply to certain branches of industry, such as metal work, the textile industry, the building industry, etc. The explanation of these facts is to be sought in another direction than that in which the managers of Soviet industry and the leaders of the Soviet trade unions are looking. It does not necessarily mean that wages are high because wages form a large proportion of the cost of production. For instance, the share of wages in the cost of production in Russia was 26 per cent in the year 1926–1927, and in the United States in the same year it was only from 16 to 17 per cent. But this does not signify that the Russian workers earn higher wages than the American!

The proportional part of wages in the cost of production is determined by the organic composition of industrial capital, by the extent to which a particular branch of production has been mechanised and rationalised. In any branch of production it is higher in proportion as the use of machinery is less extensive, while it is lower in proportion as the use of machinery is more extensive and the machinery used is of a more perfect type. In those branches of production which are best equipped in

[1] "From the outlook of the interests of industry, which needs that the share of wages in the cost of production should be reduced or at any rate stabilised, the increase in wages must certainly be regarded as somewhat excessive." [Control Figures of the State Planning Commission].—"To-day wages form a larger percentage of the cost of production than they did in pre-war days," writes A. Ginsburg in [Economics of Industry], Part II, p. 48.

the technical respect, wages are usually high, but productivity is so greatly increased that the expenditure on wages is relatively small. In contemporary Russia, the composition of industrial capital is not only lower than in the corresponding enterprises in other European countries, but is also lower than in Russian enterprises of pre-war days. That is why wages represent a larger proportion of the cost of production. In this matter, the backward condition of Russian industry as regards the structure of its capital finds expression. In like manner, the cause of the retarded increase in the productivity of labour in certain branches of Russian industry is by no means to be found in a decline in the discipline of labour, or in the "slackness" of the Russian worker, but in the fact that, in the year 1927–1928, the last reserves of the fixed capital of the old industrial system have been brought into use, and that this has led to a further decline in the general productivity of industry. Nor could anything else be expected, seeing that the break-down of motors, boilers, machinery, and machine tools has become a daily incident of late years, and that the hand tools with which the workers have to produce goods are almost completely worn out.[1] The decline in productivity is not to be explained by any falling-off in the intensity of labour. When discussing rationalisation in Chapter Five, I showed that the lack of means to pay for a speedy renewal of industrial machinery had compelled the managers of Soviet enterprise to effect the necessary increase in production mainly by speeding-up the labour process. Piece work on a large scale, an increase in the piece-work output, the introduction of conveyors, and various other expedients, have been employed in order to speed up labour. There are many reasons for believing that in enterprises where the machinery is able to be kept at work without unduly

[1] In the Moscow enterprises, stoppages of work during the year 1927–1928 were twice as extensive as in the previous year, those due to a lack of accessory materials being 3·2 times as extensive, those due to lack of half-manufactured goods being 5·4 times as extensive, those due to the need for repairing machinery being 0·8 times as extensive, and those due to defects in hand tools being 0·4 times as extensive.—"Trud", September 2, 1928.

frequent break-downs, and where there are no serious stoppages for want of raw materials or fuel, the intensity of labour now exceeds the pre-war level. Even communist trade unionists do not dispute this assertion.

In the matter of labour protection, some successes have been achieved during the years of the Nep. The workers are provided with overalls for use in certain occupations; ventilation, lighting, and cleansing of the works have been put upon a better footing in some instances. The protection of women's labour is even more satisfactory. A working woman who becomes pregnant has to be given a holiday for eight weeks before and eight weeks after delivery. In a number of the great industrial enterprises there are crèches, where the women workers can leave their children to be cared for during working hours. In practice, of course, such measures can only be applied in the towns, and in large-scale enterprises. And even when these reservations are made, the application is not universal. According to the calculations of the People's Commissariat for Health, there ought to be 180 vacancies in the factory crèches for every 1000 working women, but the number of actual vacancies per 1000 working women varies in different branches of industry from 14 to 76. We find, moreover, that precisely in those industries that employ most women, the need for factory crèches is most inadequately satisfied. Thus, in the textile industry, the demand is met only to the extent of 20 per cent; and in the clothing industry to 8 per cent.[1]

The problem of safeguarding industrial workers against accident is still an extremely urgent one. The worn-out condition of the machinery, the lack of financial resources, and in many instances managerial carelessness, have created a situation in which, often enough, the most elementary precautions against accident are neglected. Speeding-up during the last few years has led to a great increase in the number of accidents, so that these are now far more frequent than they used to be before the war. An enquiry into the Moscow

[1] "Trud", November 13, 1928.

T

enterprises in the year 1926 showed that in the textile factories accidents are 2·3 times as frequent, and in the metal works twice as frequent, as before the war.[1]

A calculation has been made showing the average number of accidents in all branches of production per 1000 workers for three months, this meaning the number of accidents for every 75,000 days of actual work. In the year 1925, the number was 24·4; in 1926, it was 36; and in 1927, it was 45·2. The serious extent of the increase is obvious.[2]

The workers' standard of life is gravely affected by the housing difficulty. Most working-class families are housed in one-roomed tenements, and sometimes have to share even these with another family. It is impossible, in such circumstances, for them to have any sort of healthy mental life, or to get a sufficiency of rest and sleep.[3]

During the years of the revolution, social insurance has made considerable advances in Russia. In the year 1927, when the total number of wage workers was 10·5 millions, the number of insured was 8·9 millions. There is insurance against illness, unemployment, accident, disablement, and death. The expenditure upon all branches of insurance has increased, as is shown in the following table:

	Total Disbursements in Millions of Roubles.		Disbursements per Insured Person in Roubles.	
	1924/25.	1927/28.	1924/25.	1927/28.
Expenditure upon Social Insurance—				
For temporary incapacity to work[4] ..	113·2	228·3	17·40	27·85
For disablement	31·3	125·0	4·65	13·85
For other kinds of insurance[5] ..	—	82·2	7·87	8·19

Year by year there is an increase in the number of persons

[1] "Voprosy Truda", 1927, No. 10.
[2] [Data for the Labour Protection Conference], February 1928.
[3] Refer back to the previous chapter, "The Housing Problem".
[4] Owing to illness or pregnancy.   [5] Allowance during lactation; death.

who receive payment from the insurance institutions.[1]   For
transient incapacity to work, in the year 1924–1925, the
insurance bureaus paid, per 100 insured, for 986 days of
illness; in the year 1925–1926, for 1079 days; and in the year
1926–1927, for 1282 days. Wholly or partially supported by the
insurance institutions were persons to the following number
(round figures):

	1924/25.	1925/26.	1926/27.
Permanently afflicted or disabled ..	239,000	318,000	388,000
Orphans and widows	197,000	245,000	290,000
Inmates of homes for the permanently disabled or afflicted..	16,800	17,000	12,000
Inmates of sanatoria and convalescent homes	316,000	351,000	500,000

The story of unemployment insurance is a less gratifying
one. Owing to the limitations imposed on the payment of
unemployment benefit, which is only payable to a worker who
has been in regular work for from one to three years before
becoming unemployed, and to an employee who has been
engaged in his salaried occupation for from three to five years
before becoming unemployed, out of the 2 to 2·5 millions
unemployed in the year 1927–1928, only from 550,000 to 600,000
received help from the insurance institutions. The amount
of benefit, moreover, is very small, not only in comparison
with the actual cost of living in Russia, but also in comparison
with the far more liberal unemployment benefits paid in
Germany and in Britain. In the year 1928, the average unemployment benefit for the whole Union (in Moscow and
Leningrad the benefit is somewhat higher) amounted to 14·3
roubles per month, when the average monthly income of
an employed worker was 60 roubles. In addition to the paying
of unemployment benefit, the Soviet State organises relief

[1] The figures in these tables regarding insurance relate to the entire insurance
system of Soviet Russia,

work. In the year 1926–1927, the amount spent for this purpose
was 9·4 millions of roubles; and for the year 1927–1928, a
sum of 12·5 millions of roubles was voted. On the average,
30,000 workers are engaged upon relief work. Further aid is
given to the unemployed by credits and subventions to the
productive cooperatives of unemployed. Taking it all in all,
the amount paid out of State funds and by the insurance
institutions to the unemployed was in 1924–1925, a sum of
35·5 millions of roubles; in the year 1925–1926, a sum of 57·8
millions of roubles; in the year 1926–1927, a sum of 85·4
millions of roubles; and in the year 1927–1928, a sum of
132 millions of roubles.

An aggravation of the already tragical position of the
unemployed in Russia is that most of them have no prospect
of finding employment, seeing that there is a regulation to the
effect that only trade unionists are to be engaged and that
the trade unions have ceased to enroll as members persons
who are not at work. Finding it impossible to protect the
interests of the working masses as a whole, and being dependent
upon the State, the Soviet trade unions have been compelled
in self-defence to bar their doors against unemployed workers.

If the condition of the unemployed thus borders on starvation,
we have to recognise that the position of the employed workers
of late years has improved only in respect of the satisfaction
of the most elementary material needs. Perpetual anxiety on
account of the dearth of the most necessary articles (for in
the cooperative stores there is a recurrent scarcity of one article
or another, such as butter, tea, petroleum, etc.); perpetual
fear of discharge with consequent prolonged unemployment;
the burden of being utterly dependent upon the State in
respect alike of work, housing, food supply, and education—
all these are factors in the peculiar social position of the Russian
worker.

The Soviet newspapers are fond of informing the Russian
workers that they are the actual masters of State industry.
In actual fact, however, except for small groups formed by

the members of the workers' committees and by members of the communist nuclei, the workers in general have no influence either upon the economic policy of the State or upon the conduct of the enterprises in which they are engaged. Now, as before, in most enterprises, the great majority of the workers are nothing more than sellers of the commodity labour power. Owing to the universal political pressure and to the dread of discharge, it is only in extreme cases that the workers will venture to criticise the management of an enterprise or the measures adopted by the supreme economic instruments of the State. The production conferences which were instituted in order to ensure that the workers should participate in the management of production have entirely lost their original significance, having become in most instances mere official parades or meetings for communist agitation.[1]

The nationalisation of the trade unions has robbed the workers of their independent trade-union organisations. Collective bargains entered into between the State enterprises and the trade unions (bargains whereby the working conditions are often changed for the worse) are effected behind the backs of the persons directly concerned. The "detestable alliance"[2] which has been formed in Russian industrial enterprises, the alliance between the communist manager of an enterprise and the communist trade-union leader, often gives rise to conflicts in the enterprises, or intensifies them when they already exist; and when this happens, the trade unions usually side with the manager of the enterprise against the mass of the workers. For all these reasons, the working masses are painfully aware that they have no independent organs of the class struggle. Fairly often, however, the working masses, impelled by the need for self-preservation, exercise sufficient pressure upon the workers' committees and the trade-union organisations to

[1] In Chapter Seventeen, entitled "Towards Socialism or Capitalism?", I shall return to this question of industrial democracy.
[2] The phrase "detestable alliance" to describe the situation in the Soviet trade unions was uttered in 1925 by Tomsky, the chairman of the Central Council of the Trade Unions, who at that time belonged to the opposition.

compel these to declare war against the managers of enterprise. Even if the workers' committees and the trade unions should, on such occasions, refrain from actively working on behalf of the interests of the rank and file, at least they ventilate dissatisfaction, and pave the way for a compromise. When the pressure of the rank and file has no effect in this direction, the attitude towards the nationalised trade unions becomes directly hostile. Sometimes, despite all the hindrances imposed by the police, working-class dissatisfaction eventuates in a strike, and sometimes illegal strike committees are formed. The usual result of such outbursts is that working conditions are changed for the worse, or that workers are dismissed, or arrested and deported.

CHAPTER SIXTEEN

PURPOSIVE ECONOMICS AND STATE
REGULATION

ALREADY in the days of war communism, the political activities of the Russian communists were guided by the desire to establish a purposive economic system. Careful calculation, and the formulation of a plan—these were the leading ideas of the period in which, from 1918 to 1920, the Soviet government was trying to transform the whole economy of the country into a centralised system working to secure definite economic ends. As every one knows, the attempt to centralise the whole of Russian production, including the cobblers' stalls and the smallest peasant farms, and the attempt to distribute all commodities (not excepting tooth-powder) in accordance with a deliberate plan, collapsed hopelessly in the year 1920.

So utopian a policy could not but fail, at any rate in a country which had been ruined by the war and in one where economic conditions were so backward. With the transition to the Nep, the Soviet government renounced the attempt to regulate from above every detail of economic life, but still persisted in the utopian endeavour to conduct all economic processes in accordance with a unified plan. The ever-recurring motif at all the congresses of the Communist Party of the U.S.S.R., has been the consideration of the Soviet economy as a purposive economy, the insistence that it must be carried on as an organised system contrasting with the unorganised economy of capitalist countries. The activities of all the State departments of the U.S.S.R. have been guided in accordance with this idea.

The State Planning Commission, the chief instrument of the attempt to carry on a purposive economy in the U.S.S.R., explained the nature of this purposive economy in a report issued in the year 1926. In that document we read: "Inasmuch as we are realising a purposive economy, we endeavour, first of all, to elaborate the national economy in such a way that, thanks to the coordination of the various parts and with the aid of scientific methods of production and distribution, with due adaptation to the objective material resources and to the amount of available labour power, it will be possible to combine the maximum of production with the minimum of expenditure in the shortest conceivable time. Secondly, the entire State system is so constructed that the frictionless course of the whole mechanism without crises and catastrophes will be ensured, while the whole working collectivity participates consciously in the aggregate social production and takes into account the ways by which and the extent to which dead nature can be subjected to its needs."[1]

Having reproduced this definition of a purposive economy, I should like to say at the outset that I am by no means inclined to contest its accuracy. In conformity with the Marxian view of scientific socialism, it correctly and in a very detailed way conveys an idea of the essential nature of a purposive economy in a fully established socialist society. But the problem with which we are now concerned is not within the plane of the determination of the ultimate aim (socialism, a purposive economy). Our trouble is that it is open to dispute whether the extant Soviet economy is really a purposive economy; whether the indispensable prerequisites for the establishment of such an economy exist as yet in Soviet Russia; and what limits are actually imposed by the objective conditions upon the State regulation of economic life in the Soviet Union.

For the present rulers of the Soviet State and the present leaders of Soviet economy, this purposive economy is not a remote aim, but something which they are engaged in upbuilding at the present day, or even something which has already been realised in Soviet Russia. S. Strumilin, a communist, and one of the principal members of the State Planning Commission, in the report upon the Five Year Plan drafted

[1] Quoted from the symposium [Problems of Planning], Moscow, 1926.

by him, declares that there is now better reason than ever for saying with Marx: "Philosophers have done nothing more than interpret the world; our business is to change it."[1] Again, in the organ of the Supreme Economic Council we read, in an account of the most pressing economic tasks: "The guidance of our purposive economy must be something more than a mere prevision, something more than the discovery of a conformity to law; it must also be the creative and deliberate upbuilding of a socialist economy".[2] Finally, the directives issued by the Communist Party of the U.S.S.R., when formulating the Five Year Plan at the Fifteenth Congress, stated categorically: "On the basis of the nationalisation of large-scale industry and of the other key positions, a purposive conduct of economic life has become possible. . . . The resolution concerning the Five Year Plan signifies that we are proceeding to the realisation of the expanded program of socialist reconstruction."[3] The best way of throwing light upon the scope and methods of a purposive economy in contemporary Russia, and upon the limits to its realisation, will be to undertake a survey of actual practice.

The State Planning Commission came into existence in the year 1921, and the first plan for reconstructing the whole of the Soviet economy upon the basis of the supply of energy had already been elaborated in the year 1920, in the form of the electrification scheme. Nevertheless, it was not until the currency was stabilised in the year 1924 that these schemes for a purposive economy had any notable effect upon the economic life of the U.S.S.R. Since 1924, however, there has been a change in the situation. In accordance with the resolutions of the Communist Party, serious attempts have been made to organise the whole economic life of Soviet Russia on the lines formulated by the State Planning Commission. During the

[1] [The Industrialisation of the U.S.S.R., and the Epigones of the Narodnichestvo], "Planovoye Hozyaistvo", 1927, No. 7.
"Torgovo-Promyshlennaya Gazeta", 1927, No. 209.
"Pravda", December 20, 1927.

last four years, the instruments and the methods of the Russian purposive economy have taken definite shape.

On principle, the scheme for establishing a purposive economy in the Soviet Union is constructed as follows. Each of the various republics that combine to form the Union has its own State Planning Commission, which drafts a scheme for the economic development of its own area. The general plan for the U.S.S.R. is drafted by the State Planning Commission of the Soviet Union.[1] The last-named authority is not subordinated to any of the people's commissariats; and should any difference of opinion arise between the State Planning Commission and economic commissariats, the matter has to be submitted to the highest economic authority of the Union, the Council for Labour and Defence, whose decisions are binding upon all the State authorities. The State Planning Commission of the Soviet Union, acting in accordance with the directives given by the Communist Party, and making use of the economic and statistical data at its disposal, has drafted two economic plans, a Five Year Plan and a Fifteen Year Plan. The Five Year Plan comprises the economic measures in the domain of reconstruction, new construction, industrialisation, and intensification, which cannot expect to become fully productive in so short a space of time. The Fifteen Year Plan, far more comprehensive, comprises the measures by which is to be achieved the transformation of economic life into a thoroughly socialised system.

The drafting of both plans has been guided by the following considerations: the movement of population, and the social composition of the population; the national income; the accumulation of capital; the amount of investments; production in industry and agriculture; the circulation of commodities; foreign trade; the issue of money; the budget; taxes; the total consumption; the wages of labour. All these are considered in relation to the aggregate of economic life, and in relation to

[1] In the budget for 1927–1928, 26 millions of roubles are set aside to finance the Central Statistical Bureau and the State Planning Commission.

individual departments of economic life and individual districts. The whole is elaborated into a unified system, a plan for the totality of Russian economic life. The schemes thus elaborated have an obligatory character and serve as guides.

Further, since 1924, the State Planning Commission has every year issued a directive economic plan for the current year, the so-called Control Figures of the national economy, based on the reports and schemes of the various departments. The Control Figures of the State Planning Commission, in which all the elements of the national economy are foreshadowed in detail, are to serve as directives, and are binding on the individual republics and on all the authorities of the U.S.S.R., which on their side have to conduct current economic life purposively within the range prescribed by the Control Figures. In addition, the State Planning Commission publishes monthly surveys and combined annual reports, which are to serve as bases for the drafting of economic plans.

It cannot be denied that these economic planning organisations possess an outward unity, and a formal systematisation. Nay, more, the numerous publications of the economic planning authorities of the Soviet Union certainly have a considerable theoretical value. The most notable Russian economists have, during recent years, done an immense amount of work in the way of throwing light upon the economic structure of the old and the new Russia, as well as in the way of formulating the methodology of a purposive economy. Ballod's work [The Future State], published long before the war, was already of great interest to every socialist economist, although it was nothing more than a first attempt to give a concrete picture of the structure of a socialised economy. The post-war attempts to draw up a plan for the development of the whole of Russian national economic life, to draft a balance sheet, and to make a prognosis, are unquestionably of enormous theoretical interest, whether the schemes are realisable or not.

For instance, much theoretical interest attaches to the

discussion which has arisen among the Soviet economists, in connexion with the drafting of the Five Year Plan and the Fifteen Year Plan, as to whether a genetic or a teleological method is preferable; whether the drafting of an economic plan in the epoch of transition should be effected with an eye to the goals to be attained, without regard to "secular conformity to economic law"; or whether the plan should be based upon a study of actual economic processes, their trends, and their inner conformity to law—foresight, and deliberate attempts to reach particular goals, being operative only in the form of directives which shall nowise conflict with the fundamental laws of the development of the forces of production.[1] This problem, though at first sight its formulation may seem to suggest the title of a doctorial dissertation, may ere long become a matter of immediate moment to the European proletariat when history makes it necessary for the workers to face the problem of purposive economic construction in the epoch of transition. In Russia, likewise, this problem, however far removed it may appear from reality, is of enormous importance, both as regards the methods whereby the directives for the economic instruments are elaborated, and in regard of the consequences that may ensue. It is very significant that most of the old-school Marxian (non-communist) economists— led by such distinguished experts as V. Groman and V. Bazaroff, are firmly convinced of the superiority of the genetic method; whereas the communist economists, and especially the younger ones, favour the teleological method. The former say: "We are not determinists, but we are of opinion that in Soviet Russia as well as elsewhere, economic laws impose their will on us. In drafting a plan, our first task must be to pay due heed to reality and its laws." The latter say: "Nor do we deny the necessity for paying heed to present experience and for studying the dynamic of past events; but the question of the primacy of teleology was settled for us once for all in the

[1] Discussion concerning the ways of drafting the Five Year Plan, April and May, 1928.

days of the November revolution, when we revolted against the 'eternal' laws of capitalist evolution." This formulation of the communist view is given in the words of N. Kovaleffsky.

Very great and very instructive have been the difficulties that have arisen in the drafting of the Five Year Plan and the Fifteen Year Plan. I will give a few illustrations.

A plan for the development of economic life cannot be based on mere estimates. The methodological difficulty arises from this, however, that there is no static basis to serve as a starting-point, for all the factors are in reciprocal dynamic dependence each upon the other. The factor which, from the Marxian standpoint, is determinative, namely, the development of the forces of production, is in this instance an unknown magnitude. We must naturally set out from the dynamic of the most important of the productive forces of a country—from the movement of population. But the increase of population is itself a derivative magnitude, is a function of economic, cultural, social, and ideological factors, which are themselves unknown magnitudes in this relation. No one can tell with certainty whether during the next fifteen years the recent rate of increase of population (2·3 per cent) will be retained in Russia, or whether the rate of increase may not prove as low as was that of France in the year 1913 (0·09 per cent). Besides, when considering the movement of population, we are concerned, not only with the size of the working population, but also with its quality—for the skill of the workers, their cultural level, is of no less importance than their numbers. How is it possible to forecast the working of these factors during the next fifteen years?

Again, what features have to be taken into account when we are calculating the extent of production? Are we to assume that the reconstruction of industry and agriculture and their further development are going to proceed upon a better technical basis, but only within the limits of extant technique? How is it possible to foresee for fifteen, or even only for five years, what changes may take place in industrial and agricultural technique as an outcome of various inventions and discoveries already made, but as yet little utilised? It is impossible to say what changes may result from the wireless transmission of energy to great distances; from the use of liquid fuels, synthetic benzene and synthetic rubber, new alloys, artificial fibre for the making of textiles, new chemical manures, new technical acquirements in the way of regulating the effects of meteorological influences.[1] The extant of the changes that may thus be brought about is incalculable. Once more, how is it possible to ascertain what natural resources may be discovered within the territories of the U.S.S.R. during the next few years? Not until 1926 were there discovered in the Volga region extensive deposits of potash, and this discovery will have immense influence upon the developmental prospects of agriculture. In 1928 there were new discoveries of metallic ores in the Siberian mountains.

Finally, if plans are to be drafted teleologically, in accordance with the decisions of the majority of the State Planning Commission, economic reconstruction must be conducted with an eye to securing that the whole working energy of the able-bodied population shall be utilised, that unemployment shall cease to exist. But how is it possible to forecast the changes which the economic reconstruction of the country in the course of fifteen years (or even in the course of five years) will produce in the composition and the numbers of the working masses? How much labour power will be liberated by the rationalisation of industrial technique, and how much labour power will be utilised in the new enterprises? How many persons will be squeezed out of the decaying handicrafts and

[1] In the periodical "Planovoye Hozyaistvo", 1928, No. 3, we are told that there is a proposal to invite the American physicist, Professor William Height, to visit the Soviet Union. Height has discovered a way of regulating meteorological conditions, and of promoting artificial rainfall, by the application of powerful electrical currents. Twenty-two millions of roubles are to be devoted to installing 750 apparatus in order to promote the rainfall desirable for Russian agriculture. When the Fifteen Year Plan was being drafted, the question of turning Height's plan to account came up for discussion.

petty industries, and how many of the agricultural producers will be thrown into the industrial labour market owing to the intensification of agriculture? How is the extent of production to be determined in advance? Should the calculation be based upon the greatest possible application of productive power, or upon the needs of the population? Even the greatest possible application of productive power is a variable magnitude; for instance, it may be modified by an increase in imports, or by a change in the relative proportions between various imports. Our calculations, then, must be based upon the popular needs. But how can we decide for several years in advance what will be the needs of the Russian workers and peasants at a time when their cultural and social standards are rapidly changing?

Difficulties of this kind are innumerable. That is why the State Planning Commission has just been compelled to elaborate a fourth variant of the Five Year Plan. The course of development is invalidating the theoretical calculations upon which the plan has been based, before there has been time to put in into operation.[1] As yet, moreover, the great Fifteen Year Plan has not been worked out as a unified system. For certain branches of economic life (machine construction, the transport system, electrification, etc.) and for certain areas of the Union (Ukraine, Ural, Central Asia, etc.), the Five Year Plan has been completed, but the coordination of these nineteen volumes (running to 500 pages each, without considering appendixes) to form a unified system, and the dispelling of their mutual contradictions, will involve an immense amount of work.

Nevertheless, although the validity of these schemes is no more than relative, and although they are in many respects utopian, their theoretical and directive value cannot be denied. An attempt has been made to solve hitherto unsolved problems;

[1] In June 1929, the Five Year Plan for the period 1928–1929 to 1932–1933 was adopted by the Soviet Congress. But the first year of operations, which came to an end in October 1929, has shown that the assumptions upon which the plan was based have not been justified.

our knowledge of economic phenomena has been enlarged and rendered more profound; new causal relationships between the factors of economic life have been disclosed; old statistical methods have been improved and new ones have been discovered. Even though our knowledge of the actual economic structure of contemporary Russia remains very limited, and although the forecasts and directives can by no means be regarded as endowed with true scientific validity, it is certain that the labours of the economic planning authorities of the U.S.S.R. will demand earnest consideration on the part of every economist who is henceforward to deal with the problems of a purposive economy. Just as the observations of the Assyrian astrologers and the medieval alchemists, though in many respects out of touch with reality and devoid of scientific value, became none the less the foundations of modern astronomy and chemistry respectively, so the labours of the Soviet economists, despite their utopism, must be taken into account by all whose business it will be to draft similar plans in the future.

But although economic planning is indisputably of great theoretical interest, the activities of the economic planning authorities of the U.S.S.R. have not only been unable to transform the Soviet economy into an organised purposive system, but further, in their endeavour to embrace the whole of economic life, they have hindered the State from concentrating upon the necessary and practicable regulation of the principal branches of economy and their various subdivisions. Owing to its utopism, Soviet economic planning is in many respects directly harmful to the national economic life, for it disorganises the productive forces of the country, and swings them in wrong directions.

Since the more comprehensive plans for the ensuing five and fifteen years are, as we have learned, still in their preparatory stages, and are continually being remodelled, let us turn to study what influence the plans drawn up in advance for each of the last four years, and known as the Control

Figures, have had upon the national economy of the U.S.S.R. The difficulties in the way of drafting an economic plan for one year are far less considerable than those of planning for a long series of years; but even the former far more modest scheme has proved impracticable under the conditions that prevail in the U.S.S.R. I do not say this because I think that communists plan badly, and that socialists might make a better job of it! The trouble is, as already said, that the objective prerequisites for economic planning do not exist in the U.S.S.R. The enormous magnitude of the tasks to be performed in drafting such a plan, the bureaucratic nature of the administrative apparatus, the confusion that prevails in the activities of the leading economic instruments (see above, Chapter Six)—these and similar influences play a great part in rendering futile any attempts to draft a valid economic plan. But, apart from the defects of the Russian administrative system, the task is objectively impracticable.

Above all, there is a lack of the necessary knowledge of the most important factors of the country's economic structure. Statistical data are incomplete and inaccurate, and a number of relevant economic phenomena have never been studied at all. How is it possible to set to work upon the construction of a unified economic system when there is no accurate information concerning the size of the national income or concerning the extent of social differentiation in the rural districts; when no adequate light has been thrown on the problem of agrarian over-population, upon that of the reproduction and accumulation of capital, upon that of the capacity of consumption in town and countryside, upon that of the amount and structure of fixed capital in industry, and upon that of the extent of the reserves of land still available for cultivation? Insuperable obstacles to successful economic planning, however, are imposed by the fact that the economic structure of the Soviet Union (in which a semi-natural economy and small-scale peasant farming are still mainly dominant), together with the methods of organisation of industry, the

U

disintegration of the processes of circulation, and prevailing economic traditions, make it impossible to construct a unified purposive economy. From the Marxian outlook it is obvious that a unified purposive economy can only be established upon the basis of a socialised method of production. What is known in the most advanced capitalist countries as "organised capitalism", is only the first approximation to a system of economic planning, is no more than a purposive economic oasis in the midst of a capitalist system whose essential nature it is to be unorganised. The huge monopolist economic organisms of the trusts and combines are steps towards the organisation of economic life, and their activity sometimes embraces whole branches of production and distribution. But they do not suffice to make the capitalist economy a purposive one. The struggle between the various branches of industry, between the banks and the industrial producers, between national and international economic entities, continues. Furthermore, the class struggle is assuming a form which, though somewhat more organised than of old, is often more accentuated than of old.

Even these germs of an economic plan, these first essays at the organised regulation of certain branches of production or distribution, have only become possible at a very high level of the development and organisation of economic life. The concentration of enterprises, their amalgamation into trusts and combines, the interweaving of financial and industrial capital, great advances in technique, huge natural resources, far-reaching and stable commercial relationships, long-standing organisational achievements—these multiple factors of a developed capitalism have made it possible to introduce certain elements of economic planning into the aggregate of economic life.

The Russian communists believe that in the U.S.S.R., owing to the nationalisation of industry, the banks, the transport system, home and foreign trade, etc., there are "special advantages in respect of the organisation of a purposive economy"; and they are unable to understand why their plans go awry. But even in the nationalised "sector" of the Russian economy, the one in which the possibilities of economic planning are most favourable, failure is often inevitable owing to the immensity of the tasks which the State sets itself to perform. Failure arises because of the endeavour to amalgamate great numbers of enterprises in accordance with a unified scheme, though these enterprises have not been trustified or syndicated as the outcome of a tedious process of development, but have merely been mechanically unified at short notice by order of the Soviet authorities.

Even in industry and commerce, the possibilities for a purposive economy are by no means great in Russia. They are mainly limited by the inseparable dependence of Russian economic life upon the spontaneous energies of peasant agricultural production and upon a disintegrated home market, but also by the increasing closeness of the ties with the world economy. A plan for the development of the Russian national economy must in respect alike of quantities and of values, be able to foresee the reciprocal relations between the Soviet Union and the world economy for one or several years. But is such foresight, is a stable purposive guidance of this kind, possible, when, owing to the scarcity of fluid financial resources in the homeland, the speed and the forms of industrialisation and the extent of production are thus dependent to a decisive extent upon conditions which are quite beyond the control of the State Planning Commission—such conditions, for example, as the extent to which the U.S.S.R. will be granted long-term credits in Germany or America? The amount of Russian imports and exports, the degree to which Russian foreign trade can be made to pay, and consequently the tempo of the development of the most important factors of the Russian national economy, are dependent upon the rapidly vacillating prices that obtain in the world market (such as the price of grain), upon the policy of the international combines that are interested in cotton, rubber, and petroleum, or upon the activity of demand in the world market for timber or for manganese ores.

But the main point is that the prerequisites for a purposive organisation do not exist in the most important branch of Russian economy, namely agriculture. The million-headed peasant masses live, produce, sell, and consume without any regard to the directives of the State Planning Commission. They are actuated by the laws of the commodity market, which are the same in Russia as in all capitalist countries.

The fact that 65 per cent of all the production of the country takes place under the conditions that obtain in a disintegrated private economy, and that 80 per cent of the population works under the conditions of an extremely primitive kind of commodity exchange, is enough to impose narrow limits upon economic plans and forecasts. A lack of organisation—spontaneity—is imposed upon Russian economic life as a whole by the spontaneity of an individualist peasant economy. Russian industry is connected by a thousand threads with Russian agriculture, and for this latter the decisive question is whether the harvest is a good one or a bad one. The primitive character of the Russian peasant economy, in its turn, makes the amount of the harvest depend almost exclusively upon meteorological conditions, and these cannot so far, be controlled by economic experts. Yet two-thirds of the raw materials needed by Russian industry are provided by Russian agriculture; and, furthermore, the main consumer of Russian industrial products is the Russian peasant. Thus it comes to pass that the amount of grain finding its way to the market, the prices of food and raw materials, the amount of exports and imports, react upon the rate at which industry can expand, impose limits upon its expansion, and modify its technical reorganisation in various ways.

It is not surprising, therefore, that even in industry and large-scale trade (where concentration and nationalisation have prepared the ground for purposive regulation) in practice only trifling results have been achieved. No doubt, considerable approximations have been made towards fulfilling the program of production in various branches of economic activity. The financing of industry is more effective than it was, calculations are more accurate, the prices of certain commodities have been satisfactorily regulated; but these achievements have only succeeded in introducing a certain measure of elementary order into the nationalised economy, and do not amount to a centralised purposive guidance of the national economy as a whole. Nay, more, notwithstanding the monopolisation and nationalisation of industry, the Soviet authorities are, as regards the management of particular enterprises, as regards the preventing of needless competition between these, as regards hindering the secret storage of supplies, etc., often far less able to take effective action than are many private combines in European countries.[1] This is because those who guide the Soviet economy are not accurately acquainted with the needs of the various branches of production, because the hetero-geneous constituents of a trust have not become interconnected in virtue of a lengthy organic process, because the technical and administrative personnel of industrial enterprises is not sufficiently skilled, and because the private commodity market exerts a corrupting and disturbing influence upon the activities of the State economic instruments. The private and local interests of the managers of the various State enterprises often conflict with the demands of a purposive economy, while the fierce competition between the various enterprises results in the directives issued from above being forgotten—and, often enough, even the citadels of the purposive economy in the State enterprises are swamped by the waves of the market.

There is even less prospect of effectively applying the purposive principle to the 25 millions of peasant farms, to private trade in its aggregate, and to the general systems of domestic and handicraft production. How can it be possible to talk of economic planning in respect of these millions of

[1] Refer back to the contrast between a Soviet trust and the Allgemeine Elektrische Gesellschaft in Chapter Six.

detached petty enterprises, whose economic horizon hardly ever extends beyond the cares of the morrow, whose production is exclusively subjected to the blind forces of nature, and the disposal of whose products is controlled by the blind forces of the market? Economic experience in Russia since the Soviet government rose to power has shown that, notwithstanding the best endeavours of the authorities, notwithstanding the issue of innumerable circulars and instructions, notwithstanding the drafting of an ostensibly impeccable balance sheet to function as a unified plan for the ensuing economic year [1]— notwithstanding the existence of all these outward and visible signs of a well-thought-out system, there is no real purposive economy in the U.S.S.R., nor can there be in view of the extant economic structure of the country.

Of course, this does not mean that the attempts of the State to formulate an economic plan are merely the work of theoretical experts who cannot see beyond the walls of their studies, and that the schemes have no bearing on practical life. Even in capitalist countries, the economic policy of the State, its deliberate interference with economic life, exerts a powerful influence, although capitalist countries have no purposive economic system. State endeavours to further agriculture or industry; a tariff policy; the budget; laws enacted to secure economic, social, and political ends—these things have a marked effect on economic life. Such considerations apply still more forcibly to the U.S.S.R., where the political and economic role of the State is greater than elsewhere. The Soviet government, equipped with dictatorial powers, decides the course of legislation in pursuit of economic and social ends at its own sweet will. It imposes directives for everyday policy; and conducts the current work of the nationalised industry, the banks, and home and foreign trade.

[1] It is interesting to note that the Control Figures for 1928–1929, which are supposed to regulate the aggregate economic life of the Union for a year in advance, were not officially confirmed until nine months after the beginning of that economic year.

But I have already shown that the positive achievements in this direction are by no means considerable. Even if they had been much greater than they are, they would not amount to anything more than the successes of State regulation, of stocktaking and rationalisation in the nationalised enterprises. These successes, in view of the dominance of the nationalised economy in the U.S.S.R., would certainly consolidate the purposive elements in the national economic aggregate, but would by no means transform this aggregate into a thoroughly purposive economic system. Only those plans and only that policy achieve positive results in Russia which aim either at a general control of the chief factors of the national economy or at the regulation of particular branches of industry or trade— at the same time only such plans and such a policy as pay due heed to the laws of the commodity market and allow for the spontaneous trends of the economic forces of the country.[1]

But directly the economic planning instruments of the State attempted to perform some task laid upon them by the Communist Party and one which conflicted with the laws of motion of economic life, or with the relations of power obtaining between various social factors, or with the trends of economic development, then, during the early years of the Nep, these paper plans simply remained unrealised, life passed them by; or, more recently, when the Soviet government had learned better how to manipulate the State apparatus, and was able to intensify its functioning by mobilising the local communist organisations for that purpose, such endeavours led to grave economic disturbances, as consequences of the strenuous endeavour to act in accordance with the directives prescribed by the economic plan. Sometimes evolution itself marched over the defective or injurious scheme; sometimes the spontaneous elements of economic life, not being strong

[1] V. Sarabyanoff, a communist, and one of the most noted economists in Soviet Russia, writes: "The plan worked when it was accordant with spontaneous evolution, and it failed when it was exclusively grounded upon the endeavours of an organised apparatus." [Basic Problems of the Nep]. 1926, p. 93.

enough to overcome the State authority, broke through the dam of purposive economic regulations at some other and less adequately protected point.

Let me give some illustrative examples. By a resolution of the Ninth Congress of the Communist Party, the Soviet government was, immediately after the proclamation of the Nep, "to devote itself first of all to the reconstruction of the branches of production which are concerned in the supply of the means of production", and was in the second place to devote itself "to producing the products of mass consumption". Trotsky, in supporting this resolution, said: "We shall not proceed to the production of the means of consumption until we have ensured the reestablishment of the means of production." Nevertheless, despite the best endeavours of the economic planning instruments, for five years in succession the actual results were the reverse of this. The process of production, going on in virtue of its own elementary forces, served in the first instance to satisfy the most urgent needs of mass consumption. The country required textiles, foodstuffs, boots and shoes; and, however wisely the economists might plan, it could not wait for the satisfaction of these needs until the blast-furnaces and the mines had been set agoing once more, or until the electrical power station Volhvostroi had been completed. Not until the year 1925–1926, when the economy of the Soviet Union and especially the Russian peasant economy had been to some extent consolidated, did there arise in the market an effective demand for metals and machinery, so that thenceforward rapid progress could be made in the reconstruction of heavy industry.

Nay more, with the aid of the funds which the State obtained by the sale of articles of mass consumption, it was now possible to finance heavy industry and make it stand on its own feet. When analysing this problem, the distinguished Soviet economist V. Sarabyanoff admitted: "During the years of reconstruction, the spontaneity of economic life played an extremely important role in industry, whereas the State Planning Commission played a very small role indeed."[1]

In earlier pages I have referred to the disregard of economic principles during the reconstruction of industry. The significance of the plans for improving the technique of production and for starting new enterprises can be judged by the following facts. The economic plan for the year 1927-1928 was not drafted so as to take account of the introduction of three shifts in various branches of industry. The introduction of a third shift led to an acute shortage of raw materials, fuel, and labour power, with the result that, in various respects, the schemes for production were nullified.

The plans for the technical reorganisation of the chemical industry and the metal industry had been carefully elaborated by the Soviet statisticians and economists. The result was that the chemists and other scientists and the working engineers found it necessary to send a memorial to the chairman of the Council of People's Commissaries asking that the scheme should be reconsidered, for in its original form it ignored the most recent discoveries, and paid no heed to the revolution that had taken place in applied chemistry during the post-war period. The technicians besieged the Supreme Economic Council with representations to the effect that: "The plans for the new metal works do not correspond to the demands of the modern technique of capitalist countries, and the concentration of production and the creation of huge combines is a prehistoric and antiquated way of organising production."[2] Even the plans for the extension of so important a branch of heavy industry as smelting underestimated the demand for crude metal, so that in the beginning of the year 1928 a shortage of metals was already apparent, a shortage which had a disturbing and hindering effect upon the further development of the metal industry as a whole. Upon instructions from the Supreme Economic Council, in the year 1928 scrap metal was collected

[1] [Basic Problems of the Nep], Moscow, 1926, p. 112.
[2] "Torgovo-Promyshlennaya Gazeta", July 6, 1928.

from all over the country, although in the year 1925–1926 there had been an increased export of scrap metal.

The rationalisation of production has been going on in Russian enterprises for five years now, but at the Congress of the Workers' and Peasants' Inspection in September 1928 it was unanimously agreed that this rationalisation had been conducted "without a plan, chaotically, without guidance or method".[1] Several of the communist speakers took the opportunity of alluding, as an example to the U.S.S.R., to the great successes in the domain of rationalisation secured of late years by capitalist Germany, which had succeeded better than Russia "notwithstanding all the advantages of the economic planning system of the U.S.S.R.".[2]

The economic plans for the circulation of commodities have been equally out of touch with reality. In the year 1925–1926, an exceptionally good harvest was expected. Very small prices were to be paid to the peasants for the grain bought by the State. The plans for export, import, the expansion of production, the circulation of commodities, the circulation of money, etc., were based on this supposition. But the actualities of life frustrated the plan. Those who had drafted it had made two gross errors of calculation, for, first of all, they had overestimated the size of the harvest, and, in the second place, seeing that the prices of industrial products were so high, the peasants refused to sell grain to the State at the stipulated low prices. In May, the price of grain had already increased by 50 per cent. Export did not pay, and industrial enterprises lacked the most essential financial resources. A crisis of "commodity famine" set in, after the good harvest, and the relation between the prices of industrial products and agrarian products established by the peasants had greatly increased the peasant demand in the commodity market. The demand for industrial

[1] "Pravda", September 1, 1928.
[2] In the year 1924, F. Dzerzhinsky wrote: "I must say that when I read of our advantages and possibilities in this matter of the rationalisation of production, I feel positively sick."—Reported by Shuhgalter, in "Torgovo-Promyshlennaya Gazeta", August 26, 1928.

products exceeded the supply very greatly. All the calculations upon which the economic plan for the year 1925–1926 had been based had proved erroneous.

For the year 1926–1927, therefore, the Control Figures anticipated a "considerable increase in the scarcity of commodities". But in the first half of that year, despite all the expectations of the Soviet economists, there was a steady falling-off in the circulation of commodities, for the peasants, having satisfied their most urgent needs, preferred to hoard their surpluses of agricultural produce, in order (as they had been used to do before the war) to safeguard themselves against a failure of the crops and other disastrous possibilities. After the State had been compelled, at short notice, to discard its plans, and to come to the help of industry and trade with subventions, this masked inflation led to a turbulent increase in the marketing of commodities, until a scarcity of commodities once more became a phenomenon of daily occurrence. Again the plans had proved out of touch with reality.

In the middle of the year 1927–1928, the history of 1925–1926 repeated itself. The peasants again refused to sell grain to the State at the low prices fixed by the purchasing departments. This time the resistance of the peasants was so stubborn that even the compulsory levying of grain failed to produce a sufficient supply, and the export of grain had to be prohibited. Not only had all the plans to be torn up, but the normal functioning of the industrial apparatus was endangered. The State had to beat a retreat, and was compelled to pay higher prices for grain.

As a no less crying example of the unsatisfactoriness of Soviet plans and forecasts, I may refer to the disproportion between the projected and the actual emission of paper money. In the year 1925–1926, whereas the plan had provided for the issue of 200 millions of roubles, the actual issue amounted to 570 millions, and the country suffered from a bad attack of inflation fever. In the year 1926–1927, 115 millions of roubles were to have been issued, but the actual note issue anounted to 285·2 millions of roubles, so that again there was a crisis of inflation. Once more, in 1927–1928, whereas the plan had looked for an issue of 170 millions of roubles, the actual issues amounted to 343 millions of roubles.

Two important "campaigns" undertaken by the Soviet government during the last few years have been defeated by the elementary movement of the market; the campaign to reduce the cost of industrial production; and the campaign to lower prices. The worn-out condition of the machinery, the scarcity of commodities in the market, and the increased issue of paper money, combined to raise prices.

It would take us too far afield were we to study examples of errors of calculation in the plans for particular branches of industry, for foreign trade, for the provision of raw materials, for the building trade, or for various other elements of the national economy. Enough to say that in actual practice Russian economic life can furnish innumerable such instances.

The question whether the Soviet economy is a purposive economy should be considered, also, from another point of view. For socialists the most important task of a purposive economy is to prevent the crises which are inevitable in a capitalist economy. L. Eventoff, one of the Soviet economists, maintains that "the Soviet economic system has enabled us to bridle the periodic crises". In this, he says, "consists the advantage of the new system as compared with a capitalist economy".[1] The facts show, however, that the economic system of Soviet Russia has not succeeded in "transforming the forces of production from demon masters into willing servants".[2]

The nature of a typical economic crisis under capitalism consists in this, that owing to the disorganisation of the capitalist economy there are periodical crises of over-production, gluts in one or more departments of the national economic life. In

[1] "Ekonomicheskaya Zhizn", September 13, 1927.
[2] The phrase was used by Engels in Herrn Eugen Dührings Umwälzung der Wissenschaft, p. 301.

the post-war period, the crises that have occurred in various countries have failed to exhibit all the phenomena that were characteristic of the typical crises. Above all, the sometime periodicity has disappeared. In England, for instance, the crisis has been of much longer duration than of old, lasting several years; whereas in Germany, a brief boom was followed by a slump which gave place within a few months to a new but transient boom. Most characteristic, however, of the post-war crises is that crises in the monetary circulation, crises due to a scarcity of capital, and crises due to economic disproportions, have been superadded to market crises.

A similar situation has been observable in Russia. If we leave the period of war communism out of consideration, we find that during the seven years since the introduction of the Nep, there have already been two market crises in Soviet Russia, the first in the year 1923–1924, and the second in the year 1926–1927. The former was characteristic, and assumed extensive proportions. V. Sarabyanoff described the crisis of 1923–1924 in the following terms: "The demand of the peasants shrank to the uttermost (owing to the disproportion between the prices for industrial products and agrarian products respectively), and a market crisis ensued, affecting all branches of our economic life."[1]

The market crisis in the first half of the year 1927 was less acute. Still, it was a serious one, as was shown by the fact that the turnover of commodities in Moscow and in the provinces from January to June 1927, fell off by 70 per cent from that of the last quarter of 1926, and by 25 per cent as compared with the turnover in the same months of the previous year.

Crises of this nature, typical market crises, should be all the less likely to occur in Russia seeing that in that country there are no objective causes for their development. Industrial production is at a very low level, the home market has a high capacity of absorption, and in years when the harvests are

[1] [Economics and Applied Economics in the U.S.S.R.], State Publishing House, 1926, p. 339.

good, the demand of the peasants, who are the chief consumers, is potentially very great. The main trouble of Soviet Russia is a scarcity of commodities, so that the market crises which do actually occur must be wholly ascribed to the forcible control of economic life by the Soviet Government.

But besides these typical market crises, there has been a rapid succession of crises of disproportion, affecting Russia more grievously than any other country. They take the form of crises of inflation, fuel crises, grain crises, raw-material crises, crises in the supply of metals, transport crises, crises of export and import, crises in respect of the accumulation of capital, and so on. There is not one single branch of Russian economic life which does not again and again exhibit a disproportion between its own structure and the functioning of other departments of economic life. The process of reconstruction is not being carried out in accordance with the dictates of a purposive economy, but goes its own spontaneous course; and the process of mutual assimilation, when it occurs, also occurs spontaneously, in respect alike of amount and speed. But mutual assimilation does not occur to a sufficient degree. The essential characteristic of the post-revolutionary economy of the U.S.S.R. is a disproportion between the capacity for industrial production and the demands of agriculture, for there is a persistent lack of capital for industrial reproduction together with a chronic scarcity of commodities.

Surely it is preposterous to speak of the economy of Soviet Russia as being free from crises when year by year thousands of workers and employees are being dismissed,[1] when the number of unemployed is continually increasing, and when from the countryside there are perpetually streaming into the towns millions upon millions of hungry persons who can find no work to do upon the land. All the "errors of calculation", all the "disproportions", all the "failures of plan"—what

[1] According to the official reports of the Supreme Economic Council, during the crisis of 1923, 37,000 workers were dismissed, and during the crisis of 1925, 46,000 workers.

are they but Soviet euphemisms for phenomena which elsewhere are usually termed economic crises?

The most serious charge that must be brought against the Russian economic system, the plainest proof that the Soviet economy is not a purposive one, is that the present system keeps the country in a condition of chronic crisis, that it hampers productive energies at a time when, freed by the revolution, their spontaneous tendency is towards a rapid expansion.

Is there a purposive economy in Russia? Let us consider once more the definition of a purposive economy that has been given by the State Planning Commission, the definition I quoted in the third paragraph of the present chapter.

Is there a mutual coordination and assimilation of production and consumption? Is there a precise knowledge and appropriate use of material resources and human labour power? Can we say that the greatest possible production is secured with the smallest expenditure and in the shortest time? Does the whole economic mechanism work without friction, without crises, and without stoppages? The answer to these questions show that a purposive economy of such a kind does not exist in Soviet Russia.

Even such State regulation as that for which the objective prerequisites actually exist in Russia, fails to give satisfactory positive results owing to the utopism which guides it, owing to the unduly far-reaching nature of the plans, and owing to the bureaucratic character of the administration. And yet the State regulation of economic life might be one of the most important factors of economic reconstruction in a country which has got beyond the period of intense revolutionary disturbance.

CHAPTER SEVENTEEN

TOWARDS SOCIALISM OR CAPITALISM?

To every one interested in contemporary Russia, the question
what is the social and economic significance of the extant
Soviet system and what are the tendencies of its development
is of fundamental importance. Are we watching the initial
stages of the first socialist community; or is the socialist
phraseology current to-day in Soviet Russia nothing more than
the mask disguising a bourgeois revolution occurring at a
late hour in the epoch of advanced capitalism? Is what we see
in Russia really nothing more than a revolution occurring at a
time when a peculiarly elaborate historical masquerade was
needed in order to induce a proletariat already awakened to its
own political significance to undertake (instead of the bourgeoisie) the eradication of the vestiges of feudalism? Whereas
in the eighteenth century, illusory hopes of realising liberty,
equality, and fraternity, sufficed to encourage the French
workers to perform the historical tasks properly belonging
to the bourgeoisie, was it perhaps essential that in the twentieth
century an illusion that socialism could be immediately realised
should be operative in order to make the workers of Russia or
of China run the risks of revolution? If the former supposition
be correct, then the terrorism practised by the bolsheviks,
and their economic blunders, have been nothing more than the
fruit of an excess of zeal, have been merely the illnesses of
childhood, the maladies natural to a socialist order born
somewhat prematurely and the first of its kind in history.
Then the task of all socialists, of all members of the working
class, would be to participate actively in the upbuilding of
this new world. But if we are only the spectators of a great
historical puppet-show; if behind the socialist façade the
features of a society which, though new, though born out of
the revolution, is fundamentally capitalist, are disclosing
themselves more plainly day by day—then we must do our

utmost to dispel the illusion that this revolution is a socialist one, so that the working class (hitherto deceived) may be enabled to hold at least the second line of its revolutionary position, and may escapè being crushed politically and morally as soon as the nature of the masquerade becomes plain to all the world.

What, let us ask once more, is the actual nature of the extant Soviet system?

Even communists give contradictory answers to this question. When they are disputing among themselves at a party congress, they are ready enough to declare that the Soviet system in its present form contains only "decisive factors of socialism," in the form of socialised industries; but when they are talking to the masses, in the Soviet press, and in the agitational propaganda of the Communist International in foreign countries, they declare that a socialist society and the Soviet system are substantially identical.[1] Contemporary Russia terms itself "a union of socialist Soviet republics". The Soviet system is contrasted, as a socialist system, with the capitalist system that obtains in Britain, Germany, or elsewhere. The Russian workers have been deprived of the right to carry on the class struggle and must put up with the increasing exploitation of labour, and the trade unions must accept subordination to the State, because the Soviet Union is a socialist country. Militarism, the subjugation of Georgia, the conquest of Azerbaidjan to minister to the Russian petroleum interests, the reintroduction of capital punishment—all these things are justified by the communists on the ground that Russia is a socialist country.

But whatever the bolsheviks may say, it is plain to all men's sight that the Soviet Union is not a country where socialism

[1] When, for a time, Zinovieff went over to the opposition, he protested vigorously against such attempts of the communist majority to depict Russia as a socialist country. He said: "Here in Russia, people are now trying to explain the Nep as a manifestation of socialism. This signifies the idealisation of the Nep, the idealisation of capitalism."—[Concerning Imaginary and Real Differences of Opinion in our Party], Leningrad, 1925.

has been fully established. Social inequality, unemployment, exploitation, and prostitution, which are widespread in contemporary Russia, afford indisputable proofs of this. But it is not so easy to say whether or not the U.S.S.R. is a country in which socialism is on the way to be inaugurated.

According to the dicta of scientific socialism, the chief characteristics of a socialist society are as follows. The means of production, the factories, the mines, and the land, have been socialised. The exploitation of man by man has been abolished. The national economy has been organised and is conducted purposively, in such a way as at one and the same time to promote the highest possible development of the forces of production and the most complete satisfaction of the needs of the population at large. The social relations entered into in the process of production have been reorganised upon the basis of the cooperation of the great commonwealth of the active workers. The political functions of the community are wholly under the control of all these active workers.

As to whether the conquest of the powers of State by the working class can only be effected by revolutionary means, and whether (as the revolutionary social democrats believe) it is only along this line that the proletariat can fight successfully for the establishment of socialism; or whether, on the other hand (as the reformists among the social democrats declare), the transference of State power into the hands of a majority at length grown fully conscious of their own interests will proceed along evolutionary paths—this is a question hotly disputed in socialist circles.

So much at least, however, is a matter of general acceptance among socialists of all ways of thinking, that the establishment of a socialist society will be a long and complicated process. A socialist society will not be born all at once in a definite form, so that all the elements of the new social order will spring to life at one and the same moment in a condition of perfect mutual harmony. No, a socialist society will be the outgrowth of a dialectical process. Foreshadowings and factors of socialism are already arising and developing within the womb of the capitalist process of production. During the first phase of a socialist society, therefore, many vestiges of capitalism will persist; and conversely, in the epoch of highly developed capitalism, there will be discoverable many intimations of the forthcoming socialist society.

For us to be entitled, therefore, to describe a method of production as socialist, it is not enough that this method should contain elements which, superficially regarded, can be held to be appropriate to the socialist ordering of society. The essential question is, what is the real nature of the social relations of production, behind the masquerade of forms and words; and no less essential is it to ascertain what are the developmental trends of an extant mode of production, guiding it in the direction of a fully socialised society. It is by the light of these principles that we must judge the state of affairs in contemporary Russia.

In the U.S.S.R., industry as a whole has been almost completely nationalised. But nationalisation, however comprehensively effected, is not of itself a decisive criterion of the socialisation of the means of production. In countries where capitalism is far advanced, we often see the State assuming the role of industrial entrepreneur. In Germany, for instance, State enterprises are predominant in a number of the branches of economic life; and even in tsarist Russia there were numerous and important State factories and mines. Certainly there is no other country in the world in which the nationalisation of industry has gone so far as in the Soviet Union; and nevertheless it is perfectly conceivable that the epoch of advanced capitalism may be an epoch of the extensive nationalisation of economic life, in so far as the leading capitalists (pushing a stage farther the already obvious fusion of the State with the organisations of the capitalist class) regard such nationalisation as a useful mask for capitalist dictatorship. Finally, we learn from the study of history that even in the remote past there have been such States as that of Peru in the

days of the conquistadors, when, under Inca rule, a thoroughgoing nationalisation of production went hand in hand with
the exploitation of enslaved peasants. In and by itself,
nationalisation is not necessarily a factor of the upbuilding of
socialism. The decisive questions are: the configuration of the
social relations of production in the actual work of production;
and who actually holds political power.

Now, in Russia, the means of production have been
nationalised, but they have not been socialised. The
management of industry is not carried on by persons or
organisations empowered to carry it on in virtue of free
organisation or free election; it is not carried on by the self-
governing organisations of the active workers; but it is carried
on by a bureaucratic State apparatus. A worker in a Soviet
enterprise does not play any active part in the management
of the process of production, being merely a seller of the
commodity labour power who is paid very little for his ware.
In actual practice, industrial democracy does not exist in
Russia. Even its most primitive form, the control of production
by the working masses, was abolished during the first years
of Soviet rule. The substitute for industrial democracy
subsequently called into being in the form of production
conferences, has become a mere farce,[1] and there do not exist
in the U.S.S.R. any democratic bodies for the control of
industry to which consumers and producers can send repre-

[1] The trade-union conference called in November 1928 to consider the
problems of economic work among the masses, referred to these productive
conferences in the following terms: "They are in a state of decay. The
work of the productive conferences is experiencing a crisis; . . . directives,
circulars, instructions, and occasional visits on the part of instructors from
the Central Council of the Trade Unions of the U.S.S.R. and from the
central committees of the various unions—these comprise the main bases
of trade-union management of the economic mass work in the enterprises."
The delegates to the conference adduced data to show that in the largest
enterprises productive conferences were held only at long intervals, every
six or ten months; that not only the rank-and-file workers, but also the
members of the workers' committees abstained from attending these conferences; that the resolutions passed at the productive conferences remained
void of effect; and so on.—"Ekonomicheskaya Zhizn", November 20, 1928,

sentatives as well as the State. Actual details of economic policy, the extent of production, the prices of commodities, the ways in which enterprises are managed, rates of wages, and the like, are decided by the instruments of the State, without the workers having a word to say in the matter. At a communist meeting held in Moscow in the year 1926, Rykoff, the veteran communist, chairman of the Council of People's Commissaries, spoke in a tone of honest pessimism: "I regret to say that I have not learned in a single meeting of workers that the working class really believes the moment to have come when the foundation stones of the new socialist society are being laid."[1] These words involve a drastic indictment of the Soviet system. The example of Soviet Russia gives a striking confirmation of the truth of what Otto Bauer wrote in 1919, that the nationalisation of industry often results, not in the socialisation of production, but in the establishment of a bureaucratic and authoritarian economy.[2]

The idea that the definitive destruction of the capitalist class in Russia would be effected by the bolshevik revolution has proved illusory. It is true that the thoroughgoing "expropriation of the expropriators" destroyed the economic basic of the old capitalists, and that the reign of terror made an end of many of the individual members of the capitalist class. But it was impossible to destroy this class as a class in a period when a monetary economy, a commodity market, and private enterprise in industry and commerce, were being restored. Both in the town and in the countryside, during the years of the Nep, there has come into existence a new, post-revolutionary bourgeoisie, not very numerous, but tenacious and predatory. Some of these new capitalists are at work openly, having complied with the requirements of the Soviet laws; others are at work in nooks and crannies of the new system, masking part of their business as the fulfilment of State orders, and withdrawing the other part from the scrutiny of the law.

---

[1] A. Rykoff [New Tasks], 1926, p. 42.
[2] Otto Bauer, Der Weg zum Sozialismus, 12th ed., p. 10.

In addition to these Russian bourgeois, there are the foreign concessionaries and the representatives of foreign commercial firms, characteristic specimens of colonial enterprise whose leading slogan is, "High risk, high profits!" [1]

The communists, however, declare that in the nationalised industry of the U.S.S.R. the exploitation of the workers has been done away with, that the workers are no longer compelled to hand over a considerable amount of surplus value to capitalist entrepreneurs. It is doubtless true that in a socialist society (in so far as we can foresee its characteristics from our present outlook) the worker will not be able to receive the full product of his labour. Some of it will have to be reserved by the State in order to maintain persons who are not directly productive; to keep the State apparatus going; to provide for scientists, teachers, medical practitioners, etc. This is a necessary outcome of the application of the principle of the division of labour to human society at large.

The only question is, how big this proportion of the labour product must be, how much of the workers' labour must be unpaid labour, and for what purposes the fruit of this unpaid labour is to be expended. Unquestionably in a socialist society the amount of unpaid labour will be comparatively small, seeing that its fruit will be expended exclusively upon socially necessary purposes. In capitalist society, the amount is very large, for its fruit is expended upon paying capitalist profit as well as upon the satisfaction of general social needs. In the Soviet system, within the domain of the nationalised economy, there is no possessing class, and the State, therefore, need only appropriate surplus value to the extent necessary for an

[1] In his struggle with the "right deviation" in the Communist Party of the U.S.S.R. (represented by Rykoff, Kalinin, etc.), Stalin found it necessary in October 1928 to make the following admission: "As long as we have not been able to grub up the roots of capitalism, it will continue to have a more solid economic basis than communism. This may seem strange, Comrades, but it is a fact."—Stalin was speaking in the Plenum of the Moscow Committee and the Moscow Control Commission of the Communist Party of the U.S.S.R., and was reported in "Pravda", October 23, 1928.

expanding reproduction [1] and for the maintenance of the State apparatus. But the main defect of the Soviet system is that the organisation of the State administration, the expansion of production, the current management of enterprise, and the maintenance of the machinery of trade, are effected in so costly and uneconomic a manner that a very large proportion of the surplus value withheld from the workers is not utilised for genuinely social purposes. We see this plainly enough in the circumstance that in Russia, notwithstanding the abolition of the capitalist class, real wages have barely regained the pre-war level, and are far lower than the wages earned by the workers elsewhere in Europe or in America. Furthermore, in Russia (just as in countries where the system of private capitalism continues) that part of surplus value which is assigned to an expanding reproduction is assigned without foresight, without regard to social needs, with the result that crises are perpetually recurring. Agreed that the fruit of unpaid labour in Russia does not go to enrich private owners or shareholders as it does in capitalist society, for it flows into the State coffers. But when we remember that the nationalised industry of the U.S.S.R. is unable out of its own resources to ensure the expanding reproduction of industrial capital, so that hundreds of millions of roubles have to be provided annually for this purpose by taxation; when we remember how inadequate is the provision in Russia for education and for the public-health service; when we recall the fact that there are two million unemployed; when we think of the sufferings of the land-hungry peasants,

[1] Under the capitalist system of production, likewise, the capitalist refrains from devoting all his profit to private and unproductive purposes. He invests a considerable proportion of it in the expansion of old enterprises or in the organisation of new ones, but nevertheless the proletariat has to pay through the nose for the luxuries and the superfluities of the capitalist class. The fundamental cause of this latter phenomenon, is, in the last analysis, the lack of a purposive allotment of the part of surplus value that goes to expanding reproduction to the various departments of social production, so that this allotment is effected in an unorganised and irrational way which leads to crises of disproportion, when the share of the aggregate surplus value assigned to the payment of new wages falls off unduly.

and of the innumerable shelterless children—we cannot but recognise that the abolition of the capitalist class in Russia has not, so far, resulted in providing the expected social benefits.

The truth is that, by thousands of channels, some of them open and some of them hidden away underground, surplus value flows away from production to enrich State dignitaries, to pay the highly-salaried directors and advisers, to support the inflated official staffs, to satisfy the appetites of the huge army of "red" traders, brokers, and purveyors, and to provide funds for corruption, for excesses, and for peculations. In these nationalised enterprises, there are no capitalist owners; but they have to support thousands of persons who are economically superfluous and many of whom are entirely parasitic—persons who can use the State apparatus to secure for themselves a share in the surplus value created by the workers. When the worker is thus exploited, it matters little to him whether the exploiter is a private capitalist or a parasite of some other kind. "In contemporary Russia", wrote L. Martoff a few years ago, "the workers are once more engaged in producing surplus value for other classes".[1]

Moreover, the prospects of being able to maintain the nationalised industry at its present level are extremely unfavourable. The communists, wishing to show that socialisation has been a success in Russia, are fond of tabulating statistics to prove that there has been a growth in the "socialised sector", that is to say in the aggregate nationalised and co-operative economy. According to official figures (whose accuracy is, however, disputed by many of the Soviet economists), in the year 1926–1927, the socialised sector comprised 49·3 per cent of the entire national property, and in the year 1927–1928, this sector increased to 49·8 per cent, thus showing an increase of 0·5 per cent in a year.[2] But even if this growth of the

[1] [Dialectic of the Dictatorship], "Sotsialistichesky Vestnik", 1922, No. 3.
[2] In illustration of what is said above, I give here data to show the amount of national property, and its appurtenance to various sectors of economic

"socialised sector" is really taking place, what evidence does it afford as to the vitality of the "socialised" economy, when the increase is due, not to the speedy and healthy development of the nationalised economy, but only to special measures adopted as the expression of the "swing to the left"—this meaning that the apparent growth of the socialised sector is due to a confiscation of the property of private industrialists in the towns and of the well-to-do peasants in the countryside?

life. The figures are taken from the [Control Figures of the National Economy for 1927–1928], being calculated for the 1st of October in each year in millions of chervonets roubles according to the prices of 1925–1926. (The figures for 1928 are only provisional.)

A. NATIONAL PROPERTY IN VARIOUS DEPARTMENTS OF ECONOMIC LIFE

	1925.	1926.	1927.	1928.
1. Agriculture	24·10	25·19	26·29	27·53
2. Industry	6·68	7·88	7·88	8·82
3. Large-scale Electrical Power Stations	0·25	0·35	0·47	0·68
4. Transport system	10·80	10·18	11·05	11·45
5. Trade	0·54	0·72	0·93	1·09
6. Municipal enterprise	2·25	2·30	2·37	2·47
7. Urban dwellings	10·10	10·08	10·22	10·45
8. Property of the administration and social and educational institutions	1·40	1·51	1·69	1·91
9. Posts and Telegraphs	0·22	0·23	0·26	0·29
Aggregate National Property	56·34	58·44	61·16	64·69

B. NATIONAL PROPERTY IN SECTORS

	1925.	1926.	1927.	1928.
(a) State	27·20	28·07	29·50	31·59
(b) Cooperatives	0·62	0·73	0·90	1·11
(c) Private	28·52	29·64	30·76	31·99
Aggregate National Property	56·34	58·44	61·16	64·69

The figures in the foregoing table are based upon extremely dubious estimates, and not upon an accurate compilation of statistics, so that it gives no more than a vague notion of the national property of the U.S.S.R. The allotment to the various "sectors" has been made in an extremely arbitrary way, as we learn from the discussions in the Soviet press.

As I have already shown, what is happening in these cases is, not that the State replaces a private economy, but simply that it destroys that economy, and thus upsets the balance of economic life throughout the country!

Apart from such "successes" as these, which are mainly due to the activity of the political police, we have to recognise that the Soviet government, in its endeavours to satisfy the most elementary needs of the population, finds itself compelled to go backwards rather than forwards in this matter of the nationalised economy. Owing to the lack of productive accumulation, Russian industry finds itself in a blind alley. Insufficiency of financial resources and the acute scarcity of commodities have once more compelled the Soviet State to seek salvation in an appeal to private capital and private initiative. Without adopting the one measure essential to the national economy as a whole, namely a radical restriction of the scope of the nationalised economy within the limits of what is economically practicable, the government is unsystematically retreating all along the line. One day it offers special privileges to private persons who will undertake to build houses; another, it proposes to hand over to foreign concessionaries, not only the most important industrial enterprises, but also various municipal enterprises, such as waterworks, tramways, and electrical power stations (enterprises which everywhere else in Europe are public concerns, and have always been public concerns in Russia). At the same time, a peasant economy still dominates the countryside, for the peasants, despite all communist endeavours to foster cooperative agricultural production, cling stubbornly to their system of small-scale individual farming, and regard with increasing hostility the nationalised industry, which produces so little, so badly, and so expensively.

During the first years of the Nep, the leaders of the Russian communists were well aware that in the struggle between a private capitalist economy and a socialised economy, the latter could only be victorious if it were able to convince the masses of the population, and above all the peasants, that it was really a better method—that under a socialist system production would expand more rapidly, would be cheaper, and would be better. "If capitalism is to be deprived of its basis," wrote Lenin, "individualist small-scale enterprise in town and countryside must be placed upon a new technical foundation, upon the technical foundation of modern large-scale production."[1] Again, at the Eleventh Congress of the Communist Party of the U.S.S.R., held in the year 1922, in support of his contention that the communists must learn from private entrepreneurs how to produce and how to trade, Lenin said: "Unless we can show the peasants that we are able to ensure them a supply of industrial products, they will send us to the devil."

In his book [Who is Beating Whom?] Trotsky showed that the U.S.S.R. would only escape being swallowed up by the encircling capitalist system if it were able to develop the forces of production more rapidly than they were being developed in capitalist countries. These thoroughly sound arguments have now been forgotten, and although, since the foundation of the Soviet State, Russia has been in the throes of one crisis after another, and although the Soviet government in the eleventh year of its existence finds itself compelled to enlarge the domain of private capitalist economy, the leaders of the Communist Party of the U.S.S.R. are still trying to persuade the Russian workers that the upbuilding of socialism is making victorious advances in Russia.

The actual course of evolution has shattered these utopian dreams. It has shown that the economic and social conditions prevailing in Russia make it impossible to overleap the capitalist phase of development.

The communists declare that their attempts to develop a purposive economic system in Russia furnish additional proof that the Soviet economy is a socialist one. But in the previous chapter I showed that there is no organised purposive economy

[1] [Collected Works], Vol. XVII, pp. 427-428.

in the Soviet Union. I showed that all we can find there are certain isolated elements of a purposive guidance, and that this restricted amount of State regulation of the national economy can only achieve positive results when it is carried on in accordance with the laws of the capitalist market.

Besides, these purposive elements are not peculiar to a socialist society. A far-reaching purposive management, organisation, and rationalisation of economic life, is likewise characteristic of the epoch of highly developed capitalism; and the distinction between the last phase of capitalism (in which there are already numerous elements of a purposive economy) and the initial stages of socialism (wherein the elements of a purposive economy have not yet been fused to form a thoroughly purposive economic system) is not to be found in the amount of purposive economic experiments in one system or the other, but in the social content of the purposive economy. From this outlook it is highly significant that, although the Soviet government is not an instrument of the possessing classes, the social content of its purposive economic policy often runs counter to the interests of the working classes. The reduction of the workers' wages in order to reduce the purchasing power of the working class, the policy of buying grain from the peasants at a price below that which obtains in the open market, and the Soviet protectionist policy, are three among many instances which might be given of the way in which the purposive economic policy of the Soviet State is often directly anti-social.

Most important, and indeed decisive, for our judgment of the character of the Soviet system, is the problem of the social content of the Soviet State. Although, in the first years after the revolution, the Soviet authority was not based exclusively upon the working class, but also upon the soldiers who were craving for peace and upon the peasants who had set their hopes upon the general redistribution of the land, the proletarian nature of the State power at this epoch was unquestionable. Under the slogan of the "enfranchisement of labour", the great bulk of the workers, fired with the revolutionary illusion, were ardent supporters of Soviet rule. But in the long run, a social class cannot be deceived. The distribution of social forces in Russia at that time was of such a nature that it was impossible, even for a party which had recourse to the terrorist use of force, to maintain itself in power when it continued to pursue a utopian policy which alienated the peasants as a whole by depriving them of the possibility of carrying on productive work. The attempt to realise socialism forthwith had to be renounced, and the New Economic Policy became the order of the day.

Under the terrorist regime of the dictatorship, the Soviet government has drawn farther and farther away from the working class. Repressive measures against socialist parties; the suppression of independent working-class organisations; the forcible expulsion, now of right-wing and now of left-wing opposition elements—these and similar measures have progressively narrowed the social stratum upon which bolshevism is grounded. Since the rulers of the State found it objectively impracticable to conduct the totality of the nationalised industry in a reasonable way, and since they had nevertheless assumed the role of industrial entrepreneurs, they soon found it necessary, partly in order to expand the scale of industry, and partly in order to increase production, to exercise a more and more vigorous pressure upon the masses of the workers, and to speed up the labour process, in this way widening the breach between the Soviet State and the proletarian masses. Further difficulties arose from the unceasing pressure exercised by the peasants, who demanded from the State the possibility of a normal economic development. The rise of the new bourgeoisie, notwithstanding reiterated attempts to keep it down; permeation of the leading circles of the Communist Party by new post-revolutionary elements longing for tranquillity and order; the gradual entanglement of the rank-and-file communists in the meshes of a comfortable petty-bourgeois existence; and, finally, the marked conservatism which, in small matters as in large, has become more and more characteristic of the essential framework of the contemporary Soviet State, the official stratum of the State employees, of the party, and of the trade unions—these factors have combined to bring about an almost imperceptible but slowly-progressive relapse of the communists in the direction of a post-revolutionary transformation. The differences of opinion within the Communist Party, and the appearance of oppositional trends, are to a great extent the expression of the despair with which the revolutionary elements of the Communist Party of the U.S.S.R. are contemplating the social transformation of the Communist Party and the Soviet State. This process of social transformation, of course, has not yet reached its term, and it moves in a zigzag rather than in a continuous straight line.

Meanwhile, there has developed a very remarkable situation, one in which the bolshevik State power, which objectively regarded has already ceased to be the State power of the working class, is subjectively in perfect honesty attempting to swim against the stream and to continue its utopian policy of socialisation. Although the Soviet power is not the State power of the workers, it has not yet become the governmental instrument of another class than the working class, and will never become this as a whole.

Naturally, so anomalous a situation cannot last. But it often happens in periods of transition, that there is an apparent severance of the State authority from its social foundation.[1] This happened in the great French revolution, just before Thermidor. It happened, too, in Russia, in the year 1917. The Kerensky government, subjectively, was beyond question a government wishing to base its power upon the working masses, and closely related to them both ideologically and by its origin; but the circumstances of historical evolution compelled it to

[1] See, for instance, Friedrich Engels, The Origin of the Family, Private Property, and the State, translated by Ernest Untermann, Kerr, Chicago, 1902, pp. 206 et seq.

fulfil the policy of the possessing classes, and thus to bring about its own destruction.

The past record of the leaders of the Soviet government makes it impossible for them, subjectively, to accept the transformation of the State power they control into the power of an owning class; and nevertheless the social structure of the country and the vital interests of economic life imperiously demand that the State should completely renounce the old utopian policy; they demand a partition of the power with the peasants, and a consolidation of the positions which the peasants have won during the revolution. Moreover, the terrorist regime of dictatorship, which has hitherto made it possible for the Soviet government to retain power, is now turning against the dominant party.

The various social classes of post-revolutionary Russia, having no means of expressing their demands in any other way, manifest their will inside the only legal political organisation, that of the Communist Party, doing this, sometimes through the instrumentality of a "left" opposition, and sometimes through the instrumentality of the "right". In this way they are decomposing and transforming the Communist Party. No doubt the Soviet dictatorship tries again and again to effect a synthesis of these social contradictions, and, by making minor concessions, to postpone the hour when a historical balance sheet will have to be drawn up. But from year to year it becomes more and more obvious that an equilibrium between the social content of the State authority, on the one hand, and the condition of the social forces in the country, on the other, cannot be secured without a radical breach with the past. There appear to be three possible ways in which this breach might be effected. A democratic State authority might be set up; or part of the Communist Party might be transformed into a party of the possessing classes (Thermidor); or, finally, there might be a Bonapartist or reactionary coup d'état. No one can foresee which course development will take. This much, however, is certain, that

the party which now rules in the U.S.S.R. is no longer a party
of the working class; is not a party which can carry out a policy
of socialisation; is not even a party competent to promote in
any consistent or enduring fashion the interests of the working
class.

We have seen that the nationalisation of industry in Russia
has not produced a socialist economy, but only a bureaucratic
and badly-functioning State capitalism, and we know that a
further extension of private capitalist production is imminent.
We have learned, moreover, that the State authority, though
it styles itself socialist, is in its daily activities compelled by
objective conditions, either to strive for the realisation of
utopian measures foredoomed to failure (the "swing to the
left"); or else to work for the realisation of the policy of
classes estranged from, and indeed hostile to, the proletariat.

To a Marxian observer it must be plain that under the
social, economic, and cultural conditions obtaining in Russia,
that country, even in the first years of the revolution, had no
prospect of achieving an independent and immediate socialist
transformation. But the revolutionary movement in Central
Europe and the economic convulsions of the post-war years
aroused natural hopes that there would be a socialist revolution
in countries where industrial development was more advanced.
That was what gave a substantial ground for the theory that
the social and economic development of Russia might be speeded
up, and even for the belief that with the aid of the proletariat
of the revolutionary industrial lands of the west, Russia might
be able to overleap the normal developmental phases of
capitalism.

But when the stabilisation of capitalism took place in Central
and Western Europe, when the situation had ceased to be
revolutionary, when capitalism had moved from the defensive
to the offensive, the hope that Russia would be able to persist
in her policy of forcible socialisation until the social revolution
had occurred in the chief industrial countries of Europe
became illusory, and even disastrous in its utopism.

During these years, the Russian communists began to discuss the possibility of "socialism in one country alone". The resolutions and theses of the Comintern, and the books and pamphlets of the Russian communists, voiced the contention that socialism in one country is possible. So abstract a formulation as this is, of course, utterly foreign to the Marxian way of looking at things. Countries whose outward political aspect is identical in the matter of State sovereignty, may be very, very different economically and structurally. It would, therefore, be absurd to suppose that the possibilities of an isolated establishment of socialism are identical in the United States, in China, in Germany, and in Russia, respectively. What may be possible for great countries which have become economically independent and where industry is highly developed, may be utterly impossible for countries which are backward economically and culturally.

Russia, though its territories are enormous and its natural resources very great, is not one of the countries in which such an isolated socialism can be established. To the Russian social democrats, this conclusion seems to be a necessary inference from the theory of scientific socialism. When we turn to practice, we see that the eleven years of Soviet rule have given a convincing, nay a cruel demonstration of the impossibility of establishing an isolated socialism in Russia. The utopian endeavours to overleap historically inevitable stages of economic evolution have been shipwrecked.

Notwithstanding all the heroism displayed by the Russian revolutionists, and notwithstanding all the sacrifices made by the Russian working class, the Soviet State has not been able to stand the Russian economic system upon its head, has not been able to force Russia through a narrow chink into the realm of socialism.

CHAPTER EIGHTEEN

ECONOMIC BALANCE SHEET

THE great revolution through which Russia has passed gave us every reason to expect a speedy blossoming of Russian economic life. The overthrow of tsarism, the appropriation of the estates of the great landlords by the peasants, the abolition of the vestiges of feudalism, the possibility of replacing a primitive system of agriculture by more intensive methods of culture, the abundance of natural resources (favourable to the development of industry, and alluring to foreign capital), the increased activity and initiative of the masses of the population as a result of the stimulating influences of the revolution—all these factors encouraged expectations that the prosperity of the country and of the population at large would rapidly increase.

Historical evolution, however, has taken another course. Russia has suffered from all the storms of the civil war and of foreign intervention; during the period of the bolshevik attempts to establish communism in the twinkling of an eye and by force, there was an immense and unprecedented destruction of the fundamental capital of industry; the peasants were impoverished, and millions died from famine and from epidemic diseases. After the inauguration of the Nep, the conditions for reconstruction and for the further development of production in town and countryside became somewhat more favourable. But even after the abandonment of war communism, the policy of the Soviet government, being dominated by utopian aspirations, continued to hinder the recovery of the national economy, deprived the population of all incitements towards productive work, reduced to a minimum the accumulation of capital, and prevented the influx of capital from abroad. After eleven years of revolution, Russia has, with infinite labour and pains, regained the pre-war level of economic evolution, a level of peace production which is lower than that of any other of the great European countries. In the economic respect, Russia is now farther than ever behind the advanced industrial lands. And this is the state of affairs at a time when the development of the youthful capitalism of South America and of Asia is proceeding with giant strides.

In the foregoing chapters I have more than once pointed out that a rapid improvement in the industry of the Soviet Union could only be achieved by reestablishing the pre-revolutionary reserves of fixed capital,[1] and that Russian industry under Soviet rule is still unable to satisfy the most elementary needs of the population. As soon as the last reserves of the pre-war fixed capital are exhausted, as soon as the extant enterprises have been exploited to the utmost limit, as soon as the old plants are kept at work without interruption (whenever this is possible), it is inevitable that the speed of industrial expansion must slacken to a lamentable extent, unless the normal essentials for an expanded reproduction are provided.[2] But the most basic requisites for the expansion

---

[1] The fact that in Germany, after the period of inflation of the currency, production in certain branches of industry expanded by from 30 to 40 per cent per annum, suffices to show that the rapid reconstruction of Russian industry in the early years after the inauguration of the Nep was not due to any special advantages of the Soviet system.—See Statistisches Jahrbuch für das Deutsche Reich, 1927.

[2] Writers in the Soviet press declare that the reconstruction period of Russian industry came to an end in the year 1926–1927. In my opinion, however, the expansion of industry is still going on at the expense of the using up of the reserves from the old regime. The well-known political economist, V. Bazaroff, says, quite rightly, in this connexion: "Capitalism, owing to its inherent tendency to restrict the effective demand of the masses of the population, never exploits to the utmost the productive capacity of its enterprises; and for this reason, under capitalism, the economic limit of the capacity for exploitation of a plant is always lower than the technically possible limit. There can be no doubt that the rapidity of the increase of production during recent years has been partly due to the exploitation of the fixed capital inherited from the capitalist system, and this to an extent beyond what was desirable in the interests of reconstruction."— "Ekonomicheskoye Obozreniye", 1928, No. 6.—The Soviet economists, Demirchoglyan and Kvasha, who have been studying the problem of the utilisation of the fixed capital of industry, come to the following conclusion: "The data of recent years lead us to assume that the extant machinery of

of reproduction are that there should be an accumulation of capital in the country for productive purposes, and an influx of foreign capital for the same end. At present, however, in the U.S.S.R. neither the one nor the other is taking place. There is no accumulation of capital going on in the nationalised industry or in the nationalised system of trade, which are dependent upon large subventions and long-term credits; and there is very little accumulation of capital in private industry and private trade, for private entrepreneurs are in continual danger of arrest and of confiscation of their property.

The only branch of economic life in which, since the inauguration of the Nep, the accumulation of capital has to some extent taken place, is agriculture. In the previous chapters we learned that, by the expedients of high prices, taxation, inflation, and the "scissors", the Soviet government has extracted from peasant agriculture many hundreds of millions of roubles in order to provide industry with the possibility of expansion, although only within the limits of mere reconstruction. Economists hostile to the working class, contemplating these phenomena, draw the conclusion that in Russia "the workers are having a good time of it at the expense of the peasants". The inference is erroneous. In the U.S.S.R., the workers receive minimal wages for extremely hard work. Their existence is not a burden on any other class, for in Russia parasitic elements live upon the labour of the workers. If, however, instead of considering the workers as individuals and as a class, we turn to consider industry as a branch of the national economy, then it is correct to say that industry—because it is nationalised to an extent that is quite impracticable for Russia, and because under the bolshevik regime the costs of production are unduly high—does in Russia actually thrive at the expense of agriculture. The fact is so obvious that none of the Russian communists dispute it. Some of them, those

industry has not yet [1928] been completely used up, and that there still remains a possibility of expanding production at the expense of the aforesaid fixed capital."—"Statisticheskoye Obozreniye", 1928, No. 3.

of the left who are led by Preobrazhensky,[1] have formulated a complete theory of "socialist accumulation", according to which, during the period of socialist upbuilding, the proletariat has to extract from the rural population the means required to finance expanded reproduction—this being a process analogous to that in virtue of which the capitalists have included the colonies in the capitalist nexus. Others, those who belong to Stalin's group, declare that, while it is true that means must be extracted from the rural population, the process of extraction must be a more moderate one. Thus the only dispute is as to the amount of "permissible robbery".

Nevertheless, both these groups of communists have formulated the problem in a wrong way. The matter at issue is not whether, in the interests of industrialisation, much should be taken from agriculture or little. Obviously, an accelerated industrialisation is essential to Russia's future. In no other way can there be effected a rapid development of the productive forces of the country, an intensification of agriculture, a solution of the problems of unemployment and agrarian over-population, a rapid cultural advance, and an increase in general wellbeing, an increase of the share of the workers in the social and economic advantages of the country, and a consolidation of the proletariat as a class. The interests of town and countryside alike urgently demand advance along these lines. If, then, during the period when the technical basis of industry is undergoing expansion, there is need for extensive financial resources, in the interests of the national economy any and every government must do its utmost to mobilise all the accumulations of capital in the homeland, and will endeavour in the first instance to attract capital from agriculture to industry. But two basic demands must be fulfilled if such a policy is to be pursued rationally and purposively. First of all, since agriculture is to be called upon to finance industry, agriculture itself must be provided with conditions favourable to its own advance and to the

[1] [The New Economics], Moscow, 1924.

accumulation of capital. In the second place, the investments of capital in industry must be such as will produce the greatest possible effect in the shortest possible time. Now, these two preliminary conditions are not fulfilled in Russia. The Russian communists fail to recognise that it must be made possible for the peasants to turn to economic account the land acquired by them during the revolution; that the land survey must be completed with the utmost speed; that opportunities for getting on in the world, opportunities for accumulating capital, must be guaranteed to the peasants. In no other way is a rapid advance of industrialisation in Russia possible. Were it only for political reasons, such measures are indispensable, for otherwise the peasants will be driven into the camp of the counter-revolution. But they are no less indispensable for economic reasons. The whole structure of the Russian national economy is one which demands that the development of industry and the development of agriculture should proceed equably side by side. But to-day in the U.S.S.R., whilst more than a milliard of roubles are invested year by year in industry, agriculture receives no more than a few dozen millions of roubles per annum—if we leave out of account the expenditure upon utopian experiments such as "Soviet farms" and "collective farms". Even if for a few years to come industry were to suffer a little because, during these years, agriculture were to receive the most indispensable assistance from the State (in order to complete the land survey, and in order to provide the necessary ploughs, separators, artificial manures, textiles, and leather goods, either by way of more extensive imports or by way of increased manufacture at home), the advance in agriculture that would thus be achieved, the increase in the harvests, the expansion of imports, and the rise in the purchasing power of the population, would soon react favourably upon industry, and would promote industrialisation in a way of which the communists, thinking of industrialisation exclusively, never venture to dream. Owing to the wrong-headed policy of the Soviet government towards the peasants, of late years these latter have had all their savings extracted from them, and the persecution of the "kulaks" has deprived them of any stimulus to improve their condition. On the other hand, the one-sided and clumsy promotion of industrialisation has had very little effect, so that there has been an extremely slow increase in industrial production, and the peasants have not been provided with agricultural machinery and implements in the desired quantities. By the year 1928, the position had become extremely critical. At the very moment when, after the exhaustion of the old reserves, industry was more than ever in need of being financed at the cost of peasant agriculture (in order to promote the expansion of production), a decline in agriculture became obvious. The area under cultivation was reduced, the harvests were smaller, and famine was imminent in large areas of the countryside.[1]

No less wrong-headed is the policy of the Soviet government as regards the second possible source of means for financing industry, namely foreign capital. At a time when the great capitalist countries are eagerly seeking a market for the investment of their superfluous capital, Russia, a land with such remarkable economic possibilities, should surely be able to attract foreign capital in large quantities. No one would venture to deny the tendency of the capital of imperialist countries to reduce to a colonial or semi-colonial status any region into which it sends its commodities or which it finances in one way or another; but at the present day in matters of foreign policy the interests of the great powers are so conflicting and their need for opening up economic relations with the U.S.S.R. is so great, that it ought not to be difficult for any Russian government, when attracting foreign capital into the country, to insist upon guarantees that in return for the high profits that can be earned, these countries should renounce

[1] At the Plenum of the Central Committee of the Communist Party of the U.S.S.R. held in the middle of November 1928, Finance Commissary Frumkin, representing the "right", announced that Russian agriculture had had a setback owing to the policy of recent years.—"Pravda", November 24, 1928.

all attempts at political or economic interference with the independence of Soviet Russia. Surely an intelligent government in Russia could easily do what tsarist Russia was able to do notwithstanding the abundant influx of foreign capital, and what even contemporary Turkey and contemporary Afghanistan can do.

The policy of the Soviet government is, however, of such a character that Russia, during the decade that has elapsed since the revolution, has been unable to procure the investment of any considerable sums of foreign money in Russian industrial production. The country has everything calculated to attract foreign capital: extensive natural resources, cheap labour power, a large and growing home market. Nothing but the gross errors of Soviet policy, nothing but the fear of excessive risks, can account for the fact that foreign capital, which would like to come to Russia, foreign capital, which seeks investment in the deserts and forests of Africa, refrains from flowing into Russia.

In all countries alike, the reconstruction of economic life after the war was attended with difficulties and exhibited morbid manifestations. But for the most part the difficulties have been overcome, and the phenomena of morbidity have disappeared. Soviet Russia is the only great country in the world in which "crisis fever" has persisted unrelieved for eleven years.

As if under the influence of some mysterious spell, the Soviet government precipitates itself, now in one direction, now in another. Sometimes, large sums of money are devoted to the reconstruction or expansion of industry in a way that is not adapted to economic possibilities, with the result that the scarcity of commodities is increased and the stability of the currency undermined. Sometimes, "extraordinary measures" against petty peasant farming are announced, and great national "grain factories" (the Soviet farms) are set agoing side by side with a nationalised industry which has already proved too much for the State to cope with. Sometimes there is renewed talk of the alliance between the workers and the peasants, and it is proposed to give economic help to those peasants who will improve and enlarge their farms. One day, the authorities stubbornly insist upon the maintenance of nationalised industry on the present scale, although experience has shown that scale to be out of relation to extant possibilities; the next, we hear of proposals to hand over even the key industries to foreign capital upon a concessionary basis. One day, we are told that the monopoly of foreign commerce will be maintained in its present form at all hazards; the next, we hear of frantic demands for foreign credits. So it goes, first a swing to the right, then a swing to the left, and then back to the right again. Always the economics of the country are getting more hopelessly involved in a blind alley.

But if the productive forces of the country were to be freed from the trammels which now hamper their working, Russian economic life would speedily recover, and Russia, like all the countries where capitalism is in its youth, would rapidly overtake the old industrial lands which have hitherto led the way. If this is to happen, the first and most important step must be a radical change in economic policy. The objective conditions of to-day are such as make it necessary that the economic development of Russia should take place mainly within the framework of a capitalist economy. The extent of nationalised industry must be reduced to the limits of the practical; the government must renounce the monopolisation of economic life; and conditions must be created under which private industry, private trade, and peasant farming can flourish. Only by such a development of the productive forces of the country, and by an expansion of the technical basis of industry, can the most urgent needs of the working class be satisfied, and favourable conditions created for the class struggle of the proletariat.

But no mere change of economic policy, however radical it may be, will suffice, seeing that the development of the productive forces of a country presupposes the existence of specific political conditions. Just as the economic development of Russia during the last years before the fall of tsarism was restricted by the limitations imposed by the absolutionist State, so the development of the productive forces in contemporary Russia is restricted by the barriers of the Soviet dictatorship. No matter in which direction we look when we contemplate the realities of Soviet life, we see that the fundamental defects cannot be overcome by minor political reforms. The Soviet government has devoted a great deal of energy to the campaign against bureaucracy, official venality, and the crimes of those in high places. A parade is made of legal proceedings; there is much "self criticism"; the Party and the Soviet apparatus are thoroughly cleansed. But all is in vain, under existing auspices. As long as the dictatorship by a minority continues, as long as the communists form a privileged caste, and as long as it is impossible for public opinion to express itself freely in Russia, there will continue to exist a medium in which corruption, the abuse of power, and the caprice of satraps will flourish.

For example, the Soviet government has been vainly trying for several years to ensure that the process of economic reconstruction shall be actively supported by scientists, technicians, and skilled operatives. But how can production be expected to develop, how can the initiative and activity essential to technical advance show themselves, in a country where the population in general has no political rights; in one where the engineer or the man of science who for political reasons is out of favour with the authorities, is liable to be prosecuted without rhyme or reason; in a country where the holding of opinions distasteful to those in authority will lead to dismissal from the service?

The arbitrary use of power on the part of the rulers, and the lack of rights among the ruled, paralyse also the initiative of private men of business. To-day an enterprise will be leased to a private entrepreneur, or a private trader will be allowed to carry on business, and to-morrow, owing to a new turn in policy, their enterprises will be suppressed, and they will be banished to some place adjoining the arctic circle. To-day, private credit institutions will be permitted; to-morrow, upon the ground that a formality has been infringed, they will be told to close their doors. A decree will be issued, demunicipalising dwellings which cannot be made to pay, and then, a few years later, when private owners have got them into working order, and have made them commercially profitable, they will be taken over once more by the municipality. The mining trial has given plain proof that a foreign concessionary cannot carry on in a country in which there exist neither elementary legal guarantees nor independent law courts nor political liberties.

The interdependence of politics and economics is especially disastrous to the Russian peasant. He is wholly in the power of the higher and lower authorities. He has no fixity of tenure of the land he farms, for he may be deprived of it at the next redistribution; he does not know what taxes he will have to pay, since they are changed from time to time in the most arbitrary way; nor does he know the prices at which he will be compelled to sell his produce to the State, or the moment at which it may please the local authorities to stigmatise him as a "kulak" and thus transform him into a pariah and an outlaw. How can he be expected to do productive work under such conditions?

Finally, the Russian worker, although the dictatorship is exercised in his name, does not possess the minimum of political rights which might enable him to protect his own interests. He has no right to say a word when piece-work rates are being fixed or lowered, nor any right to a voice in the decision of great political issues. These Russian workers, who for decades under the rule of the tsars were fighting for freedom of the press, free speech, the right of public meeting, these Russian workers who were banished in their thousands because they strove to secure the right of combination, are now deprived of the possibility of influencing governmental policy by the free election of their representatives, have no right to join the

Social Democratic Party, may not form independent trade unions to represent their class, and have neither freedom of the press nor the right of public meeting. The Soviet government, by justifying the regime of a terrorist dictatorship on the plea that in Russia a working-class party holds power, and by justifying the nationalisation of the proletarian organisations on the plea that there are no capitalist employers in Russia, condemns the Russian proletariat to a truly tragical fate; for the workers, now faced with the inevitable reestablishment of private capitalism, have to encounter the enemies of their class disarmed, impotent, and disorganised. Year by year, the Soviet government loses touch more and more with the working class. More and more extensive become the concessions which the State, despite all "swings to the left", has to make to the private capitalist elements—has to make in order to maintain the dominance of the Communist Party. More and ever more inevitable becomes a complete political and economic collapse of the present policy. Meanwhile the working class, when the reestablishment of its class enemies in power seems at hand, has forgotten the methods of the class struggle, has lost its class consciousness, and has ceased to possess political and trade-union organisations.

Thanks to the recurrent crises, to the ever-renewed manifestations of arbitrary authority, and to the regime in which the great majority are devoid of political rights, the economic life of the country is continually coming into fiercer collision with its political life. Under the Soviet dictatorship, a normal development whether of industry or of agriculture has proved to be impossible. If the Soviet dictatorship (foredoomed to perish) is not to be ousted by a reactionary regime which, while giving privileges to the bourgeoisie, will once again enslave the working class—if it is to be replaced by the only regime which can be beneficial to the working masses in town and countryside, the regime of democracy—it is essential that the workers should fight actively for political rights and for the freedom of organisation, and should, furthermore, enter into an effective and close alliance with the peasants.

An exit from the economic blind alley can only be found if, under pressure of the steadily increasing dissatisfaction of the masses, the absolutist regime of the dictatorship be liquidated, the political system be democratised, and the present utopian economic policy be radically changed.

Unless an end be put to the present regime along these lines, there seems to be no prospect for contemporary Russia but the continuance of stagnation and depression, or else the occurrence of grave economic and political disturbances.

For Product Safety Concerns and Information please contact our EU
representative GPSR@taylorandfrancis.com
Taylor & Francis Verlag GmbH, Kaufingerstraße 24, 80331 München, Germany

www.ingramcontent.com/pod-product-compliance
Lightning Source LLC
Chambersburg PA
CBHW061127220326
41599CB00024B/4196

* 9 7 8 1 0 3 2 4 8 8 9 7 4 *